STUDENT BOOK

Houghton
Mifflin
Harcourt

W9-CMM-429

STECK-VAUGHN
SOCIAL STUDIES
TEST PREPARATION FOR THE 2014 GED® TEST

Civics and Government

United States History

Economics

Geography and the World

Social Studies Practices

POWERED BY
PAXEN

Houghton
Mifflin
Harcourt

POWERED BY

PAXEN

Acknowledgments

For each of the selections and images listed below, grateful acknowledgment is made for permission to excerpt and/or reprint original or copyrighted material, as follows:

Text

63 From *The New York Times*, October 17, 2004. © *The New York Times*. All rights reserved. Used by permission and protected by the Copyright Laws of the United States. The printing, copying, redistribution, or retransmission of the Material without express written permission is prohibited. **65** Used with the permission of *Encyclopedia Britannica*. **67** From *The New York Times*, December 15, 1990. © *The New York Times*. All rights reserved. Used by permission and protected by the Copyright Laws of the United States. The printing, copying, redistribution, or retransmission of the Material without express written permission is prohibited. **77** Used with the permission of the © *Chicago Tribune*. **80** Used with the permission of *Encyclopedia Britannica*. **82** From *The New York Times*, October 13, 2012. © *The New York Times*. All rights reserved. Used by permission and protected by the Copyright Laws of the United States. The printing, copying, redistribution, or retransmission of the Material without express written permission is prohibited.

Images

Cover (bg) © Vito Palmisano/Photographer's Choice/Getty Images; **cover** (inset) © Ellen Rooney/Robert Harding World Imagery/Getty Images. **Blind** Courtesy of the U.S. Department of State. **1** iStockphoto. **20** © Neal Preston/CORBIS. **21** iStockphoto. **21** iStockphoto. **44** Used with the permission of James M. Kelly/Globe Photos, Inc. **45** iStockphoto © webking. **58** A Prohibition Party political cartoon. Circa 1920. **59** A Herbert Hoover political cartoon by Clifford K. Berryman. Circa 1929. **59** Used with permission of the Herb Block Foundation. **73** David J. Frent/Political Americana. **75** Used with the permission of © Tribune Media Services. **82** Kaiser/Franklin Delano Roosevelt Archives. **82** Saalburg/University of Minnesota libraries. **86** Copyright by Bill Mauldin (1962). Courtesy of the Bill Mauldin Estate LLC. **88** © Dana Edmunds; reproduced with permission. **89** Getty Images © Ariel Skelley.

Copyright © 2013 by Paxen Learning Corp.

All rights reserved. No part of this work may be reproduced or transmitted in any form or by any means, electronic or mechanical, including photocopying or recording, or by any information storage and retrieval system, without the prior written permission of the copyright owner unless such copying is expressly permitted by federal copyright law. Requests for permission to make copies of any part of the work should be addressed to Houghton Mifflin Harcourt Publishing Company, Attn: Contracts, Copyrights, and Licensing, 9400 Southpark Center Loop, Orlando, Florida 32819-8647.

Printed in the U.S.A.

ISBN 978-0-544-27430-3

3 4 5 6 7 8 9 10 0877 22 21 20 19 18 17 16 15 14

4500460774   A B C D E F G

If you have received these materials as examination copies free of charge, Houghton Mifflin Harcourt Publishing Company retains title to the materials and they may not be resold. Resale of examination copies is strictly prohibited.

Possession of this publication in print format does not entitle users to convert this publication, or any portion of it, into electronic format.

Social Studies

Table of Contents

About the GED® Test

Welcome to the first day of the rest of your life. Now that you've committed to study for your GED® credential, an array of possibilities and options—academic, career, and otherwise—await you. Each year, hundreds of thousands of people just like you decide to pursue a GED® credential. Like you, they left traditional school for one reason or another. Now, just like them, you've decided to continue your education by studying for and taking the GED® Test.

Today's GED® Test is very different from the one your grandparents may have taken. Today's GED® Test is new, improved, and more rigorous, with content aligned to the Common Core State Standards. For the first time, the GED® Test serves both as a high-school equivalency degree and as a predictor of college and career readiness. The new GED® Test features four subject areas: Reasoning Through Language Arts (RLA), Mathematical Reasoning, Science, and Social Studies. Each subject area is delivered via a computer-based format and includes an array of technology-enhanced item types.

The four subject-area exams together comprise a testing time of seven hours. Preparation can take considerably longer. The payoff, however, is significant: more and better career options, higher earnings, and the sense of achievement that comes with a GED® credential. Both employers and colleges and universities alike accept the GED® credential as they would a high school diploma. On average, GED® graduates earn at least $8,400 more per year than those with an incomplete high school education.

The GED® Testing Service has constructed the GED® Test to mirror a high school experience. As such, you must answer a variety of questions within and across specific subject areas. For example, you may encounter a Social Studies passage on the Reasoning Through Language Arts Test, and vice versa. The following table details the content areas, quantity of items, score points, Depth of Knowledge (DOK) levels—the cognitive effort required to answer a given item—and total testing time.

Subject Area Test	Content Areas	Items	Raw Score Points	DOK Level	Time
Reasoning Through Language Arts	**Informational texts**—75% **Literary texts**—25%	*51	65	80% of items at Level 2 or 3	150 minutes
Mathematical Reasoning	**Algebraic Problem Solving**—55% **Quantitative Problem Solving**—45%	*46	49	50% of items at Level 2	90 minutes
Science	**Life Science**—40% **Physical Science**—40% **Earth/Space Science**—20%	*34	40	80% of items at Level 2 or 3	90 minutes
Social Studies	**Civics/Government**—50% **U.S. History**—20% **Economics**—15% **Geography and the World**—15%	*35	44	80% of items at Level 2 or 3	90 minutes

* Number of items may vary slightly by test.

Because the demands of today's high school education and its relationship to workforce needs differ from those of a decade ago, the GED® Testing Service has moved to a computer-based format. Although multiple-choice questions remain the dominant type of item on the new, computer-based GED® Test series, they've been joined by a variety of new, technology-enhanced item types: drop-down, fill-in-the-blank, drag-and-drop, hot spot, short answer, and extended response items.

The table to the right illustrates the various item types and their distribution on the new subject-area exams. As you can see, all four tests include multiple-choice, drop-down, fill-in-the-blank, and drag-and-drop items. Some variation occurs with hot spot, short answer, and extended response items.

2014 ITEM TYPES

	RLA	Math	Science	Social Studies
Multiple-choice	✓	✓	✓	✓
Drop-down	✓	✓	✓	✓
Fill-in-the-blank	✓	✓	✓	✓
Drag-and-drop	✓	✓	✓	✓
Hot spot		✓	✓	✓
Short answer			✓	
Extended response	✓			✓

Items on each subject-area exam connect to three factors:

- **Content Topics/Assessment Targets:** These topics and targets describe and detail the content on the GED® Test. They tie to the Common Core State Standards, as well as state standards for Texas and Virginia.
- **Content Practices:** These practices describe the types of reasoning and modes of thinking required to answer specific items on the GED® Test.
- **Depth of Knowledge (DOK):** The Depth of Knowledge model details the level of cognitive complexity and steps required to arrive at a correct answer on the test. For the new GED® Test, there are three levels of DOK complexity:
  - **Level 1:** Test takers must recall, observe, question, or represent facts or simple skills. Typically, they must exhibit only a surface understanding of text.
  - **Level 2:** Test takers must process information beyond simple recall and observation to include summarizing, ordering, classifying, identifying patterns and relationships, and connecting ideas. Test takers must scrutinize text.
  - **Level 3:** Test takers must explain, generalize, and connect ideas by inferring, elaborating, and predicting. Test takers must summarize from multiple sources, and use that information to develop compositions with multiple paragraphs. Those paragraphs should feature a critical analysis of sources, include supporting positions from the test takers' own experiences, and reflect editing to ensure coherent, correct writing.

Approximately 80 percent of items across all four content areas will be written to DOK Levels 2 and 3, with the remainder at Level 1. Writing portions, such as the extended response item in Social Studies (25 minutes) and Reasoning Through Language Arts (45 minutes), are considered DOK Level 3 items.

Now that you understand the basic structure of the GED® Test and the benefits of earning a GED® credential, you must prepare for the GED® Test. In the pages that follow, you will find a recipe of sorts that, if followed, will guide you toward successful completion of your GED® credential. So turn the page. The next chapter of your life begins right now.

GED® Test on Computer

Along with fresh item types, the 2014 GED® Test also unveils a new, computer-based testing experience. The GED® Test will be available on computer and only at approved Pearson VUE Testing Centers. Along with content knowledge and the ability to read, think, and write critically, you must perform basic computer functions—clicking, scrolling, and typing—to succeed on the test. The screen below closely resembles a screen that you will experience on the GED® Test.

The **INFORMATION** button contains material vital to the successful completion of the item. Here, by clicking the Information button, a test taker enables a map about the American Revolution. On the Mathematical Reasoning exam, similar buttons for **FORMULA SHEET** and **CALCULATOR REFERENCE** provide information that will help learners like you answer items that require use of formulas or the TI-30XS calculator. You may move a passage or graphic by clicking and dragging to a different part of the test screen.

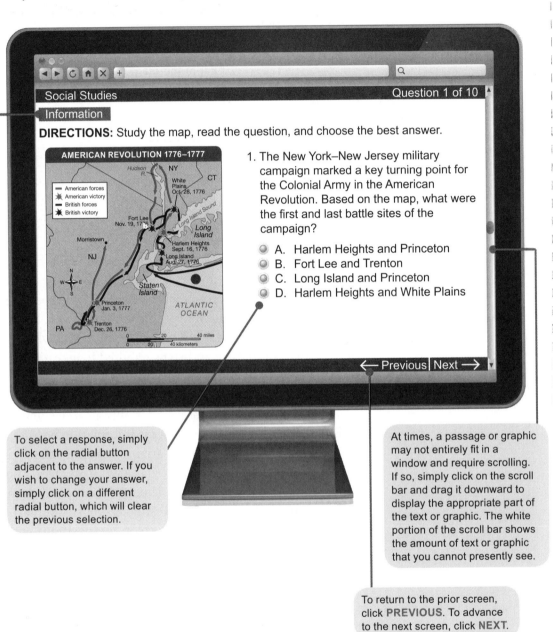

To select a response, simply click on the radial button adjacent to the answer. If you wish to change your answer, simply click on a different radial button, which will clear the previous selection.

At times, a passage or graphic may not entirely fit in a window and require scrolling. If so, simply click on the scroll bar and drag it downward to display the appropriate part of the text or graphic. The white portion of the scroll bar shows the amount of text or graphic that you cannot presently see.

To return to the prior screen, click **PREVIOUS**. To advance to the next screen, click **NEXT**.

Some items on the new GED® Test, such as fill-in-the-blank, short answer, and extended response questions, will require you to type answers into an entry box. In some cases, the directions may specify the range of typing the system may accept. For example, a fill-in-the-blank item may allow you to type a number from 0 to 9, along with a decimal point or a slash, but nothing else. The system also will tell you keys to avoid pressing in certain situations. The annotated computer and keyboard below provide strategies for entering text and data for fill-in-the-blank, short answer, and extended response items.

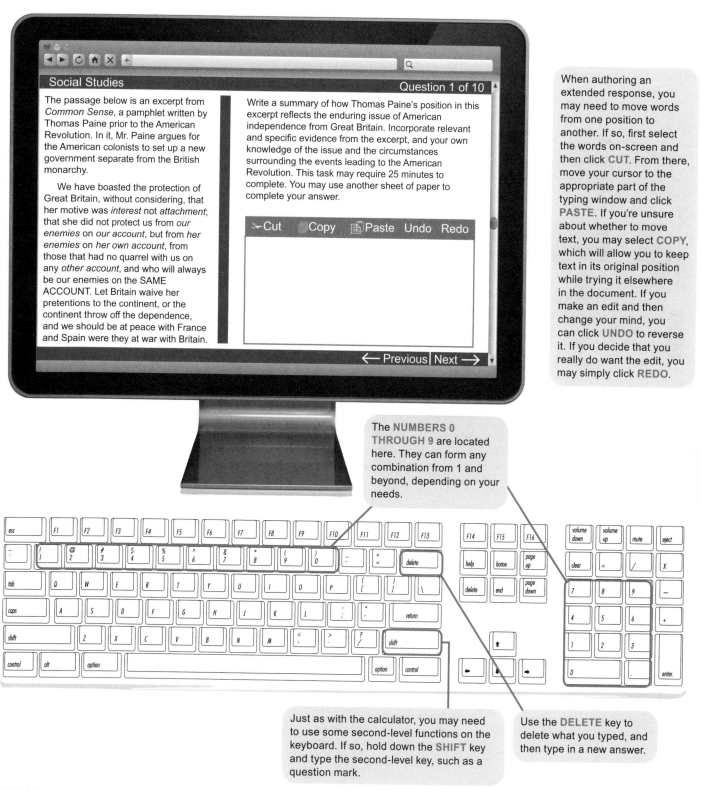

Social Studies   Question 1 of 10

The passage below is an excerpt from *Common Sense*, a pamphlet written by Thomas Paine prior to the American Revolution. In it, Mr. Paine argues for the American colonists to set up a new government separate from the British monarchy.

We have boasted the protection of Great Britain, without considering, that her motive was *interest* not *attachment*; that she did not protect us from *our enemies* on *our account*, but from *her enemies* on *her own account*, from those that had no quarrel with us on any *other account*, and who will always be our enemies on the SAME ACCOUNT. Let Britain waive her pretentions to the continent, or the continent throw off the dependence, and we should be at peace with France and Spain were they at war with Britain.

Write a summary of how Thomas Paine's position in this excerpt reflects the enduring issue of American independence from Great Britain. Incorporate relevant and specific evidence from the excerpt, and your own knowledge of the issue and the circumstances surrounding the events leading to the American Revolution. This task may require 25 minutes to complete. You may use another sheet of paper to complete your answer.

✂ Cut   📋 Copy   📋 Paste   Undo   Redo

← Previous | Next →

When authoring an extended response, you may need to move words from one position to another. If so, first select the words on-screen and then click **CUT**. From there, move your cursor to the appropriate part of the typing window and click **PASTE**. If you're unsure about whether to move text, you may select **COPY**, which will allow you to keep text in its original position while trying it elsewhere in the document. If you make an edit and then change your mind, you can click **UNDO** to reverse it. If you decide that you really do want the edit, you may simply click **REDO**.

The **NUMBERS 0 THROUGH 9** are located here. They can form any combination from 1 and beyond, depending on your needs.

Just as with the calculator, you may need to use some second-level functions on the keyboard. If so, hold down the **SHIFT** key and type the second-level key, such as a question mark.

Use the **DELETE** key to delete what you typed, and then type in a new answer.

GED® Test on Computer

About *Steck-Vaughn*
Test Preparation for the 2014 GED® Test

Along with choosing to pursue your GED® credential, you've made another smart decision by selecting *Steck-Vaughn's Test Preparation for the 2014 GED® Test* as your main study and preparation tool. Our emphasis on the acquisition of key reading and thinking concepts equips learners like you with the skills and strategies to succeed on the GED® Test.

Two-page micro-lessons in each student book provide focused and efficient instruction. For those who require additional support, we offer companion workbooks, which provide *twice* the support and practice exercises. Each lesson in the series includes a *Spotlighted Item* feature that corresponds to one of the technology-enhanced item types that appear on the GED® Test.

The **LEARN THE SKILL** section provides information about the skill to be studied.

Each lesson includes correlations to subject-area **CONTENT TOPICS** and **PRACTICES** that will help focus your studies.

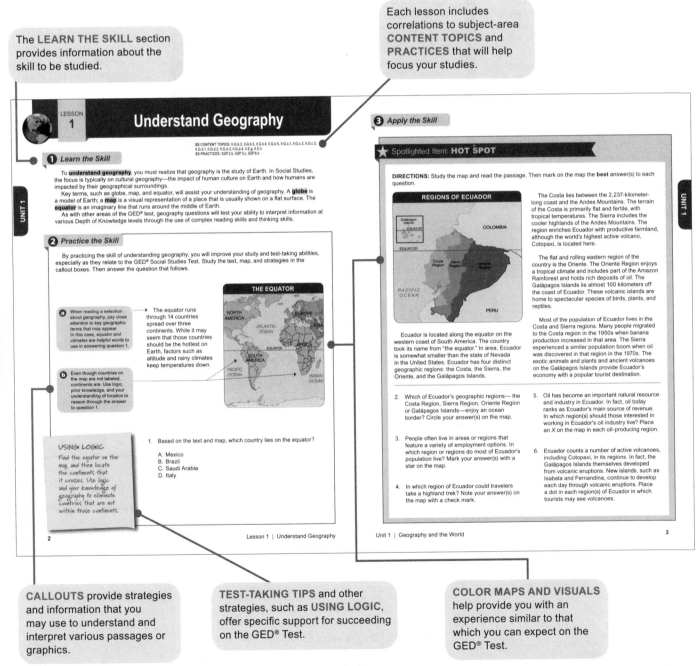

CALLOUTS provide strategies and information that you may use to understand and interpret various passages or graphics.

TEST-TAKING TIPS and other strategies, such as **USING LOGIC**, offer specific support for succeeding on the GED® Test.

COLOR MAPS AND VISUALS help provide you with an experience similar to that which you can expect on the GED® Test.

Unit Reviews and Answer Keys

Every unit opens with the feature GED® Journeys, a series of profiles of people who earned and used their GED® credential as a springboard to future success. From there, you receive in-depth instruction and practice through a series of linked lessons, all of which tie to Content Topics/Assessment Targets, Content Practices, and Depth of Knowledge levels.

Each unit closes with an eight-page review that includes a representative sampling of items, including technology-enhanced item types, from the lessons that comprise the unit. You may use each unit review as a posttest to gauge your mastery of content and skills and readiness for that aspect of the GED® Test.

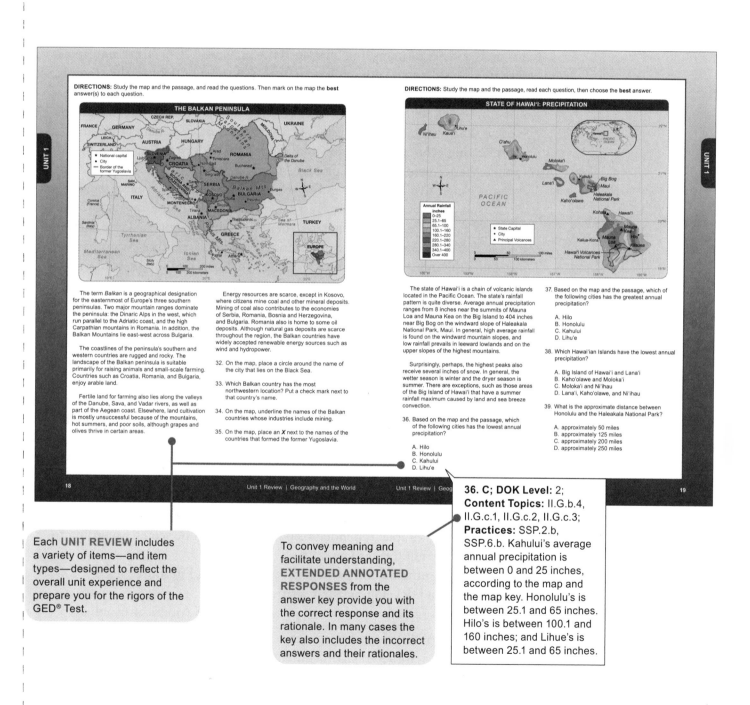

DIRECTIONS: Study the map and the passage, and read the questions. Then mark on the map the **best** answer(s) to each question.

THE BALKAN PENINSULA

The term *Balkan* is a geographical designation for the easternmost of Europe's three southern peninsulas. Two major mountain ranges dominate the peninsula: the Dinaric Alps in the west, which run parallel to the Adriatic coast, and the high Carpathian mountains in Romania. In addition, the Balkan Mountains lie east-west across Bulgaria.

The coastlines of the peninsula's southern and western countries are rugged and rocky. The landscape of the Balkan peninsula is suitable primarily for raising animals and small-scale farming. Countries such as Croatia, Romania, and Bulgaria, enjoy arable land.

Fertile land for farming also lies along the valleys of the Danube, Sava, and Vadar rivers, as well as part of the Aegean coast. Elsewhere, land cultivation is mostly unsuccessful because of the mountains, hot summers, and poor soils, although grapes and olives thrive in certain areas.

Energy resources are scarce, except in Kosovo, where citizens mine coal and other mineral deposits. Mining of coal also contributes to the economies of Serbia, Romania, Bosnia and Herzegovina, and Bulgaria. Romania also is home to some oil deposits. Although natural gas deposits are scarce throughout the region, the Balkan countries have widely accepted renewable energy sources such as wind and hydropower.

32. On the map, place a circle around the name of the city that lies on the Black Sea.

33. Which Balkan country has the most northwestern location? Put a check mark next to that country's name.

34. On the map, underline the names of the Balkan countries whose industries include mining.

35. On the map, place an **X** next to the names of the countries that formed the former Yugoslavia.

DIRECTIONS: Study the map and the passage, read each question, then choose the **best** answer.

STATE OF HAWAI'I: PRECIPITATION

The state of Hawai'i is a chain of volcanic islands located in the Pacific Ocean. The state's rainfall pattern is quite diverse. Average annual precipitation ranges from 8 inches near the summits of Mauna Loa and Mauna Kea on the Big Island to 404 inches near Big Bog on the windward slope of Haleakala National Park, Maui. In general, high average rainfall is found on the windward mountain slopes, and low rainfall prevails in leeward lowlands and on the upper slopes of the highest mountains.

Surprisingly, perhaps, the highest peaks also receive several inches of snow. In general, the wetter season is winter and the dryer season is summer. There are exceptions, such as those areas of the Big Island of Hawai'i that have a summer rainfall maximum caused by land and sea breeze convection.

36. Based on the map and the passage, which of the following cities has the lowest annual precipitation?

A. Hilo
B. Honolulu
C. Kahului
D. Lihu'e

37. Based on the map and the passage, which of the following cities has the greatest annual precipitation?

A. Hilo
B. Honolulu
C. Kahului
D. Lihu'e

38. Which Hawai'ian Islands have the lowest annual precipitation?

A. Big Island of Hawai'i and Lana'i
B. Kaho'olawe and Moloka'i
C. Moloka'i and Ni'ihau
D. Lana'i, Kaho'olawe, and Ni'ihau

39. What is the approximate distance between Honolulu and the Haleakala National Park?

A. approximately 50 miles
B. approximately 125 miles
C. approximately 200 miles
D. approximately 250 miles

18   Unit 1 Review | Geography and the World   Unit 1 Review | Geog...   19

Each **UNIT REVIEW** includes a variety of items—and item types—designed to reflect the overall unit experience and prepare you for the rigors of the GED® Test.

To convey meaning and facilitate understanding, **EXTENDED ANNOTATED RESPONSES** from the answer key provide you with the correct response and its rationale. In many cases the key also includes the incorrect answers and their rationales.

36. C; DOK Level: 2; **Content Topics:** II.G.b.4, II.G.c.1, II.G.c.2, II.G.c.3; **Practices:** SSP.2.b, SSP.6.b. Kahului's average annual precipitation is between 0 and 25 inches, according to the map and the map key. Honolulu's is between 25.1 and 65 inches. Hilo's is between 100.1 and 160 inches; and Lihue's is between 25.1 and 65 inches.

About the GED® Social Studies Test

The new GED® Social Studies Test is more than just a set of dates and events. In fact, it reflects an attempt to increase the rigor of the GED® Test to better meet the demands of a 21st-century economy. To that end, the GED® Social Studies Test features an array of technology-aided item types. All of the items are delivered via computer-based testing. The items reflect the knowledge, skills, and abilities that a student would master in an equivalent high school experience.

Multiple-choice questions remain the majority of items on the GED® Social Studies Test. However, a number of technology-enhanced items, including fill-in-the-blank, drop-down, drag-and-drop, hot spot, and extended response questions—will challenge learners like you to master and convey knowledge in deeper, fuller ways. For example:

- Multiple-choice items will assess virtually every content standard as either discrete items or as a series of items. In contrast to the previous GED® Test, multiple-choice items on the new series will include four answer options (rather than five), structured in an A./B./C./D. format.

- Fill-in-the-blank items allow test takers to type in one-word or short answers. For example, test takers may be asked to identify a particular data point on a chart reflecting economic trends or to demonstrate understanding of an idea or vocabulary term mentioned in a passage.

- Drop-down items will include a pull-down menu of response choices, enabling test takers to complete statements. Test takers may encounter drop-down items on the GED® Social Studies Test that ask them to identify a conclusion drawn from text-based evidence or make a generalization based on an author's argument.

- Drag-and-drop items involve interactive tasks that require test takers to move small images, words, or numerical expressions into designated drop zones on a computer screen. They may assess how well test takers make comparisons between concepts or data or how well they classify or order information. For example, test takers may be asked to place labels on a map to indicate commodities produced in various regions. Other items may ask test takers to place data points or labels drawn from a brief passage onto a graph or chart.

- Hot spot items consist of a graphic with virtual sensors placed strategically within it. They allow you to demonstrate understanding of geographic concepts with regard to mapping. Other uses of hot spot items may involve selecting data or points in a table, chart, or graph that support or refute a given conclusion stated in the text.

- An extended response item on the GED® Social Studies Test will be a 25-minute task that requires test takers to analyze one or more source texts in order to produce a writing sample. Extended response items will be scored according to how well learners fulfill three key traits:
    - analyzing arguments and gathering evidence found in source texts
    - organizing and developing their writing
    - demonstrating fluency with conventions of Edited American English

You will have a total of 90 minutes in which to answer about 35 items. The social studies test is organized across four main content areas: civics and government (50 percent of all items), United States history (20 percent), economics (15 percent), and geography and the world (15 percent). All told, 80 percent of the items on the GED® Social Studies Test will be written at Depth of Knowledge Levels 2 or 3.

About *Steck-Vaughn Test Preparation for the 2014 GED® Test: Social Studies*

Steck-Vaughn's student book and workbook help unlock the learning and deconstruct the different elements of the test by helping learners like you build and develop core reading and thinking skills. The content of our books aligns to the new GED® social studies content standards and item distribution to provide you with a superior test preparation experience.

Our *Spotlighted Item* feature provides a deeper, richer treatment for each technology-enhanced item type. On initial introduction, a unique item type—such as drag-and-drop—receives a full page of example items in the student book lesson and three pages in the companion workbook. The length of subsequent features may be shorter depending on the skill, lesson, and requirements.

A combination of targeted strategies, informational call-outs and sample questions, assorted tips and hints, and ample assessment help to clearly focus study efforts in needed areas.

In addition to the book features, a highly detailed answer key provides the correct answer and the rationale for it so that you know exactly why an answer is correct. The *Social Studies* student book and workbook are designed with an eye toward the end goal: Success on the GED® Social Studies Test.

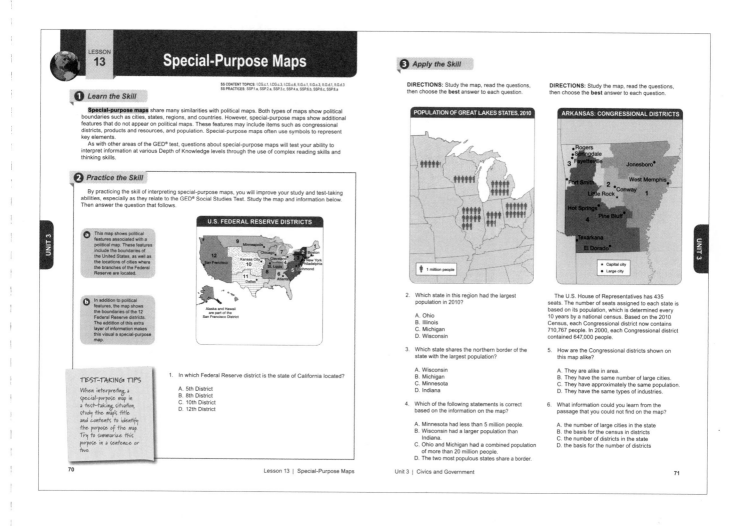

Calculator Directions

Certain items on the GED® Mathematical Reasoning Test allow for the use of a calculator to aid in answering questions. That calculator, the TI-30XS, is embedded within the testing interface. The TI-30XS calculator will be available for most items on the GED® Mathematical Reasoning Test and for some items on the GED® Science Test and GED® Social Studies Test. The TI-30XS calculator is shown below, along with callouts of some of its most important keys. A button that will enable the calculator reference sheet will appear in the upper right corner of the testing screen.

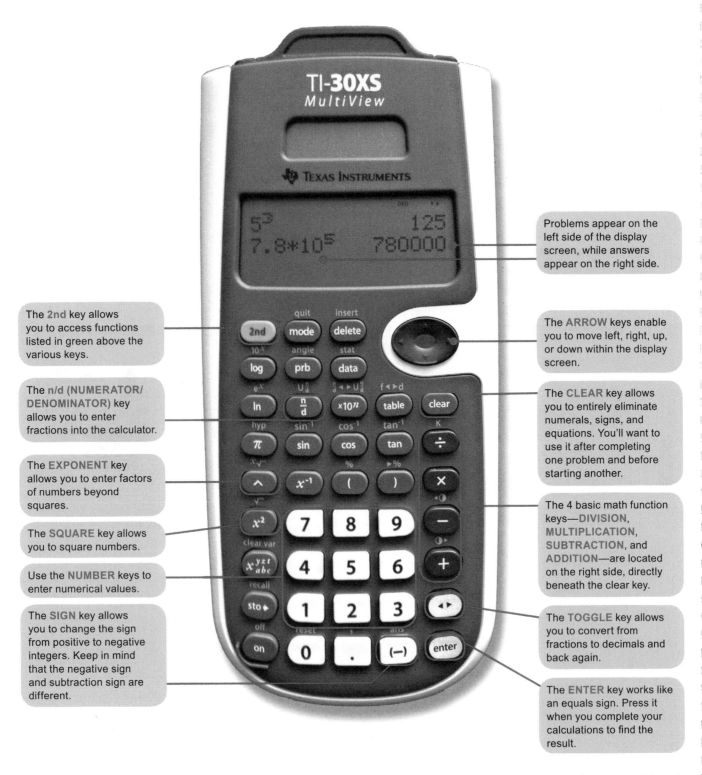

The **2nd** key allows you to access functions listed in green above the various keys.

The **n/d (NUMERATOR/DENOMINATOR)** key allows you to enter fractions into the calculator.

The **EXPONENT** key allows you to enter factors of numbers beyond squares.

The **SQUARE** key allows you to square numbers.

Use the **NUMBER** keys to enter numerical values.

The **SIGN** key allows you to change the sign from positive to negative integers. Keep in mind that the negative sign and subtraction sign are different.

Problems appear on the left side of the display screen, while answers appear on the right side.

The **ARROW** keys enable you to move left, right, up, or down within the display screen.

The **CLEAR** key allows you to entirely eliminate numerals, signs, and equations. You'll want to use it after completing one problem and before starting another.

The 4 basic math function keys—**DIVISION, MULTIPLICATION, SUBTRACTION,** and **ADDITION**—are located on the right side, directly beneath the clear key.

The **TOGGLE** key allows you to convert from fractions to decimals and back again.

The **ENTER** key works like an equals sign. Press it when you complete your calculations to find the result.

Getting Started

To enable the calculator on a question that allows it, click on the upper left-hand portion of the testing screen. If the calculator displays over top of a problem, you may move it by clicking and dragging it to another part of the screen. Once enabled, the calculator will be ready for use (no need to push the **on** key).

- Use the **clear** key to clear all numbers and operations from the screen.
- Use the **enter** key to complete all calculations.

2nd key

The green **2nd** key is located in the upper left corner of the TI-30XS. The **2nd** key enables a second series of function keys, which are located above other function keys and noted in green type. To use the 2nd-level function, first click the numeral, next click the **2nd** key, and then click the 2nd-level function key you need. For example, to enter **25%**, first enter the number [**25**]. Then click the **2nd** key, and finally click the 2nd-level **%** key (1st-level *beginning parenthesis* sign).

Fractions and Mixed Numbers

To enter fractions, such as $\frac{3}{4}$, click the **n/d** (**numerator/denominator**) key, followed by the numerator quantity [**3**]. Next, click the **down arrow** button (upper right corner of the calculator), followed by the denominator quantity [**4**]. To calculate with fractions, click the **right arrow** button and then the appropriate function key and other numerals in the equation.

To enter mixed numbers, such as $1\frac{3}{8}$, first enter the whole number quantity [**1**]. Next, click the **2nd** key and the **mixed number** key (1st level **n/d**). Then enter the fraction numerator [**3**], followed by the **down arrow** button, and the denominator [**8**]. If you click **enter**, the mixed number will convert to an improper fraction. To calculate with mixed numbers, click the **right arrow** button and then the appropriate function key and other numerals in the equation.

Negative Numbers

To enter a negative number, click the **negative sign** key (located directly below the number **3** on the calculator). Please note that the negative sign key differs from the subtraction key, which is found in the far right column of keys, directly above the plus (+) key.

Squares, Square Roots, and Exponents

- **Squares:** The x^2 key squares numbers. The **exponent** key (^) raises numbers to powers higher than squares, such as cubes. To find the answer to 5^3 on the calculator, first enter the base number [**5**], then click the exponent key (^), and follow by clicking the exponent number [**3**], and the **enter** key.
- **Square Roots:** To find the square root of a number, such as 36, first click the **2nd** key, then click the **square root** key (1st-level x^2), then the number [**36**], and finally **enter**.
- **Cube Roots:** To find the cube root of a number, such as **125**, first enter the cube as a number [**3**], followed by the **2nd** key and **square root** key. Finally, enter the number for which you want to find the cube [**125**], followed by **enter**.
- **Exponents:** To perform calculations with numbers expressed in scientific notation, such as 7.8×10^9, first enter the base number [**7.8**]. Next, click the **scientific notation** key (located directly beneath the **data** key), followed by the exponent level [**9**]. You then have 7.8×10^9.

Test-Taking Tips

The new GED® Test includes more than 160 items across the four subject-area exams of Reasoning Through Language Arts, Mathematical Reasoning, Science, and Social Studies. The four subject-area exams represent a total test time of seven hours. Most items are multiple-choice questions, but a number are technology-enhanced items. These include drop-down, fill-in-the-blank, drag-and-drop, hot spot, short answer, and extended response items.

Throughout this book and others in the series, we help learners like you build, develop, and apply core reading and thinking skills critical to success on the GED® Test. As part of an overall strategy, we suggest that you use the test-taking tips below and throughout the book to improve your performance on the GED® Test.

➤ **Always thoroughly read directions so that you know exactly what to do.** As we've noted, the 2014 GED® Test has an entirely new computer-based format that includes a variety of technology-aided items. If you are unclear of what to do or how to proceed, ask the test provider whether directions can be explained.

➤ **Read each question carefully so that you fully understand what it is asking.** Some items, for example, may present information beyond what is necessary to correctly answer them. Other questions may use boldfaced words for emphasis (for example, "Which statement represents the **most** appropriate revision for this hypothesis?").

➤ **Manage your time with each question.** Because the GED® Test is a series of timed exams, you want to spend enough time with each question, but not *too* much time. For example, on the GED® Mathematical Reasoning Test, you have 90 minutes in which to answer approximately 46 questions. That works out to an average of about 2 minutes per item. Obviously, some items will require more time than that and others will require less, but you should remain aware of the overall number of items and amount of testing time. The new GED® Test interface may help you manage time. It includes an on-screen clock in the upper right corner that provides the remaining time in which to complete a test.

You may also monitor your progress by viewing the **Question** line, which will give you the current question number, followed by the total number of questions on that subject-area exam.

➤ **Answer all questions, regardless of whether you know the answer or are guessing.** There is no benefit in leaving questions unanswered on the GED® Test. Keep in mind the time that you have for each test and manage it accordingly. If you wish to review a specific item at the end of a test, you may click **Flag for Review** to mark the question. When you do, the flag will display in yellow. At the end of a test, you may have time to review questions you've marked.

➤ **Skim and scan.** You may save time by first reading each question and its answer options before reading an accompanying passage or graphic. Once you understand what the question is asking, review the passage or visual for the appropriate information.

➤ **Note any unfamiliar words in questions.** First attempt to re-read the question by omitting any unfamiliar word(s). Next, try to substitute another word in its place.

➤ **Narrow answer options by re-reading each question and re-examining the text or graphic that goes with it.** Although four answers are *possible* on multiple-choice items, keep in mind that only one of them is *correct*. You may be able to eliminate one answer immediately; you may need to take more time or use logic or assumptions to eliminate others. In some cases, you may need to make your best guess between two options.

➤ **Go with your instinct when answering questions.** If your first instinct is to choose **A** in response to a question, it's best to stick with that answer unless you know that answer is incorrect. Usually, the first answer someone chooses is the correct one.

Study Skills

You've already made two very smart decisions in studying for your GED® credential and in purchasing *Steck-Vaughn Test Preparation for the 2014 GED® Test: Social Studies* to help you to do so. Following are additional strategies to help you optimize success on the GED® Test.

4 weeks out ...

➤ **Set a study schedule for the GED® Test.** Choose times in which you are most alert and places, such as a library, that provide the best study environment.

➤ **Thoroughly review all material in *Steck-Vaughn Test Preparation for the 2014 GED® Test: Social Studies*, using the *Social Studies Workbook* to extend understanding of concepts in the *Social Studies Student Book*.**

➤ **Keep notebooks for each of the subject areas that you are studying.** Folders with pockets are useful for storing loose papers.

➤ **When taking notes, restate thoughts or ideas in your own words rather than copying them directly from a book.** You can phrase these notes as complete sentences, as questions (with answers), or as fragments, provided you understand them.

2 weeks out ...

➤ **Take the pretests, noting any troublesome subject areas.** Focus your remaining study around those subject areas.

The day before ...

➤ **Map out the route to the test center, and visit it a day or two before your scheduled exam.** If you drive, find a place to park at the center.

➤ **Get a good night's sleep the night before the GED® Test.** Studies have shown that students with sufficient rest perform better in testing situations.

The day of ...

➤ **Eat a hearty breakfast high in protein.** As with the rest of your body, your brain needs ample energy to perform well.

➤ **Arrive 30 minutes early to the testing center.** This will allow sufficient time in the event of change to a different testing classroom.

➤ **Pack a sizeable lunch,** especially if you plan to be at the testing center most of the day.

➤ **Remember to relax.** You've come this far and have spent weeks preparing and studying for the GED® Test. Now, it's your time to shine!

UNIT
1

Jon M. Huntsman

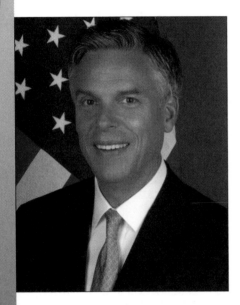

Jon Huntsman attended Highland High School in Salt Lake City, Utah, and became an Eagle Scout at age 15. He then left school to pursue a musical career and obtained his GED® certificate.

Jon M. Huntsman understood the value of hard work at an early age. As a child, he helped his father sell goods to grocery stores and started his own lawn mowing business. In school Huntsman wanted a career in music, dropping out to play in a rock band. He then earned his GED® certificate and went to college, studying international politics. During his college years, Huntsman also served as a missionary in Taiwan, where he learned to speak Mandarin Chinese.

In the 1980s, Huntsman worked for President Ronald Reagan, then moved to Taiwan to oversee his family's manufacturing company. In 1992, at the age of 32, he became the U.S. Ambassador to Singapore. Back home, Huntsman directed the Huntsman Cancer Foundation, where he promoted cancer awareness and raised funds for cancer patients.

Yet, politics still beckoned. Huntsman was elected governor of Utah in 2004, winning re-election by a landslide in 2008. He left the governorship in 2009, when President Barack Obama asked him to become the U.S. Ambassador to China, a post he held until 2011. In June of that year, Huntsman campaigned for President of the United States, highlighting his goal to increase national economic growth. Although he failed to receive his party's nomination, Huntsman remains prominent in both business and politics.

"One thing I've learned is that your life will never be complete until you find your most deep-rooted passion. And you'll never find your passion until you learn to follow your heart."

CAREER HIGHLIGHTS: *Jon M. Huntsman*

- Born in Palo Alto, California
- Speaks fluent Mandarin Chinese
- Served as a missionary in Taiwan while in college

- Twice elected governor of Utah
- Helps lead No Labels, an organization dedicated to solving U.S. political issues

Geography and the World

Unit 1: Geography and the World

Geography shapes the world in which we live. Throughout history, geographic features influenced important aspects of people's lives. Regions throughout the world have natural geographic barriers such as mountains, oceans, and rivers, and have thus been separated by cultural, economic, and language differences. The world today, however, *is* becoming a smaller place, due to technologies such as various forms of satellite and wireless communications, thereby enabling people to bridge geographic barriers and study and experience other cultures. Geography plays a major role in discovering your place in today's ever-changing world.

The importance of geography and the world around you also extends to the GED® Social Studies Test, making up 15 percent of all questions. As with other areas of the GED® Tests, questions about geography and the world will test your ability to read, analyze, and interpret various types of maps and to answer questions about them. Unit 1 will help you prepare for the GED® Social Studies Test.

Table of Contents

Architects, surveyors, engineers, teachers, and various other occupations depend on employees with geographic knowledge and skills.

Understand Geography

SS CONTENT TOPICS: II.G.b.2, II.G.b.3, II.G.b.4, II.G.b.5, II.G.c.1, II.G.c.2, II.G.c.3,
II.G.d.1, II.G.d.2, II.G.d.3, II.G.d.4, II.E.g, II.E.h
SS PRACTICES: SSP.2.b, SSP.3.c, SSP.6.b

UNIT 1

1 Learn the Skill

To **understand geography**, you must realize that geography is the study of Earth. In Social Studies, the focus is typically on cultural geography—the impact of human culture on Earth and how humans are impacted by their geographical surroundings.

Key terms, such as globe, map, and equator, will assist your understanding of geography. A **globe** is a model of Earth; a **map** is a visual representation of a place that is usually shown on a flat surface. The **equator** is an imaginary line that runs around the middle of Earth.

As with other areas of the GED® test, geography questions will test your ability to interpret information at various Depth of Knowledge levels through the use of complex reading skills and thinking skills.

2 Practice the Skill

By practicing the skill of understanding geography, you will improve your study and test-taking abilities, especially as they relate to the GED® Social Studies Test. Study the text, map, and strategies in the callout boxes. Then answer the question that follows.

a When reading a selection about geography, pay close attention to key geographic terms that may appear. In this case, *equator* and *climates* are helpful words to use in answering question 1.

The equator runs through 14 countries spread over three continents. While it may seem that those countries should be the hottest on Earth, factors such as altitude and rainy climates keep temperatures down.

b Even though countries on the map are not labeled, continents are. Use logic, prior knowledge, and your understanding of location to reason through the answer to question 1.

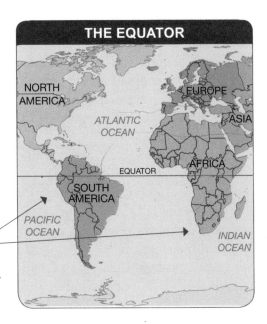

THE EQUATOR

ASK About This one

USING LOGIC

Find the equator on the map, and then locate the continents that it crosses. Use logic and your knowledge of geography to eliminate countries that are not within those continents.

1. Based on the text and map, which country lies on the equator?

   A. Mexico
   B. Brazil
   C. Saudi Arabia
   D. Italy

UNIT 1

★ Spotlighted Item: **HOT SPOT**

DIRECTIONS: Study the map and read the passage. Then mark on the map the **best** answer(s) to each question.

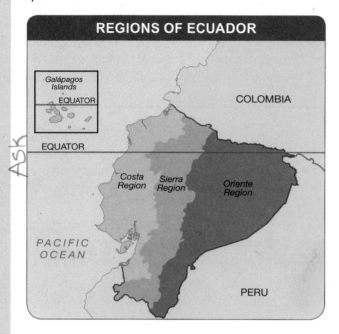

REGIONS OF ECUADOR

Galápagos Islands
EQUATOR

COLOMBIA

EQUATOR

Costa Region   Sierra Region   Oriente Region

PACIFIC OCEAN

PERU

Ecuador is located along the equator on the western coast of South America. The country took its name from "the equator." In area, Ecuador is somewhat smaller than the state of Nevada in the United States. Ecuador has four distinct geographic regions: the Costa, the Sierra, the Oriente, and the Galápagos Islands.

The Costa lies between the 2,237-kilometer-long coast and the Andes Mountains. The terrain of the Costa is primarily flat and fertile, with tropical temperatures. The Sierra includes the cooler highlands of the Andes Mountains. The region enriches Ecuador with productive farmland, although the world's highest active volcano, Cotopaxi, is located here.

The flat and rolling eastern region of the country is the Oriente. The Oriente Region enjoys a tropical climate and includes part of the Amazon Rainforest and holds rich deposits of oil. The Galápagos Islands lie almost 100 kilometers off the coast of Ecuador. These volcanic islands are home to spectacular species of birds, plants, and reptiles.

Most of the population of Ecuador lives in the Costa and Sierra regions. Many people migrated to the Costa region in the 1950s when banana production increased in that area. The Sierra experienced a similar population boom when oil was discovered in that region in the 1970s. The exotic animals and plants and ancient volcanoes on the Galápagos Islands provide Ecuador's economy with a popular tourist destination.

2. Which of Ecuador's geographic regions— the Costa Region, Sierra Region, Oriente Region or Galápagos Islands—enjoy an ocean border? Circle your answer(s) on the map.

3. People often live in areas or regions that feature a variety of employment options. In which region or regions do most of Ecuador's population live? Mark your answer(s) with a star on the map.

4. In which region of Ecuador could travelers take a highland trek? Note your answer(s) on the map with a check mark.

5. Oil has become an important natural resource and industry in Ecuador. In fact, oil today ranks as Ecuador's main source of revenue. In which region(s) should those interested in working in Ecuador's oil industry live? Place an *X* on the map in each oil-producing region.

6. Ecuador counts a number of active volcanoes, including Cotopaxi, in its regions. In fact, the Galápagos Islands themselves developed from volcanic eruptions. New islands, such as Isabela and Fernandina, continue to develop each day through volcanic eruptions. Place a dot in each region(s) of Ecuador in which tourists may see volcanoes.

Understand Map Components

SS CONTENT TOPICS: II.G.b.1, II.G.b.3, II.G.b.5, II.G.c.1, II.G.c.3, II.G.d.3, II.G.d.4
SS PRACTICES: SSP.2.b, SSP.6.b

UNIT 1

1 Learn the Skill

When you begin to analyze maps, you must first **understand map components.** Maps often include the following components: 1. **Scales** have small marks that stand for miles and kilometers. Scales help measure real distances on Earth. 2. **Lines of longitude** and **lines of latitude** are used to find exact, or absolute, locations of places. Lines of longitude run north-south, while lines of latitude run east-west. Relative location describes the position of a place in relation to other places. 3. **Symbols**, such as dots for cities, stars for capital cities, or icons for special events such as battles, can help you understand details on a map. Symbols are explained in the **map key**. Different types of maps use different symbols. Map titles, compass roses, and labels also are useful tools on a map.

2 Practice the Skill

By mastering the skill of understanding map components, you will improve your study and test-taking skills, especially as they relate to the GED® Social Studies Test. Analyze the map below, study the boxed information to the left of the map, and then answer the question that follows.

a When you start to analyze a map, examine all of the components, such as the title and key. This will help you determine the purpose of the map.

b Use the map scale to measure distances between cities.

a

NEW JERSEY: MAJOR CITIES

NY

Paterson
East Orange • Newark
Elizabeth • Jersey City
Edison

PA

NEW JERSEY

ATLANTIC OCEAN

★ Trenton

Beachwood
Camden

N
W ⬥ E
S

a
★ State capital
• Major city

DE

Cape May

b
0   25   50 miles
0   25   50 kilometers

USING LOGIC

A compass rose "⬥" is a map symbol you may use to determine direction. Along with cardinal directions (north, south, east, west), it includes intermediate directions (e.g., northwest).

1. Which area of New Jersey has the most major cities?

   A. northwest
   B. west
   C. northeast
   D. south

DIRECTIONS: Study the map, then choose the **best** answer to each question.

DIRECTIONS: Study the map, then choose the **best** answer to each question.

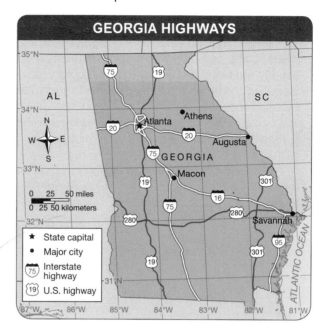

2. Based on the map, which statement about Sydney is accurate?

   A. Sydney is the capital of Australia.
   B. Sydney is located on the west coast of Australia.
   C. Sydney is east of 150°E longitude.
   D. Sydney is north of 30°S latitude.

3. Based on the map, what can you assume about Australia?

   A. Most of the cities are located north of 15°S.
   B. Most of the cities are located along the coast.
   C. Most of the cities are located between 105°E and 120°E.
   D. Most of the cities are located between 0 and 15°S.

4. According to the map, which two cities in Australia are located the farthest apart?

   A. Perth and Adelaide
   B. Perth and Melbourne
   C. Melbourne and Sydney
   D. Sydney and Darwin

5. Which interstate highway runs through Georgia's capital?

   A. 19
   B. 95
   C. 16
   D. 75

6. Which city is near Interstate Highway 16 and Interstate Highway 95?

   A. Atlanta
   B. Augusta
   C. Savannah
   D. Macon

7. Which city's absolute location is closest to 81°W, 32°N?

   A. Savannah
   B. Athens
   C. Atlanta
   D. Macon

8. Which part of Georgia has the highest population density?

   A. north
   B. north-central
   C. south
   D. east

Physical Maps

SS CONTENT TOPICS: II.G.b.2, II.G.b.3, II.G.b.4, II.G.b.5, II.G.c.1, II.G.c.2, II.G.c.3, II.E.c.7
SS PRACTICES: SSP.2.b, SSP.3.c, SSP.4.a, SSP.6.b, SSP.6.c

UNIT 1

1 Learn the Skill

A **physical map** shows the geographic land and water features of an area, such as mountains, plains, rivers, gulfs, and oceans. Physical maps also can show **climate** and **elevation** of an area. Physical maps usually will have shading or different colors for elevation and climate, and symbols for features that can be identified using the map key. Scientists study physical maps for settlement and migration patterns.

2 Practice the Skill

By practicing the skill of analyzing physical maps, you will improve your study and test-taking abilities, especially as they relate to the GED® Social Studies Test. Study the map and information below. Then answer the question that follows.

a To identify a physical map, look for landforms and bodies of water such as rivers or oceans.

b Use the map key to learn more about the meaning of the shading on a map.

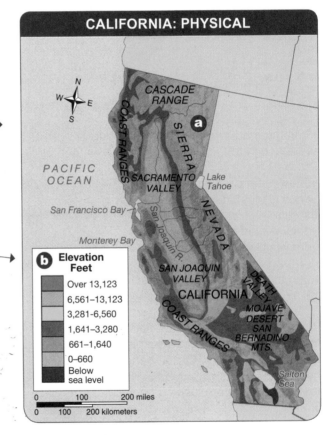

CALIFORNIA: PHYSICAL

MAKING ASSUMPTIONS

You might assume that physical maps do not show national or state boundaries, but they usually do. However, keep in mind that physical features can cross over many borders.

1. Based on information on the map, which statement about the land in California is correct?

   A. The land is mostly low-lying with some hills.
   B. The land on the coast is very low.
   C. The land is mostly mountainous on the coast.
   D. The land is a mixture of lowland, hills, and mountains.

Lesson 3 | Physical Maps

⭐ Spotlighted Item: **HOT SPOT**

DIRECTIONS: Study the map and read the passage. Then mark on the map the **best** answer(s) to each question.

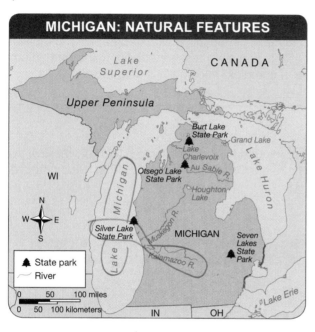

Michigan has more than 11,000 lakes and ponds. Bordering the state are the Great Lakes of Huron, Ontario, Michigan, Erie, and Superior (sometimes recalled as "HOMES" for their first initials). Several of Michigan's more than 90 state parks are located near bodies of water, where visitors can swim, fish, and enjoy the state's natural beauty.

2. The Kalamazoo River joins which Great Lake? Circle the name of the lake on the map.

3. On which river is Otsego Lake State Park located? Underline the name of the river on the map.

DIRECTIONS: Study the map, read the questions, and choose the **best** answer to each question.

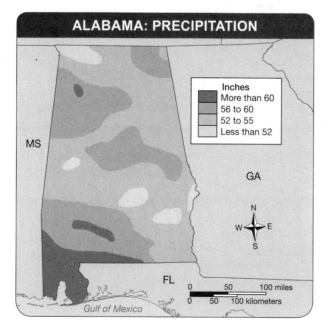

4. In general, where is the wettest area of Alabama?

   A. in the north
   B. in the southeast
   C. the coastal area
   D. in the west

5. What is the least amount of precipitation that occurs along the border of Alabama and Florida?

   A. less than 52 inches
   B. 52 to 55 inches
   C. 56 to 60 inches
   D. more than 60 inches

6. Peanut farming contributes more than $200 million each year to Alabama's economy. Peanuts thrive in warm, dry climates with well-drained sandy soils. Where would be the **best** location for a peanut farm?

   A. in coastal Alabama
   B. in northeastern Alabama
   C. in southeastern Alabama
   D. in central Alabama

Political Maps

SS CONTENT TOPICS: II.G.b.1, II.G.c.1, II.G.c.2, II.G.c.3, II.G.d.3, II.G.d.4
SS PRACTICES: SSP.2.b, SSP.3, SSP.6.b, SSP.6.c

UNIT 1

① Learn the Skill

A **political map** shows how humans have divided the surface of Earth. It shows **borders** between counties, states, territories, and countries. A political map can also show **human-made features** such as roads, buildings, and cities. Some political maps use shading or dots to illustrate areas where people live. This is known as **population density**. Areas with fewer dots or lighter shading generally are less populated.

Understanding the information presented in political maps, and how that information connects with present-day life or a period in history, will enable you to make connections with geography and the world. As with other areas of the GED® test, questions about political maps will test your ability to interpret information at various Depth of Knowledge levels through the use of complex reading skills and thinking skills.

② Practice the Skill

By practicing the skill of understanding information presented in a political map, you will improve your study and test-taking abilities, especially as they relate to the GED® Social Studies Test. Study the map and information below. Then answer the question that follows.

ⓐ Political maps usually do not show physical features such as elevations, landforms, or waterways.

ⓑ Political maps show different levels of political boundaries, including county and state borders.

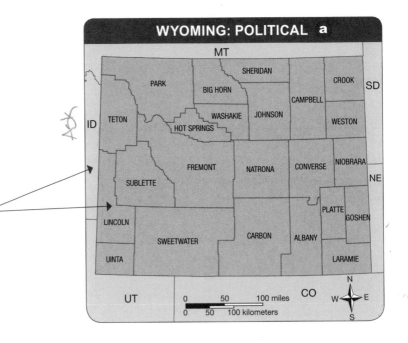

WYOMING: POLITICAL ⓐ

TEST-TAKING TIPS

Map keys change depending on the map. Some maps, such as the one above, lack a key. It does, however, feature a map scale and compass rose, which provide information about distance and direction.

1. Which of the following best describes the information on this map?

A. the counties of Wyoming
B. the counties of Wyoming and border states
C. the counties of Wyoming, elevation, and border states
D. the counties and elevation of Wyoming

3 Apply the Skill

DIRECTIONS: Study the map, read each question, and choose the **best** answer.

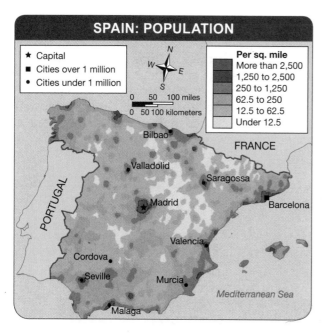

SPAIN: POPULATION

DIRECTIONS: Study the map, read each question, and choose the **best** answer.

ARIZONA: POLITICAL

2. In which areas of Spain are the population densities the greatest?

   A. between Madrid and Saragossa
   B. along the French border
   C. between Madrid and Cordova
   D. near most major cities

3. Based on the map, which statement about Spain is accurate?

   A. Madrid has the highest population.
   B. Seville is larger than Barcelona.
   C. Few people live along the Mediterranean coast.
   D. Murcia has areas with more than 2,000 people per square mile.

4. If you wanted to vacation in a place with lower population and less population density, which city would offer the best choice?

   A. Madrid
   B. Bilbao
   C. Barcelona
   D. Cordova

5. What does the symbol next to Tucson probably represent?

   A. small city and county seat
   B. large city and county seat
   C. large city and state capital
   D. state capital and county seat

6. Based on the map, which area of the state is least populated?

   A. Maricopa County
   B. far northern Arizona
   C. Pima County
   D. southeastern Arizona

7. Based on the map, what can be assumed about Arizona?

   A. Most of the population is near the California border.
   B. The state's population is evenly distributed across all counties.
   C. Coconino County has the largest population.
   D. Maricopa County has the largest population.

LESSON 5

Movement on Maps

SS CONTENT TOPICS: II.G.b.1, II.G.b.2, II.G.b.4, II.G.c.1, II.G.c.2, II.G.d.1, II.G.d.2, II.G.d.3, II.E.g
SS PRACTICES: SSP.2.b, SSP.3.a, SSP.3.c, SSP.6.b

UNIT 1

1 Learn the Skill

To understand **movement on maps**, it is important to know the symbols and map elements that are commonly used to show movement. In the map key, symbols such as **arrows** or **lines** can show the movement, direction, or route of people, goods, or ideas. Colors, shading, and patterns such as dots or solid lines can show when movements occur or illustrate forces or factors that cause the movements.

For that reason, you should first examine the map key prior to studying the map itself. Some maps that show movement are considered special-purpose maps, which are discussed more in Unit 3. Movement, or migration, is an important factor in understanding the connections between geography and the world.

2 Practice the Skill

By practicing the skill of understanding movement on maps, you will improve your study and test-taking abilities, especially as they relate to the GED® Social Studies Test. Study the map and information below. Then answer the question that follows.

a Study the arrows to understand the direction of movements presented on the map.

b When studying movement on maps, be sure to note the geographic areas involved. Which areas are the movements going to, or from, or between? What do you know about those areas during the time period specified on the map?

ATLANTIC SLAVE TRADE ROUTES

Key:
- Slave traders' routes early 1500s
- Slave traders' routes 1600s
- Slave traders' routes after 1619
- Gathering areas for enslaved people
- Major concentration of enslaved people

NORTH AMERICA
Great Lakes
Mississippi R.
ATLANTIC OCEAN
Gulf of Mexico
CUBA HISPANIOLA
EUROPE
AFRICA
SOUTH AMERICA
PACIFIC OCEAN

N W E S

0 1,000 2,000 miles
0 1,000 2,000 kilometers

Ask

TEST-TAKING TIPS

Use the map key to determine the meaning of the map's different colors and shadings. Map keys provide information about movement on maps, such as who or what group is moving to or from which direction.

1. Jamestown Colony was founded in Virginia in 1609. According to the map, what changes occurred after the founding of Jamestown Colony?

   A. The slave-gathering areas of Africa increased.
   B. Areas with major concentrations of enslaved people moved from South America to Africa.
   C. More enslaved people were sent from South America.
   D. The trade routes extended to North America.

DIRECTIONS: Study the map and passage, read each question, and choose the **best** answer.

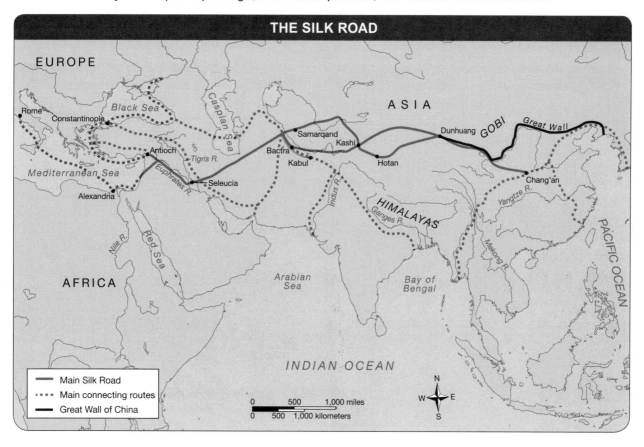

THE SILK ROAD

The Silk Road was not just one road. It was a series of ancient trade routes that stretched more than 4,000 miles from the Far East to the West. The main overland route extended from China to the Mediterranean Sea. Travelers on the Silk Road did not solely trade in silk. Traders from China in the Far East also exchanged ideas, philosophies, and culture with their counterparts traveling from the West.

2. Why was the Silk Road important?

   A. It boosted the economy of Africa.
   B. It prevented the cultural exchange between the Far East and the West.
   C. It provided silk to wealthy Asians.
   D. It allowed for goods and ideas to be exchanged between Asia and Europe.

3. How might goods from Alexandria have reached Kabul?

   A. via Rome and Constantinople
   B. via Seleucia and Bactra
   C. across the Great Wall of China
   D. via Antioch and Samarqand

4. What connection can you make about the cities of Samarqand, Bactra, Kashi, and Kabul?

   A. These cities were not located on the main connecting routes of the Silk Road.
   B. These cities were located north of the Great Wall of China.
   C. These cities were centrally located on the Silk Road.
   D. Kashi and Kabul were west of Bactra and Samarqand.

5. How is it likely that traders from Rome reached the Silk Road?

   A. by wagon
   B. by horse
   C. by foot
   D. by boat

Unit 1 Review

DIRECTIONS: Study the map, read each question, then choose the **best** answer.

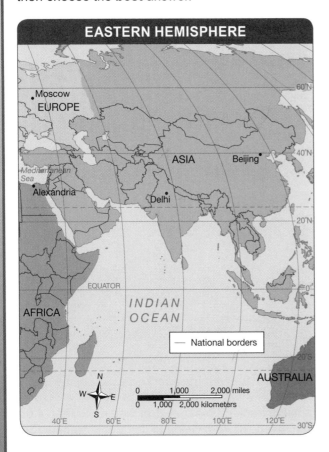

EASTERN HEMISPHERE

1. Based on information on the map, what is the relative location of Beijing, China?

   A. west of Moscow
   B. northeast of Delhi
   C. 40°N, 80°E
   D. 40°S, 80°W

2. What tool could you use to find the absolute location of a place?

   A. a map scale
   B. a map key
   C. map symbols
   D. latitude and longitude

3. Which continent falls fully within the Southern Hemisphere?

   A. Africa
   B. Asia
   C. Australia
   D. Europe

DIRECTIONS: Study the map, read each question, then choose the **best** answer.

OHIO: EARLY SETTLEMENT

(1789) Date city was founded
~~~ Rivers

4. Based on information on the map, which of the following statements is accurate?

   A. Settlements were mostly in the interior of the Ohio territory.
   B. Settlements fell mostly along Lake Erie.
   C. Portsmouth was the westernmost settlement.
   D. Settlements were built along waterways.

5. Soon after which historical event were most of the settlements in the Ohio Territory founded?

   A. the American Revolution
   B. the French and Indian War
   C. the War of 1812
   D. the Civil War

6. Which of the following settlements was founded after all of the others?

   A. Cleveland
   B. Portsmouth
   C. Chillicothe
   D. Zanesville

DIRECTIONS: Study the map, read each question, then choose the **best** answer.

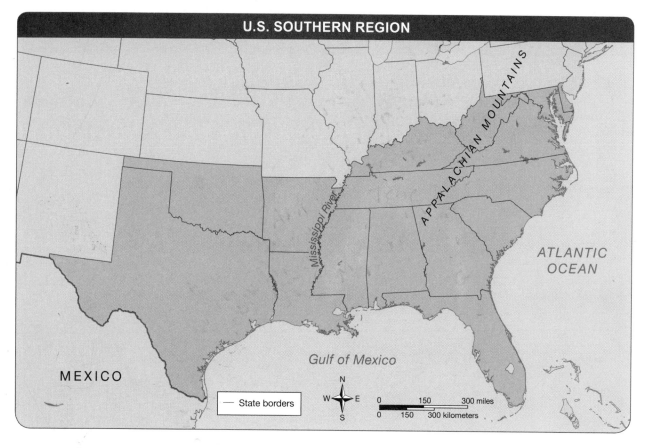

U.S. SOUTHERN REGION

7. Based on the map, which of the following statements is accurate?

   A. The U.S. Southern region includes all states east of the Mississippi River.
   B. The U.S. Southern region includes Virginia, but not West Virginia.
   C. The U.S. Southern region includes all states that feature the Appalachian Mountains.
   D. The U.S. Southern region includes all states that border the Gulf of Mexico.

8. Which of the following cities is located in the U.S. Southern region?

   A. Nashville
   B. Cincinnati
   C. St. Louis
   D. Wichita

9. Which of the following states borders a state in the U.S. southern region?

   A. Iowa
   B. Pennsylvania
   C. Colorado
   D. Michigan

10. About how far away are east Texas and west South Carolina?

    A. about 300 miles
    B. about 500 miles
    C. about 700 miles
    D. about 900 miles

11. Which Southern state shares a border with seven other states in the Southern region?

    A. Arkansas
    B. Georgia
    C. Mississippi
    D. Tennessee

12. Which of the following is true about the Southern region?

    A. West Virginia is the smallest state in the region.
    B. Most of the states border either the Atlantic Ocean or the Mississippi River.
    C. The states in the region also formed the Confederacy in the Civil War.
    D. The Southern Region occupies approximately half the land area of the United States.

DIRECTIONS: Study the map, the passage, and read the questions. Then mark on the map the best answer(s) to each question.

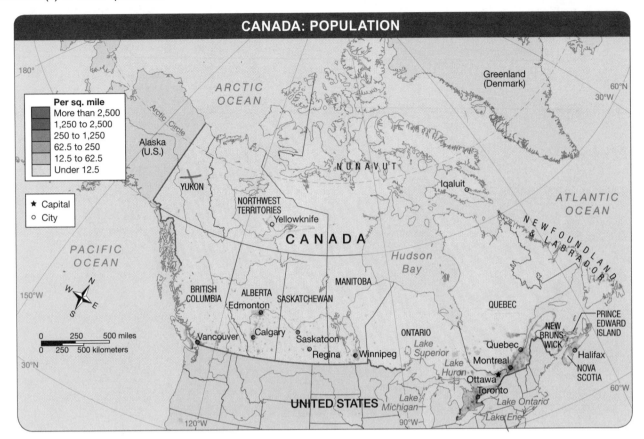

CANADA: POPULATION

On January 1, 2012, the majority (86%) of people in Canada lived in Ontario, Quebec, British Columbia, and Alberta. Between 1992 and 2012, the percentage of Canada's population living in Ontario, Alberta, and British Columbia increased, while the percentage living in all other provinces declined. The population in the territories remained stable.

The proportion of Canadians who live in urban areas has increased steadily since it gained its independence from Great Britain. In 2011, more than 27 million Canadians (81%) lived in urban areas, a reversal from more than a century ago. Also in 2011, the three large urban areas in Canada—Toronto, Vancouver, and Montréal—made up just more than a third (35%) of Canada's entire population.

The urban-rural distribution was uneven across the provinces and territories. Ontario, British Columbia, and Alberta all had populations with urban proportions higher than the national level. Conversely, some provinces and territories had rural populations significantly higher than the national average, ranging from 28% in Manitoba to 53% in Prince Edward Island.

13. Where is most of Canada's population located? Circle the area on the map.

14. On the map, place a check mark beside the name of a city in the Nunavut Province.

15. On the map, underline the names of provinces that share a border with the United States.

16. Which Canadian province is the farthest north: Yukon, Ontario, Quebec, or British Columbia? Place an **X** next to a name of that province.

17. On the map, place a double-underline beneath the name of the city whose absolute location is closest to 60°N, 120°W.

18. On the map, place a star symbol next to Canada's largest inland waterway.

19. On the map, place two star symbols next to two of the provinces that were home to rural populations that were much higher than the national average.

DIRECTIONS: Study the map and the passage, read each question, then choose the **best** answer.

U.S. AVERAGE ANNUAL PRECIPITATION

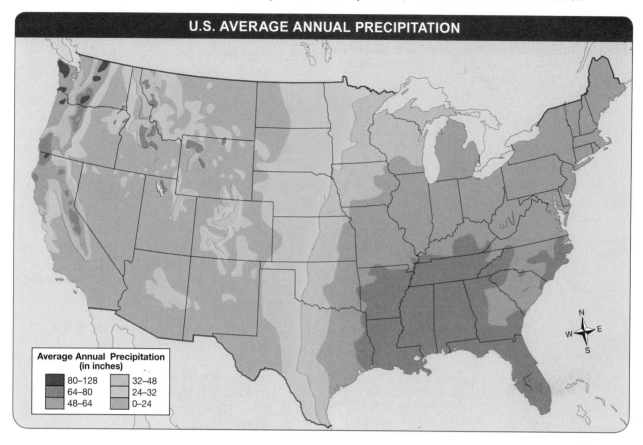

Average Annual Precipitation (in inches)

- 80–128
- 64–80
- 48–64
- 32–48
- 24–32
- 0–24

Even though the United is a large country, it features many different types of climates. The average annual precipitation, including rainfall and snowfall, is one way to view those differences.

Rain forms when small cloud drops become too heavy for the cloud, thus falling toward Earth as rain. Rain can also begin as ice crystals that collect and form large snowflakes. As the snow falls toward Earth through warmer air, the flakes melt and collapse into raindrops. Snowflakes are clumps of ice crystals that collect as they fall toward Earth. Since snowflakes do not fall through a layer of air warm enough to cause them to melt, they remain intact and reach the ground as snow.

20. Based on the map and the passage, which of the following states has the lowest annual precipitation?

   A. Idaho
   B. Nevada
   C. Texas
   D. Arizona

21. Which area of the United States probably has the most diverse climate?

   A. the Pacific Coast
   B. the Atlantic Coast
   C. the Midwest
   D. the Northeast

22. Which of the following states receives between 0 and 128 inches in annual precipitation?

   A. New Mexico
   B. California
   C. Colorado
   D. Wisconsin

23. Which of the following states has the highest annual precipitation?

   A. Florida
   B. Kansas
   C. North Dakota
   D. West Virginia

DIRECTIONS: Study the map and the passage, read each question, then choose the **best** answer.

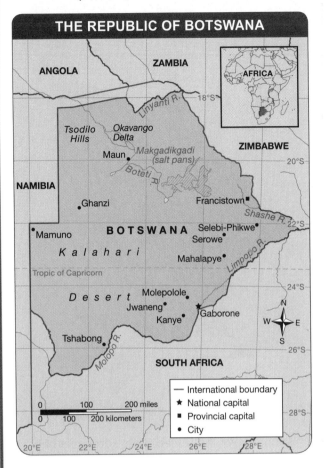

THE REPUBLIC OF BOTSWANA

ANGOLA
ZAMBIA
AFRICA
ZIMBABWE
Linyanti R.
18°S
Tsodilo Hills
Okavango Delta
Maun
Makgadikgadi (salt pans)
Boteti R.
20°S
NAMIBIA
Ghanzi
Francistown
Shashe R.
22°S
Mamuno
BOTSWANA
Selebi-Phikwe
Serowe
Kalahari
Mahalapye
Limpopo R.
Tropic of Capricorn
24°S
Desert
Molepolole
Jwaneng
Kanye
Gaborone
Tshabong
Molopo R.
26°S
SOUTH AFRICA
28°S

0 100 200 miles
0 100 200 kilometers

— International boundary
★ National capital
■ Provincial capital
• City

20°E   22°E   24°E   26°E   28°E

The Republic of Botswana is a country in southern Africa that is slightly smaller than the state of Texas and about the same size as France or Kenya. Most of landlocked Botswana is characterized by vast and nearly level sandy basins and scrub-covered savannah. The Kalahari Desert in the southwest makes up much of the country. Botswana's sparse population is concentrated in the eastern part of the country. Most areas are too arid to sustain any agriculture other than cattle.

Botswana experiences extremes in both temperature and weather. Winter days (late May through August) are normally clear, warm, and sunny, and nights are cool to cold. In summer (October to April), rains can render the country's mostly sandy roads impassable. This is also the time of the most humidity and stifling heat. During the long days, temperatures of more than 105°F are common.

A former British colony, Botswana gained its independence in 1966. With almost 50 years of civilian leadership, progressive social policies, and significant capital investments, the Republic of Botswana enjoys one of the most dynamic economies in Africa. Diamond mining dominates the country's economic activity, but Botswana is becoming a tourist destination due to its extensive nature preserves and conservation practices.

24. Based on the map and the passage, what can you assume about Botswana?

   A. The Kalahari Desert is sparsely populated.
   B. Botswana's cities are all located along its waterways.
   C. Most of Botswana's cities are located near the salt pans.
   D. Most of Botswana's cities are located south of the Tropic of Capricorn.

25. Which of the following statements about Botswana's economy is true?

   A. Mining and tourism provide income for Botswana's citizens.
   B. Most Botswanans make their living from farming.
   C. Botswana has a failing economy.
   D. There are no tourist attractions to help support Botswana's economy.

26. Which of the following cities in Botswana is the capital?

   A. Mamuno
   B. Francistown
   C. Mahalapye
   D. Gaborone

27. Traveling west from Mamuno, into which African country would you enter?

   A. Angola
   B. Zimbabwe
   C. South Africa
   D. Namibia

DIRECTIONS: Study the map and the passage, read each question, then choose the **best** answer.

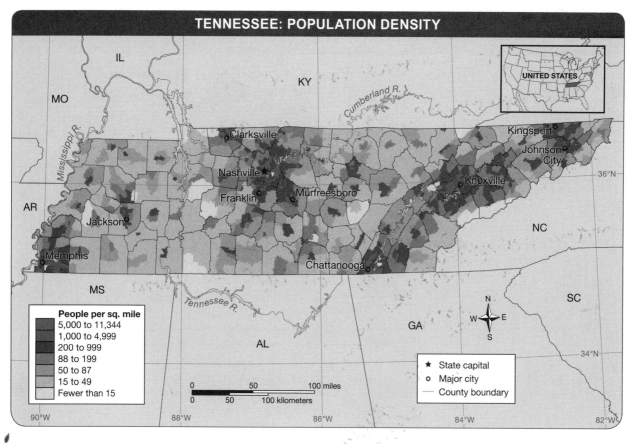

TENNESSEE: POPULATION DENSITY

Tennessee is located in the Southern region of the United States. It is the seventeenth most populous state in the United States.

The 2010 Census recorded Tennessee's population at 6,346,106 inhabitants, an increase of more than 650,000 people since 2000.

28. Based on the map and the passage, why might there be a large area of population density near the center of the state?

    A. All of Tennessee's major cities are centrally located.
    B. The Appalachian Mountains are located in the central part of the state.
    C. Nashville is located in this area.
    D. Chattanooga is located in this area.

29. Which of the following states shares a border with Tennessee and also with South Carolina?

    A. Georgia
    B. Alabama
    C. Virginia
    D. Florida

30. Based on the map, which area of the state has the lowest population density?

    A. between the counties northeast of Chattanooga and southwest of Knoxville
    B. between the counties west and southwest of Clarksville and northeast and southeast of Jackson
    C. the counties located around Nashville
    D. the counties located in the north-central part of the state

31. Based on your knowledge of geography, why do you assume there is a large population area located in the southwestern part of the state?

    A. The Tennessee River and Memphis are located in this area.
    B. The Mississippi River begins near that location of the state.
    C. Memphis is located there and is the state capital.
    D. The Mississippi River and Memphis are located in this area.

DIRECTIONS: Study the map and the passage, and read the questions. Then mark on the map the **best** answer(s) to each question.

THE BALKAN PENINSULA

The term *Balkan* is a geographical designation for the easternmost of Europe's three southern peninsulas. Two major mountain ranges dominate the peninsula: the Dinaric Alps in the west, which run parallel to the Adriatic coast, and the high Carpathian mountains in Romania. In addition, the Balkan Mountains lie east-west across Bulgaria.

The coastlines of the peninsula's southern and western countries are rugged and rocky. The landscape of the Balkan peninsula is suitable primarily for raising animals and small-scale farming. Countries such as Croatia, Romania, and Bulgaria, enjoy arable land.

Fertile land for farming also lies along the valleys of the Danube, Sava, and Vadar rivers, as well as part of the Aegean coast. Elsewhere, land cultivation is mostly unsuccessful because of the mountains, hot summers, and poor soils, although grapes and olives thrive in certain areas.

Energy resources are scarce, except in Kosovo, where citizens mine coal and other mineral deposits. Mining of coal also contributes to the economies of Serbia, Romania, Bosnia and Herzegovina, and Bulgaria. Romania also is home to some oil deposits. Although natural gas deposits are scarce throughout the region, the Balkan countries have widely accepted renewable energy sources such as wind and hydropower.

32. On the map, place a circle around the name of the city that lies on the Black Sea.

33. Which Balkan country has the most northwestern location? Put a check mark next to that country's name.

34. On the map, underline the names of the Balkan countries whose industries include mining.

35. On the map, place an **X** next to the names of the countries that formed the former Yugoslavia.

DIRECTIONS: Study the map and the passage, read each question, then choose the **best** answer.

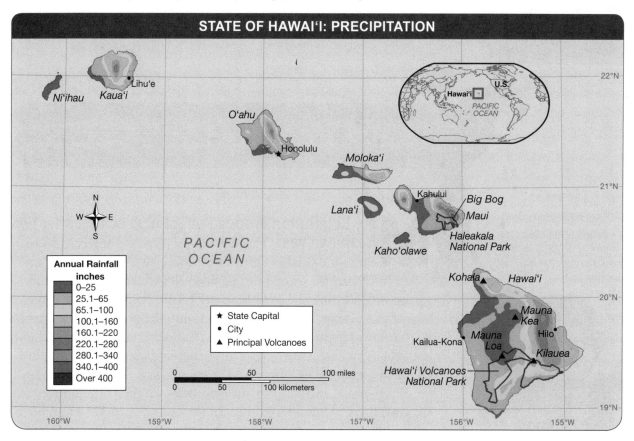

STATE OF HAWAI'I: PRECIPITATION

The state of Hawai'i is a chain of volcanic islands located in the Pacific Ocean. The state's rainfall pattern is quite diverse. Average annual precipitation ranges from 8 inches near the summits of Mauna Loa and Mauna Kea on the Big Island to 404 inches near Big Bog on the windward slope of Haleakala National Park, Maui. In general, high average rainfall is found on the windward mountain slopes, and low rainfall prevails in leeward lowlands and on the upper slopes of the highest mountains.

Surprisingly, perhaps, the highest peaks also receive several inches of snow. In general, the wetter season is winter and the dryer season is summer. There are exceptions, such as those areas of the Big Island of Hawai'i that have a summer rainfall maximum caused by land and sea breeze convection.

36. Based on the map and the passage, which of the following cities has the lowest annual precipitation?

  A. Hilo
  B. Honolulu
  C. Kahului
  D. Lihu'e

37. Based on the map and the passage, which of the following cities has the greatest annual precipitation?

  A. Hilo
  B. Honolulu
  C. Kahului
  D. Lihu'e

38. Which Hawai'ian Islands have the lowest annual precipitation?

  A. Big Island of Hawai'i and Lana'i
  B. Kaho'olawe and Moloka'i
  C. Moloka'i and Ni'ihau
  D. Lana'i, Kaho'olawe, and Ni'ihau

39. What is the approximate distance between Honolulu and the Haleakala National Park?

  A. approximately 50 miles
  B. approximately 125 miles
  C. approximately 200 miles
  D. approximately 250 miles

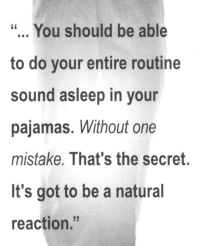

Not only did Mary Lou Retton earn her GED® certificate, she won the hearts of the nation while winning the Gold Medal in gymnastics at the 1984 Summer Olympic Games.

"... You should be able to do your entire routine sound asleep in your pajamas. *Without one mistake.* That's the secret. It's got to be a natural reaction."

GED® JOURNEYS

Mary Lou Retton

Mary Lou Retton dropped out of high school after her freshman year. This did not prevent her, however, from earning a GED® certificate—and five Olympic medals.

Retton's path to success began when she was an eight-year-old gymnast. Watching the 1976 Summer Olympics on TV, she dedicated herself to training, and left school to train. She practiced relentlessly; her hard work paid off. After winning various competitions, including both the American Cup and Japan's Chunichi Cup in 1983, Retton qualified for the 1984 Summer Olympics in Los Angeles.

But political and military tensions between the United States and the then Soviet Union were high. In response to the American boycott of the 1980 Summer Olympics in Moscow, the Soviet Union and other Eastern European countries boycotted the 1984 Summer Olympics in Los Angeles. Not allowing her recent knee operation to deter her, 16-year-old Retton became the first American woman to win a gold medal in gymnastics. Patriotic pride rose across the United States. Adding to this historic victory, she also won two silver medals and two bronze medals.

Retton retired from gymnastics in 1986, and attended the University of Texas. She has appeared in films and television programs and served as an expert commentator for gymnastics and Olympic events. Today, Mary Lou Retton works as a motivational speaker and helps encourage the benefits of exercise and healthful nutrition.

CAREER HIGHLIGHTS: *Mary Lou Retton*

- Born in Fairmont, West Virginia
- First American woman to win an Olympic gold medal in gymnastics
- Named "Sportswoman of the Year" in 1984

- Inducted into the International Gymnastics Hall of Fame in 1997
- Serves on the USA Gymnastics Board of Directors and The Children's Miracle Network

United States History

Unit 2:
United States History

Throughout its short but momentous history, the United States has defended its citizens and millions worldwide through its progressive military strength and intelligence forces. As history changes, so too does the role of our military.

Women have served in the U.S. armed forces since 1775. They nursed the wounded, laundered clothes, and cooked for the troops. In 1944, as Allied Forces fought in World War II, Women's Army Corps (WAC) units supported combat troops. But it was not until 2013 that the Defense Department authorized women to serve on an equal basis alongside their male counterparts, removing the remaining barrier to equality in the services. Recent wars such as Iraq and Afghanistan lacked real front lines and thousands of women soldiers found themselves in combat situations. By 2016, women will be fully integrated into front-line positions within the military.

American history is dynamic, ever changing with the times. The importance of understanding U.S. history extends to the GED® Social Studies Test, where it makes up 20 percent of all questions. As with other areas of the GED® Tests, U.S. history questions will test your ability to interpret text and visuals, such as tables, graphs, and timelines. Unit 2 helps you prepare for the GED® Social Studies Test.

Table of Contents

WOMEN IN OUR ARMED SERVICES

UNITED STATES 3¢ POSTAGE OF AMERICA

American history is dynamic, ever changing with the times. So, too, are your career opportunities when you successfully complete your GED® certification.

SS CONTENT TOPICS: II.G.b.1, II.G.b.5, II.G.c.1, II.G.c.2, II.G.c.3, II.G.d.1, II.G.d.2, II.G.d.3, II.G.d.4, I.USH.a.1, I.USH.b.6
SS PRACTICES: SSP.1.a, SSP.1.b, SSP.2.a, SSP.2.b, SSP.3.a, SSP.3.b, SSP.3.c, SSP.4.a, SSP.6.a, SSP.6.b, SSP.6.c

1 Learn the Skill

To understand how to **relate geography and history**, you must first analyze the context of a physical, political, or other type of map, and how that context connects with a historical period or event. All of the map skills you have learned thus far will help you make these connections.

As with other areas of the GED® test, geography and United States history questions will test your ability to interpret information at various Depth of Knowledge levels through the use of complex reading skills and thinking skills.

2 Practice the Skill

By practicing the skill of relating geography and history, you will improve your study and test-taking abilities, especially as they relate to the GED® Social Studies Test. Study the passage and the map below. Then answer the question that follows.

THE NORTHWEST ORDINANCE

In 1787, Congress created a territory west of Pennsylvania, north of the Ohio River, east of the Mississippi River, and south of the Great Lakes. The Northwest Ordinance established a government and the formation of three to five states.

"There shall be formed in the said territory, not less than three nor more than five states; and the boundaries of the states … shall become fixed and established as follows, … and it is further understood and declared, that the boundaries of these three states, shall be subject so far to be altered, … to form one or two states in that part of the said territory which lies north of an east and west line drawn through the southerly bend or extreme of lake Michigan."

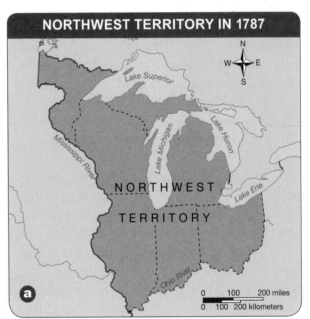

NORTHWEST TERRITORY IN 1787

a Note the details in the passage concerning the minimum and maximum number of states. How many states are described? Is there a possible exception? Now, compare and contrast this information with the information on the map.

MAKING ASSUMPTIONS

You can assume that the dotted lines shown on the map represent the present-day boundaries of the states created by the provisions of The Northwest Ordinance.

1. Ultimately, how many complete states were formed from the Northwest Territory?

A. three
B. four
C. five
D. six

★ Spotlighted Item: **FILL-IN-THE-BLANK**

DIRECTIONS: Study the map and read the passage. Then fill in your answer in the box below.

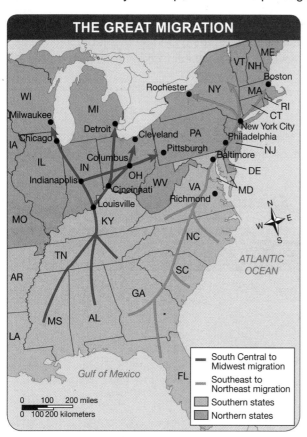

THE GREAT MIGRATION

In the early 1900s, more than one million African Americans, pushed by discrimination and poor economic conditions in the rural south, migrated north and west in an event that became known as The Great Migration. The migration began around 1916, lessened during the Great Depression, and increased again during World War II and after. Northern cities such as New York, Chicago, Cleveland, and Detroit saw the greatest African American population increases. Manufacturing and other urban jobs led African Americans to these cities. Moving to cities also caused a growth in African American literacy and an African American cultural explosion. Many southern African American artists, authors, and musicians converged on New York City because it was seen as a cultural center of the United States.

2. The easternmost state to which African Americans from Florida and Georgia migrated during The Great Migration was

_____.

DIRECTIONS: Study the map and the passage, read the question, then fill in the answer in the boxes below.

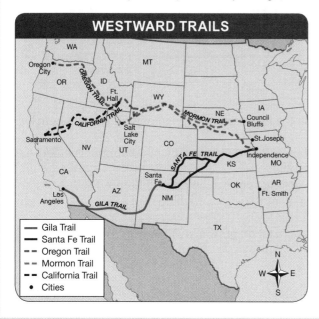

WESTWARD TRAILS

In 1845, writer John O'Sullivan proclaimed that it would be "the fulfillment of our manifest destiny to overspread the continent allotted by Providence." Proving O'Sullivan correct, settlers cut trails and pushed the boundaries of the United States west near the Pacific Ocean.

3. Settlers travelling to Los Angeles, California, from Independence, Missouri, would most

likely have used the _____

and the _____ Trails.

Interpret Tables

SS CONTENT TOPICS: I.USH.b.1, II.USH.e, II.G.b.1, II.G.b.2, II.G.b.4, II.G.b.5, II.G.d.1, II.G.d.2, II.G.d.3
SS PRACTICES: SSP.1.a, SSP.1.b, SSP.2.b, SSP.6.a, SSP.6.b

1 Learn the Skill

One way to present facts, statistics, and other details in a clear, well-organized manner is to use a **table**. Tables allow authors to visually present information that might be too lengthy or complex to describe in a narrative passage.

Tables organize information into **rows** and **columns**. Rows run across the table from the left to right. Columns run up and down the table from the top to the bottom. Reading the title of a table, as well as the headings for its rows and columns, can help you interpret and use the information presented in the table.

2 Practice the Skill

By practicing the skill of interpreting tables, you will improve your study and test-taking skills, especially as they relate to the GED® Social Studies Test. Examine the table and strategies below. Then answer the question that follows.

a The title can be found above the table, below the table, or in the first row of the table. The title identifies the subject or topic of the table.

b The headings of each column or row identify the information located in that part of the table.

a ESTIMATED POPULATION OF VIRGINIA COLONY

YEAR **b**	POPULATION **b**
1630	2,500
1650	18,700
1670	35,300
1690	53,000
1700	58,600
1720	87,800
1740	180,400
1750	231,000
1770	447,000
1780	538,000

TEST-TAKING TIPS

The headings of a table's rows and columns determine how the information is related in these sections. Notice that the year in each row corresponds to the population number to the right.

1. The details in the table support which of the following conclusions?

A. Many people left Virginia to settle in other colonies between 1700 and 1750.
B. Virginia's colonial population peaked before 1750.
C. The population of Virginia doubled every 20 years between 1630 and 1690.
D. Virginia's population grew significantly between 1630 and 1780.

Apply the Skill

Spotlighted Item: **FILL-IN-THE-BLANK**

DIRECTIONS: Study the table and read the questions. Then fill in your answers in the boxes below.

ORIGINS OF MIGRANTS TO AMERICAN COLONIES, 1700–1750

LOCATION	TOTAL
Africa	278,400
Ireland	108,600
Germany	84,500
England/Wales	73,100
England/Scotland	35,300
Other	5,900
TOTAL	**585,800**

2. Based on the table, from which location other than England did the greatest number of immigrants come?

3. The immigration of 278,400 Africans to the American colonies between 1700 and 1750 was likely due to

.

UNIT 2

DIRECTIONS: Study the information presented in the table, read the questions, then choose the **best** answer to each question.

THE AMERICAN REVOLUTION: A COMPARISON OF RESOURCES

	BRITAIN	THIRTEEN COLONIES
Population	Approximately 12,000,000	Approximately 2,800,000
Money	Richest country in the world	No money to support the war effort
Army	Large, well-trained army	Willing, but poorly-equipped, volunteer force
Leaders	Many skilled officers	Few officers capable of leading
Geography	Vast strange land without nearby supplies	Familiar land with close, but limited, supplies

4. Based on the table, which of the following looked like the most likely outcome of the war?

   A. The colonies would win.
   B. The British would win.
   C. A truce would be declared.
   D. The thirteen colonies would expand.

5. Based on the table, in what area were the colonists most prepared?

   A. They had the most people.
   B. They had the largest budget.
   C. They had many trained military officers.
   D. They easily could locate their supplies.

Main Idea and Details

SS CONTENT TOPICS: I.USH.a.1, I.USH.b.1, I.E.a, I.E.b, I.CG.a.1, I.CG.b.2
SS PRACTICES: SSP.1.a, SSP.1.b, SSP.2.a, SSP.2.b, SSP.4.a, SSP.5.a, SSP.5.c, SSP.6.b, SSP.7.a

❶ Learn the Skill

The **main idea** is the most important point of a passage or paragraph. The main idea may come at the beginning, middle, or end of a passage or paragraph. A main idea may be implied or clearly stated. If it is implied, use reasoning and supporting details to determine the main idea. If it is clearly stated, you are likely to find it within the **topic sentence**, or the first or last sentence, of a given paragraph.

Supporting details provide additional information or facts about the main idea. Such details include facts, statistics, explanations, graphics, and descriptions.

As with other areas of the GED® test, questions about the main idea and details of a passage will test your ability to interpret information at various Depth of Knowledge levels through the use of complex reading skills and thinking skills.

❷ Practice the Skill

By practicing the skill of identifying the main idea and supporting details, you will improve your study and test-taking abilities, especially as they relate to the GED® Social Studies Test. Read the excerpt and strategies below. Then answer the question that follows.

From Thomas Paine's *Common Sense* (1776):

a The main idea expresses the key point of a passage. It usually can be found in the topic sentence.

b Supporting details provide additional information about the main idea.

The infant state of the Colonies, as it is called, so far from being against, is an argument in favour of independence. We are sufficiently numerous, and were we more so we might be less united. 'Tis a matter worthy of observation that the more a country is peopled, the smaller their armies are. In military numbers, the ancients far exceeded the moderns; and the reason is evident, for trade being the consequence of population, men became too much absorbed thereby to attend to anything else. Commerce diminishes the spirit both of patriotism and military defense. And history sufficiently informs us that the bravest achievements were always accomplished in the non-age of a nation.

USING LOGIC

One way that a writer may add supporting details for a main idea is to cite examples from history that show an earlier precedent for his or her argument.

1. Which detail best supports the main idea that the colonists should seek independence from Britain?

   A. "were we more so we might be less united"
   B. "trade being the consequence of population"
   C. "bravest achievements were always accomplished in the non-age of a nation"
   D. "the more a country is peopled, the smaller their armies are"

Apply the Skill

★ Spotlighted Item: FILL-IN-THE-BLANK

DIRECTIONS: Study the table and read the information in the passage. Then fill in your answer in the box below.

COLONIES	NUMBER OF SIGNERS
Connecticut	4
Delaware	3
Georgia	3
Maryland	4
Massachusetts	5
New Hampshire	3
New Jersey	5
New York	4
North Carolina	3
Pennsylvania	9
Rhode Island	2
South Carolina	4
Virginia	7

A total of 56 men from thirteen colonies representing New England, the Middle Colonies, and the Southern Colonies signed the Declaration of Independence. The signers ranged in age from 26 to 70 and included two future presidents, John Adams and Thomas Jefferson.

2. Which two colonial regions were equally represented in the signing of the Declaration of Independence, suggesting both their power and importance?

UNIT 2

DIRECTIONS: Read the passages and the questions, then choose the **best** answers.

War between Britain and its colonies began on April 19, 1775, but few Americans wanted to break from Britain. Instead, most colonists wanted to gain rights under the British government. As the war continued, however, many Americans began to want economic freedom in addition to personal liberty.

On April 12, 1776, North Carolina's delegates voted for independence, and a month later, Virginia delegates did the same. In June 1776, a committee created a document entitled the Declaration of Independence that explained the need for independence.

From the Declaration of Independence:

We hold these truths to be self-evident, that all men are created equal, that they are endowed by their Creator with certain unalienable rights, that among these are life, liberty, and the pursuit of happiness. That to secure these rights, governments are instituted among men, deriving their just powers from the consent of the governed. That whenever any form of government becomes destructive to these ends, it is the right of the people to alter or abolish it, and to institute new government, "laying its foundation of such

principles and organizing its powers in such form, as to them shall seem most likely to effect their safety and happiness.

3. The details in the passage support which of the following main ideas?

   A. After war broke out in 1775, the colonists wanted to be independent of Britain.
   B. North Carolina's and Virginia's delegates were at odds over independence.
   C. The colonists cautiously approached independence.
   D. Virginia led the movement for independence.

4. What is the main idea in this excerpt from the Declaration of Independence?

   A. All men are endowed with unalienable rights.
   B. Life, liberty, and the pursuit of happiness are important freedoms.
   C. King George III of Britain was a tyrant.
   D. People have the right to end destructive governments and form new ones.

Categorize

SS CONTENT TOPICS: I.USH.a.1, I.USH.b.1, I.USH.b.4, I.CG.a.1, I.CG.b.3, I.CG.b.8, I.CG.b.9, II.G.b.1, II.G.d.1, II.G.d.2, II.G.d.3, II.G.d.4
SS PRACTICES: SSP.1.a, SSP.2.a, SSP.2.b, SSP.3.d, SSP.6.b

1 Learn the Skill

A good way to organize information about people, places, dates, and events is to **categorize** it. To categorize means to place information in a group of similar or related items. For instance, when learning about a particular time period in history, you might categorize events into groups such as political events, military events, and economic events.

By sorting information into categories, you can better examine how things are alike and how they are different. Categorizing information can also help you understand patterns or trends throughout social studies. When you organize specific information into larger categories, it can help you see the big picture.

As with other areas of the GED® test, questions about categorizing information will test your ability to interpret information at various Depth of Knowledge levels using complex reading and thinking skills.

2 Practice the Skill

By practicing the skill of categorizing, you will improve your study and test-taking skills, especially as they relate to the GED® Social Studies Test. Study the table and information below. Then answer the question that follows.

a The two main categories shown in this table are Federalists and Anti-Federalists. You can use the content of the table to determine whether other people or ideas should be categorized as Federalists or Anti-Federalists.

b Tables are useful tools for categorizing information. Here, information about these groups has been categorized according to views on the government, views on the United States Constitution, and leaders.

FEDERALISTS AND ANTI-FEDERALISTS

Group	Views on Government	View on Constitution	Leader
Federalists	Supported strong national government; wanted large military force; supported commerce and industry over agriculture; opposed to slavery	Supported adoption of Constitution	Alexander Hamilton
Anti-Federalists	Wanted to limit power of national government; believed states should keep as much power as possible; favored agriculture over commerce and industry; supported slavery	Opposed adoption of Constitution	Thomas Jefferson

USING LOGIC

When categorizing information, determine the most general categories into which information can be grouped. Then, you can further group each set of information into more specific categories.

1. Which of the following statements could be categorized as expressing an Anti-Federalist viewpoint?

A. The Constitution should be ratified as quickly as possible.
B. The national government must be capable of enforcing its own laws.
C. The work of the nation's farmers is more important than that of its factory workers.
D. Taxes should be raised to support industrial growth.

DIRECTIONS: Study the information in the passages, read each question, then choose the **best** answer to each question.

From "The Federalist No. 2" by John Jay:

It has until lately been a received and uncontradicted opinion that the prosperity of the people of America depended on their continuing firmly united, and the wishes, prayers, and efforts of our best and wisest citizens have been constantly directed to that object. But politicians now appear, who insist that this opinion is erroneous, and that instead of looking for safety and happiness in union, we ought to seek it in a division of the States into distinct confederacies or sovereignties.

From *Anti-Federalist Letters from the Federal Farmer to the Republican*:

There are certain unalienable and fundamental rights, which in forming the social compact, ought to be explicitly ascertained and fixed—a free and enlightened people, in forming this compact, will not resign all their rights to those who govern, and they will fix limits to their legislators and rulers.

2. Which two categories of individuals does John Jay identify in the first excerpt?

   A. his supporters and supporters of Alexander Hamilton
   B. people who believe in a strong central government and people who believe in strong state governments
   C. people of America and politicians from Great Britain
   D. supporters of state militias and supporters of a large national army

3. How might the author of the second excerpt have categorized some of the citizens of the United States?

   A. They were a group that was not free and enlightened.
   B. They were people who did not possess unalienable and fundamental rights.
   C. They were individuals who supported a strong national government.
   D. They were people who wanted limited government.

DIRECTIONS: Study the information in the passage, read each question, then choose the **best** answer to each question.

Georgia was the southernmost colony and bordered Spanish Florida. In 1739, when England and Spain were at war, colonists were successful in beating back a Spanish retaliation attack on the colony. To help to defend against the possibility of invasion, the city of Savannah, Georgia was fortified. By the time of the American Revolution, Georgia remained the least-populated colony, with its land still mostly wilderness.

After the American Revolution, many states tried to expand their territories toward the Mississippi River. In 1785, Georgia established a claim to land in what is now present-day Alabama and Mississippi. Spain had first claimed the territory and ordered the Georgian settlers to leave. In 1789, land companies purchased some of this disputed land from the Georgia legislature, further complicating the issue of ownership. At that time, Spain still claimed a portion of this territory.

4. Into which category could the future states of Alabama and Mississippi best be placed?

   A. Federalist states
   B. English colonies
   C. Spanish colonies
   D. Southern states

5. Which of the following could be a reason why Georgia categorized the Spanish a threat?

   A. Georgia was the least-populated colony at the time of the American Revolution.
   B. The land in Georgia was mostly wilderness.
   C. British and Spanish forces were at war over Georgia.
   D. Georgia bordered Florida and had been previously attacked by the Spanish.

6. Into which foreign relations category is the information in the passage best placed?

   A. Spanish-American
   B. English-Spanish
   C. English-American
   D. Georgia-Florida

UNIT 2

Sequence

SS CONTENT TOPICS: I.USH.b.2, I.USH.b.6, I.USH.b.7, II.G.c.1, II.G.c.2, II.G.d.1,
II.G.d.2, II.G.d.3, II.G.d.4
SS PRACTICES: SSP.1.a, SSP.1.b, SSP.2.b, SSP.3.a, SSP.3.b, SSP.3.c, SSP.6.b

❶ Learn the Skill

When you **sequence** events, you place them in an order, most often chronologically (from earliest to latest). By understanding the order in which events occur, you can examine how one event leads to another to produce a certain outcome. The ability to sequence further enables you to recognize how a past event might affect a current event, which could lead to a future result. In this way, **sequencing events** can help you make predictions about future outcomes.

As with other areas of the GED® test, questions about sequencing will test your ability to interpret information at various Depth of Knowledge levels through the use of complex reading skills and thinking skills.

❷ Practice the Skill

By practicing the skill of sequencing, you will improve your study and test-taking abilities, especially as they relate to the GED® Social Studies Test. Study the passage and the strategies below. Then answer the question that follows.

ⓐ The final event or outcome of a sequence of events is sometimes described at the beginning of a passage.

ⓑ Words such as *first, next, later, finally*, and so on provide clues about the order in which events occur. Times and dates also provide hints regarding sequence.

ⓐ By the 1840s, only a very small number of Native Americans remained in the southern United States between the Atlantic Ocean and the Mississippi River. Much of the Native Americans' removal from this area occurred through a series of treaties and legislation encouraged by President Andrew Jackson. After taking office in 1829, Jackson spurred Congress to pass the Indian Removal Act of 1830. This allowed Jackson to offer Native Americans territory in the west in exchange for leaving their native lands in the east. Jackson also signed many removal treaties that forced Native Americans off their homelands.

One such group, the Cherokee Nation, disputed government policies in Georgia that limited their freedoms. The Supreme Court decided in 1832 that Native American groups were not subject to state laws. **ⓑ** Later, Jackson negotiated his own removal treaty with a Cherokee chief. Congress approved the treaty in 1835. When many Cherokee resisted leaving their lands, Jackson ordered a military response. **ⓑ** Finally, in 1838, U.S. troops forced the Cherokee to the Indian Territory along what has become known as the Trail of Tears.

MAKING ASSUMPTIONS

You can assume that historical information is presented in chronological order. However, it may also be organized by themes, such as such as Native American conflicts.

1. Which of the following events occurred immediately after Jackson became President?

   A. Jackson negotiated a removal treaty with the Cherokee.
   B. The Cherokee disputed government policies that limited their freedoms.
   C. Congress approved the Indian Removal Act of 1830.
   D. U.S. troops forced the Cherokee along the Trail of Tears.

DIRECTIONS: Study the information presented in the passage, the graphic organizer, and the questions. Then choose the **best** answer to each question.

The War of 1812 began after a long period of escalating tensions between Britain and the United States. Tensions grew when British forces disrupted American ships carrying goods to Europe. However, another important cause of the conflict proved to be Americans' desire for additional lands along the frontier. Many settlers suspected that the British supported Native Americans in their conflicts with settlers. After the Battle of Tippecanoe in 1811, settlers became especially eager to remove the British from the area.

WAR OF 1812

2. Which event preceded the War of 1812?

   A. the Battle of the Thames
   B. the Battle of Tippecanoe
   C. the British attack on Washington, D.C.
   D. the Treaty of Ghent

3. Which of the following events might logically be placed last on the graphic organizer showing the sequence of events of the War of 1812?

   A. Britain ceded Canada to the United States.
   B. The British defeated Andrew Jackson's forces at the Battle of New Orleans.
   C. The United States became the most powerful nation in the world.
   D. Nationalism began to grow in the United States.

DIRECTIONS: Study the information in the passage, read the questions, then choose the **best** answer to each question.

After the War of 1812, Americans were especially interested in the lands of the West. Large areas of land, beyond that of the Louisiana Purchase that was added to the United States in 1803, still belonged to other countries. Britain claimed Oregon Territory; Mexico claimed the Southwest and Texas. Many Americans believed that all these territories should be part of the United States.

This belief added to the growing American sense of national pride. It supported the idea known as Manifest Destiny. Manifest Destiny meant that the United States had the duty to bring democracy and progress to the Western Hemisphere. Many Americans believed that the best way to achieve Manifest Destiny was to expand the territory of the United States.

4. Which of the following scenarios follows an accurate sequence of events?

   A. Manifest Destiny, Louisiana Purchase, American Revolution
   B. American Revolution, Louisiana Purchase, War of 1812, Manifest Destiny
   C. American Revolution, Manifest Destiny, War of 1812, Louisiana Purchase
   D. Manifest Destiny, Indian Removal Act, Louisiana Purchase, War of 1812

5. Which event might follow the feeling of national pride that Americans experienced after the War of 1812?

   A. Britain and the United States claimed joint ownership of the Oregon Territory.
   B. The French and Indian War was fought.
   C. A period of prolonged peace was experienced throughout the young nation.
   D. The Civil War was fought.

Cause and Effect

SS CONTENT TOPICS: I.USH.c.1, I.USH.c.2, II.G.b.1, II.G.b.3, II.G.b.4, II.G.b.5, II.G.c.1, II.G.c.2, II.G.d.3, I.E.a, I.CG.b.8, I.CG.d.2
SS PRACTICES: SSP.1.a, SSP.1.b, SSP.2.a, SSP.2.b, SSP.3.a, SSP.4.a, SSP.5.a, SSP.5.d

1 Learn the Skill

A **cause** is an action or occurrence that makes another event happen. Sometimes causes will be directly stated in text. At times, however, authors may imply the causes of certain events or occurrences. An **effect** is something that happens as a result of a cause. Without the cause, the resultant effect might never have occurred. A single cause often produces more than one effect. Similarly, multiple causes can work together to produce a single effect. By **identifying causes and effects** in social studies texts, you can better understand the connections among events and more fully comprehend what you read.

As with other areas of the GED® test, understanding cause-and-effect questions will test your ability to interpret data at various Depth of Knowledge levels through the use of complex reading and thinking skills.

2 Practice the Skill

By practicing the skill of understanding cause and effect, you will improve your study and test-taking abilities, especially as they relate to the GED® Social Studies Test. Study the passage and strategies below. Then answer the question that follows.

During the era of the American Revolution, Northern and Southern states were united behind the common goal of gaining independence from Britain. However, as time went by, differences between the two regions grew pronounced.

With the beginning of the 1800s, the South remained primarily agricultural. The Southern economy centered on plantations and the use of enslaved African laborers.

a Note the author's use of cause-and-effect signal words and phrases, such as *on the other hand.*

a The Northern economy, on the other hand, featured growing commercial and industrial sectors in addition to agriculture.
b These differences caused economic and ideological friction between the North and the South. Disputes over states' rights emerged as questions arose about the morality and legality of slavery in the United States' territories.

b Here, the author directly states that one event caused another.

USING LOGIC

Other signal words and phrases include *caused, affected, led to,* and *resulted from.* To confirm a cause-and-effect relationship, restate the events as "A" caused "B."

1. What is one effect of the regional differences that emerged between the North and the South in the early-to mid-1800s?

    A. Northern states strongly supported states' rights.
    B. The South began using the labor of enslaved people.
    C. The Northern economy became increasingly diverse.
    D. Northern farmers began establishing plantations.

Spotlighted Item: **FILL-IN-THE-BLANK**

DIRECTIONS: Study the passage, read the questions, then fill in your answer to each question in the boxes that follow.

Many people still debate why Americans fought the Civil War. Some historians claim the war was about states' rights, while others believe the war was fought over slavery. However, no confusion existed when the South fired on the North's Ft. Sumter in 1861. The Vice President of the Confederate States, Alexander Stephens, gave his famous "Cornerstone" speech in March 1861, shortly before the war started.

From Alexander Stephens's "Cornerstone" Speech:

The new constitution has put at rest, forever, all the agitating questions relating to our peculiar institution of African slavery as it exists amongst us the proper status of the negro in our form of civilization. This was the immediate cause of the late rupture and present revolution.

Jefferson in his forecast, had anticipated this, as the "rock upon which the old Union would split." He was right. What was conjecture with him, is now a realized fact. But whether he fully comprehended the great truth upon which that rock stood and stands, may be doubted. The prevailing ideas entertained by him and most of the leading statesmen at the time of the formation of the old constitution, were that the enslavement of the African was in violation of the laws of nature; that it was wrong in principle, socially, morally, and politically. It was an evil they knew not well how to deal with, but the general opinion of the men of that day was that, somehow or other in the order of Providence, the institution would be evanescent and pass away. This idea, though not incorporated in the constitution, was the prevailing idea at that time. The constitution, it is true, secured every essential guarantee to the institution while it should last, and hence no argument can be justly urged against the constitutional guarantees thus secured, because of the common sentiment of the day. Those ideas, however, were fundamentally wrong. They rested upon the assumption of the equality of races. This was an error. It was a sandy foundation, and the government built upon it fell when the "storm came and the wind blew."

Our new government is founded upon exactly the opposite idea; its foundations are laid, its corner-stone rests, upon the great truth that the negro is not equal to the white man; that slavery subordination to the superior race is his natural and normal condition. This, our new government, is the first, in the history of the world, based upon this great physical, philosophical, and moral truth. This truth has been slow in the process of its development, like all other truths in the various departments of science. It has been so even amongst us.

2. To what did President Thomas Jefferson refer as the "rock upon which the old Union would split"?

3. Stephens claims that Jefferson and other American forefathers believed slavery would cease to exist due to

.

4. The [   ], according to Stephens, guarantees that slavery will continue to exist.

5. The institution of slavery, claims Stephens, is a natural and normal condition because the white and African races are

.

UNIT 2

Interpret Timelines

SS CONTENT TOPICS: I.USH.c.3, I.USH.d.1, I.USH.d.2, I.USH.d.4, I.USH.d.5, I.CG.b.8, I.CG.c.5, I.CG.d.2
SS PRACTICES: SSP.1.b, SSP.2.a, SSP.2.b, SSP.3.b, SSP.4.a, SSP.6.b

① Learn the Skill

The ability to **interpret timelines** is an especially valuable tool when studying history. Timelines present sequences of events in a visual manner. Visualizing events in this way enables you to determine not only the order in which the events occur, but also the intervals that fall between these events. Because timelines show key events in sequence, it is possible to identify historical trends that connect those events.

As with other areas of the GED® test, questions about interpreting timelines will test your ability to interpret information at various Depth of Knowledge levels through the use of complex reading skills and thinking skills.

② Practice the Skill

By practicing the skill of interpreting timelines, you will improve your study and test-taking abilities, especially as they relate to the GED® Social Studies Test. Study the information and the timeline below. Then answer the question that follows.

ⓐ The benchmark dates on a timeline show the equivalent intervals into which the full time span of the timeline is divided. In this case, the timeline shows the period from 1890 to 1920 divided into five-year intervals.

ⓑ This timeline illustrates some of the historic events that occurred during the years leading to the ratification of the Nineteenth Amendment, which granted U.S. women the right to vote.

ⓑ SELECTED DATES IN THE FIGHT FOR WOMEN'S SUFFRAGE

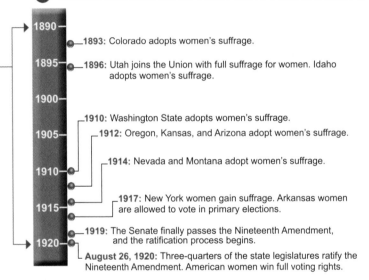

1890
1893: Colorado adopts women's suffrage.

1895
1896: Utah joins the Union with full suffrage for women. Idaho adopts women's suffrage.

1900

1910: Washington State adopts women's suffrage.
1905
1912: Oregon, Kansas, and Arizona adopt women's suffrage.

1914: Nevada and Montana adopt women's suffrage.
1910

1917: New York women gain suffrage. Arkansas women are allowed to vote in primary elections.
1915

1919: The Senate finally passes the Nineteenth Amendment, and the ratification process begins.
1920
August 26, 1920: Three-quarters of the state legislatures ratify the Nineteenth Amendment. American women win full voting rights.

Beginning in the second half of the 1800s, many women in the United States worked to gain the right to vote. Organizations such as the National Woman Suffrage Association and the American Woman Suffrage Association worked to gain this right through a national constitutional amendment and individual state constitutional amendments. Susan B. Anthony (1820–1906) served as a leader in the National Woman Suffrage Association. After a number of states granted suffrage, women began to use their new voting rights to once again push for a national amendment. In 1920, the Nineteenth Amendment granted women throughout the United States the right to vote.

USING LOGIC

Timelines typically show a trend in events. By reviewing each event and the events that occurred before and after each one, you should be able to see the trend.

1. Which of the following inferences can you make about Susan B. Anthony?

    A. She voted in the 1920 presidential election.
    B. She opposed anti-slavery and temperance amendments.
    C. She traveled and lectured on the importance of women's suffrage.
    D. She lived in one of the first states to grant women the right to vote.

★ Spotlighted Item: **FILL-IN-THE-BLANK**

DIRECTIONS: Read the information presented in the passage and the timeline. Then, read each question and write your response to it in the box that follows.

IMPORTANT DATES IN AMERICA'S JIM CROW PERIOD

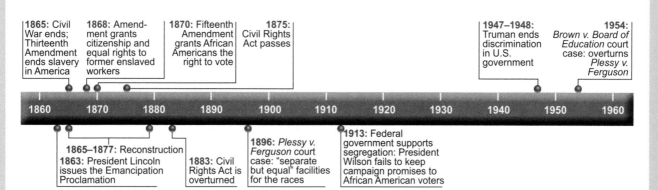

Following the Civil War most Southern states as well as some border states enacted laws that denied basic human rights to newly freed African Americans. A white minstrel, popularly known as Jim Crow, wore blackface and mocked characteristics of African Americans. The term "Jim Crow" evolved to encompass the laws, customs, and personal behavior that white people displayed in their segregation and degradation of African Americans.

Jim Crow laws and practices represented the biased racial hierarchy that was prevalent during the decades following the Civil War, with white people at the top and African Americans at the bottom.

For example, during the Jim Crow period, an African American person was expected to move from a front seat of a train or a bus to a seat in the back when a white person boarded. Segregated drinking fountains were common. Supporters of Jim Crow and racial segregation believed that if the two races shared public facilities, it might promote social equality, leading, they feared, to the destruction of American culture.

Also common during this time were separate hospitals, prisons, churches, cemeteries, public and private schools, public restrooms, and other public accommodations. In general, the facilities for African Americans were quite inferior, less

conveniently located, much older, smaller, and dirtier. In many locations, there simply were no facilities available for African Americans, including no place to eat or sit or no public restrooms.

2. African Americans from all states received the

   right to vote ☐ years after

   the Civil War ended.

3. The year ☐ was notable for

   practices of racial segregation in the U.S. government.

4. White citizens who practiced racial segregation during the Jim Crow period did not

   want ☐

   between the races.

5. Maintaining separate-but-equal public facilities between the races was ensured by the Supreme Court case

   ☐ .

UNIT 2

Unit 2 Review

DIRECTIONS: Study the information in the passage and on the map, read the questions, then choose the **best** answer to each question.

RUSSIAN REVOLUTION

   In 1917 during the late stages of World War I, social and economic conflict drove Russian society into crisis. In February 1917, Tsar Nicholas II left power and a provisional government took over. In October, the Bolsheviks, led by Vladimir Lenin, overthrew the provisional government. During the next two years, Lenin and Leo Trotsky helped to fortify the Bolshevik Russian Red Army. Opposing the Red Army, was the White Army, led by generals such as Admiral Kolchak and General Denikin. The White Army had military successes against the Red Army in 1918 and early 1919. Kolchak moved his troops across the Urals toward Moscow and Denikin pushed toward Moscow from the south.

   However, Russia's Civil War began to turn in favor of the Red Army during the summer of 1919. The Red Army, unlike the White Army, commanded strong internal communication lines and clear leadership. Ultimately, the Red Army supported the establishment of the world's first communist state, which eventually became the Union of Soviet Socialist Republics (USSR). In the decades to come, the USSR supported the spread of communism around the world. The United States viewed communism as a political and ideological threat. These political differences paved the way for a Cold War between the Soviet Union and the U.S.

1. To what did the U.S. object in the aftermath of the Russian Revolution?

   A. rise of the Red Army
   B. formation of the USSR
   C. defeat of the White Army
   D. spread of communism

2. What was one effect of the Russian Revolution on the U.S.?

   A. World War I
   B. the Civil War
   C. the Cold War
   D. World War II

DIRECTIONS: Study the table, read the questions, then choose the **best** answer for each question.

U.S. CENSUS, 1890:
ORIGIN OF IMMIGRANT CITIZENS

Northern Europe	Western Europe	Southern Europe	Eastern Europe
1. Ireland: 1,871,509	1. Germany: 2,784,894	1. Italy: 182,580	1. Russia: 182,644
2. England 908,141	2. Austria: 123,271	2. Portugal: 15,996	2. Poland: 147,440
3. Scotland 242,231	3. France: 113,174	3. Azores: 9,739	3. Czechoslovakia: 118,106
4. Wales 100,079	4. Low Countries: 107,349	4. Spain: 6,185	4. Hungary: 62,435
5. Scandinavia 933,249	5. Switzerland: 104,069	5. Greece: 1,887	5. Turkey in Europe: 1,839
Total from the Top 5 Areas in the Region: 4,055,209	3,232,757	216,387	512,464

3. By 1890, the greatest number of European immigrants had come to the U.S. from which European region?

   A. Northern
   B. Western
   C. Southern
   D. Eastern

4. After 1890, there was a regional shift in European immigration to the U.S. Which European region with the smallest number of immigrants by 1890 likely saw an increase?

   A. Northern
   B. Western
   C. Southern
   D. Eastern

DIRECTIONS: Study the table and the passage, read the questions, then choose the **best** answer for each question.

PERMANENT MEMBERS OF
THE LEAGUE OF NATIONS COUNCIL

> Great Britain
> France
> Italy
> Japan
> Germany
> USSR

The League of Nations was an international organization established after World War I. Created as part of the peace treaty that ended the war, the purpose of the League was to preserve international peace and prevent the outbreak of future conflicts. United States President Woodrow Wilson was a strong supporter of the League of Nations. However, many members of Congress opposed the idea of the United States joining the organization. The League of Nations strove to achieve its goals through the protection of permanent and member countries and their boundaries against aggressor nations, the establishment of a world court, and disarmament.

5. What can you infer based on the information presented in the passage and the table?

   A. The League of Nations allowed just Allied nations and neutral countries to join.
   B. The United States never joined the League of Nations.
   C. The League of Nations Council included just six permanent member nations.
   D. Woodrow Wilson served as a member of the League of Nations World Court.

6. What can be inferred about the long-term success of the League of Nations?

   A. It stopped invasions by aggressor nations for more than 50 years.
   B. The member nations of the Council enjoyed peaceful relations for many decades.
   C. It was taken over by the U.S. Congress.
   D. It did not achieve peace by protecting its members from aggressor nations.

DIRECTIONS: Read the passage and the questions, then choose the **best** answer to each question.

Italian Prime Minister Benito Mussolini co-wrote the following excerpt in 1932 as part of an encyclopedia entry on Fascism:

For Fascism, the growth of empire, that is to say the expansion of the nation, is an essential manifestation of vitality, and its opposite a sign of decadence. Peoples which are rising, or rising again after a period of decadence, are always imperialist; and renunciation is a sign of decay and death. Fascism is the doctrine best adapted to represent the tendencies and the aspirations of a people, like the people of Italy, who are rising again after many centuries of abasement and foreign servitude ... for never before has the nation stood more in need of authority, of direction and order. If every age has its own characteristic doctrine, there are a thousand signs which point to Fascism as the characteristic doctrine of our time.

From Benito Mussolini's (with Giovanni Gentile), "WHAT IS FASCISM?" 1932

7. Which of the following is the main idea that Mussolini and Gentile are conveying?

    A. Italy needs to rise again as a world power.
    B. Fascism is the root cause of Italy's centuries of abasement and foreign servitude.
    C. The doctrine of Fascism is equal to decadence.
    D. The doctrine of Fascism is critical to Italy's rise as a strong nation again.

8. In addition to Fascism, what other totalitarian form of government played a key role in the events of World War II?

    A. Federalism
    B. Socialism
    C. Democracy
    D. Nazism

9. Which of the following represents a reasoning error that Mussolini makes in this excerpt?

    A. He appeals to the beliefs of his audience.
    B. He makes absolute and universal claims.
    C. He focuses on the people of Italy.
    D. He defines terminology.

DIRECTIONS: Study the table and the passage, read the question, then choose the **best** answer to the question.

17 NON-SELF-GOVERNING TERRITORIES, 2013

TERRITORY	Administration	Population
AFRICA: Western Sahara	disputed	531,000
ATLANTIC & CARIBBEAN: Anguilla	United Kingdom	15,500
ATLANTIC & CARIBBEAN: Bermuda	United Kingdom	62,000
ATLANTIC & CARIBBEAN: British Virgin Islands	United Kingdom	28,103
ATLANTIC & CARIBBEAN: Cayman Islands	United Kingdom	55,500
ATLANTIC & CARIBBEAN: Falkland Islands (Malvinas)	United Kingdom	2,500
ATLANTIC & CARIBBEAN: Montserrat	United Kingdom	5,000
ATLANTIC & CARIBBEAN: St. Helena	United Kingdom	5,396
ATLANTIC & CARIBBEAN: Turks and Caicos Islands	United Kingdom	31,458
ATLANTIC & CARIBBEAN: United States Virgin Islands	United States	106,405
EUROPE: Gibraltar	United Kingdom	29,752
ASIA & PACIFIC: American Samoa	United States	55,519
ASIA & PACIFIC: Guam	United States	159,358
ASIA & PACIFIC: New Caledonia	France	252,000
ASIA AND PACIFIC: French Polynesia	France	271,000
ASIA AND PACIFIC: Pitcairn	United Kingdom	50
ASIA AND PACIFIC: Tokelau	New Zealand	1,411

From un.org, accessed 2013

When the United Nations was founded in 1945, approximately one-third of the world's population lived in colonial territories. Today, fewer than two million people live under colonial rule in the 17 remaining non–self-governing territories.

10. Which administrator governs the largest number of the remaining 17 non-self-governing colonies?

    A. United Kingdom
    B. United States
    C. France
    D. New Zealand

DIRECTIONS: Study the table and the passage, read the questions, then fill in your answers in the boxes below.

HOLOCAUST VICTIMS

Region	# Killed	Region	# Killed
Africa	526	Hungary	305,000
Albania	200	Italy	8,000
Austria	65,000	Latvia	85,000
Belgium	24,387	Lithuania	135,000
Czechoslovakia	277,000	Luxembourg	700
Denmark	77	Netherlands	106,000
Estonia	4,000	Norway	728
France	83,000	Poland	3,001,000
Germany	160,000	Romania	364,632
Greece	71,301	Soviet Union	1,500,000
Yugoslavia	67,122	TOTAL: 6,258,673	

The Nazi Party came to power in Germany in March 1933, and Adolf Hitler was Dictator of Germany. The Nazis were effective at blaming the Jewish people for Germany's economic disaster after World War I. This anti-Semitic sentiment and Hitler's absolute power enabled him to pursue what he called the "final solution."

With German victories early in World War II, Jews were trapped in Europe. By 1941, Nazi killing units swept through the Soviet Union, killing over a million Jews. In 1942, concentration and extermination camps were built throughout Europe along main rail lines. The Nazis systematically executed and cremated another 3.5 million Jews. Ultimately, more than six million Jews died at the hands of the Nazis.

11. After Poland and the Soviet Union, which region had the most Holocaust victims?

12. According to the information, how did the Nazis transport Jews to the camps?

13. How did Adolf Hitler categorize his systematic extermination of the Jewish people?

DIRECTIONS: Study the map and the passage, read the questions, then fill in your answers in the boxes below.

JAPANESE INTERNMENT CAMPS

In February 1942, President Franklin D. Roosevelt ordered all Americans of Japanese descent into internment camps. Roosevelt's decision was based on fear of espionage, racism among Americans, and concerns for national security. This action was just two months after the Japanese bombed Pearl Harbor on December 7, 1941, forcing the United States officially into World War II. More than 120,000 U.S. citizens, many of whom were born in the U.S. and had never been to Japan, were sent to one of ten military-like camps located in seven states.

14. Fear of what activity did President Roosevelt use to justify his actions in February 1942?

15. Based upon the camp locations on the map, in which part of the United States would you infer that most Japanese Americans lived in 1942?

16. What problem, still troubling America today, was motivating the hysterical outcry that supported internment?

DIRECTIONS: Study the information presented in the table and the passage, read the questions, then choose the **best** answer to each question.

THE GI BILL

Cause
Veterans returning to the U.S. from World War II faced unemployment, under-education, and poverty.

Effect
On June 22, 1944, President Franklin D. Roosevelt signed the GI Bill, which was administered by the Veterans' Administration (VA), to help veterans reassimilate into society. The bill provided for: • payments of $20 per week. • non-taxable funds for college education. • loans for homes, farms, or businesses.

The "GI Bill" has been heralded as one of the most significant pieces of legislation ever produced by the federal government—one that impacted the United States socially, economically, and politically.

17. Which of the following is the main cause for passage of the GI Bill?

  A. Franklin D. Roosevelt was responsible for bringing the United States into World War II.
  B. Unemployed veterans needed education, training, and assistance with housing.
  C. The Veterans Administration needed to add employees to its workforce.
  D. Colleges and universities were lacking sufficient numbers of students.

18. Which of the following is the most important effect of the GI Bill for veterans?

  A. The Veterans' Administration was formed.
  B. Veterans received tax benefits.
  C. Veterans received school, job, and housing benefits.
  D. President Roosevelt was re-elected.

DIRECTIONS: Study the information in the timeline, read the question, then choose the **best** answer.

THE COLD WAR (1947–1989)

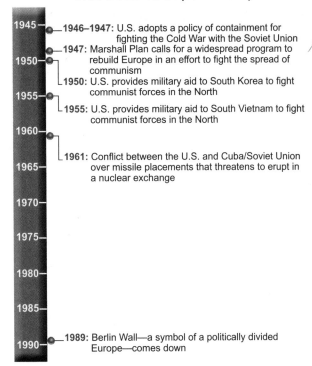

1946–1947: U.S. adopts a policy of containment for fighting the Cold War with the Soviet Union

1947: Marshall Plan calls for a widespread program to rebuild Europe in an effort to fight the spread of communism

1950: U.S. provides military aid to South Korea to fight communist forces in the North

1955: U.S. provides military aid to South Vietnam to fight communist forces in the North

1961: Conflict between the U.S. and Cuba/Soviet Union over missile placements that threatens to erupt in a nuclear exchange

1989: Berlin Wall—a symbol of a politically divided Europe—comes down

19. During the Cold War, how did the U.S. try to contain communism?

  A. It allowed the Soviet Union to place missiles in Cuba.
  B. It opposed the tearing down of the Berlin Wall.
  C. It adopted policies to isolate itself from Europe and Asia.
  D. It provided aid for European reconstruction and eastern military conflicts.

DIRECTIONS: Read the passage and the questions, then choose the **best** answer for each question.

Britain's financial and physical losses during World War I and World War II were immense, and the former world power no longer had the ability to provide monetary or military assistance to countries such as Greece and Turkey, both of which had suffered drastic losses during the wars. Greece was undergoing a civil war, and Turkey needed financial assistance. Given their proximity to the Communist Soviet Union, it seemed possible that both countries might fall under its growing regional power.

United States government officials discussed The Domino Theory, which predicted that if one nation fell to Soviet communism, weakened neighboring states would also fall. President Harry S. Truman agreed to address the issue in a joint session of Congress, which would be nationally broadcast.

On March 12, 1947, in an address now known as The Truman Doctrine, the President declared it to be America's duty to assist any country threatened by communism:

"I believe that it must be the policy of the United States to support free peoples who are resisting attempted subjugation by armed minorities or by outside pressures. I believe that we must assist free peoples to work out their own destinies in their own way. I believe that our help should be primarily through economic and financial aid, which is essential to economic stability and orderly political processes."

Truman requested $400 million to assist both Greece and Turkey. Congress approved the President's request and signed it into law on May 22, 1947.

20. What was President Truman's justification for requesting financial assistance for Turkey and Greece?

   A. The President wanted the United States to take the place of Britain as a world power.
   B. The President wanted the countries to become democratic.
   C. The countries had fallen to the Soviet Union and had become communist countries.
   D. The countries were weakened, close to the Soviet Union, and vulnerable to communism.

21. What effect of The Domino Theory worried U.S. government leaders?

   A. The U.S. might have to support countries formerly supported by Britain.
   B. If one nation fell to communism, another weak neighboring nation might also fall.
   C. If the United States provided financial assistance to one country, other weak neighboring countries would expect aid.
   D. Small countries such as Greece or Turkey could not govern themselves properly.

DIRECTIONS: Read the passage and the questions, then choose the **best** answer for each question.

The communist government of East Germany constructed the Berlin Wall in 1961 to prevent East Germans from fleeing the communist nation for the democratic nation of West Germany. East German troops heavily guarded the wall to prevent crossings. While a few citizens managed to cross this boundary, many people attempting to cross into West Berlin lost their lives. However, by the summer of 1989, the Hungarian government began to allow East Germans to travel through Hungary in order to reach Austria and West Germany. This development rendered the wall obsolete. By the fall of 1989, the East German government had nearly collapsed. On November 9, 1989, the government granted citizens the freedom to move across the boundary into West Germany. In 1990, the wall was torn down and East Germany and West Germany reunited as a single nation.

22. Which of the following statements is the main idea of the passage?

   A. The Berlin Wall was favored by most East Germans.
   B. The Berlin Wall was a hostile dividing line between communism and democracy.
   C. East Germans viewed West Germany as a hostile nation.
   D. East Germans directed their attempts to escape toward Hungary.

23. For how many years were East and West Germany divided by the Berlin Wall?

   A. 38 years
   B. 35 years
   C. 29 years
   D. 25 years

DIRECTIONS: Study the map and the passage, read the questions, then choose the **best** answer to each question.

NATO AND THE WARSAW PACT: 1949–1991

ICELAND
Norwegian Sea
U.S./CANADA (NATO Alliance)
FINLAND
NORWAY
SWEDEN
Baltic Sea
North Sea
DENMARK
U.S.S.R.
IRELAND
UNITED KINGDOM
NETHER-LANDS
EAST GERMANY
POLAND
BELGIUM
ATLANTIC OCEAN
LUXEMBOURG
WEST GERMANY (1955)
CZECHOSLOVAKIA
FRANCE
SWITZ.
AUSTRIA
HUNGARY
ROMANIA
Black Sea
YUGOSLAVIA
BULGARIA
ITALY
ALBANIA
PORTUGAL
SPAIN (1975)
TURKEY (1952)
GREECE (1952)
Mediterranean Sea

NATO Countries
Warsaw Pact Countries
Non-signing Countries

After World War II, President Truman adopted a policy of containment and built a global network of anti-communist alliances. The first network was the North Atlantic Treaty Organization, or NATO. As a result of the Soviet blockade of the city of Berlin, which was inside the Soviet-controlled part of Germany, and the resulting Berlin Airlift in June 1948, President Truman declared his intention to provide military aid to Western Europe.

The United States and Canada, along with ten West European countries, signed the North Atlantic Treaty to establish NATO on April 4, 1949, to counter the threat from the Soviet Union. The ten signatories from Europe were Belgium, Denmark, France, Iceland, Italy, Luxembourg, the Netherlands, Norway, Portugal, and the United Kingdom. The cornerstone of NATO was that all members agreed to come to each other's aid if they were attacked. NATO committed the United States by treaty to the defense of Western Europe. It also ensured that the United States would not pursue a policy of isolationism, as it had after World War I when it tried to stay out of European affairs. NATO was further expanded when Turkey and Greece joined

the original countries in 1952, the Federal Republic of Germany joined in 1955, and when Spain joined in 1975. Today, there are 28 independent member countries.

The re-militarization of West Germany was used as an excuse by the Soviet Union to form the communist equivalent to NATO, the Warsaw Pact, which was signed by Albania, Bulgaria, Czechoslovakia, the German Democratic Republic, Hungary, Poland, Romania, and the Soviet Union in Warsaw, Poland, on May 14, 1955. This military treaty bound its signatories to come to the aid of the others, should any one of them be the victim of foreign aggression. Although the Warsaw Pact was based on total equality of each nation and mutual noninterference in one another's internal affairs, it quickly became a powerful political tool for the Soviet Union. The sole legal defector after its formation was Albania, which withdrew in 1968, in protest of the Soviet invasion of Czechoslovakia. Following the diminishing power of the U.S.S.R. in the 1980s, and the eventual fall of Communism, the Warsaw Pact was officially dissolved in 1991.

24. After the original twelve, how many more countries have joined NATO?

A. 4
B. 10
C. 16
D. 28

25. The formation of NATO was in response to what threat from the Soviet Union?

A. the invasion of Czechoslovakia
B. the Berlin Airlift
C. the signing of the Warsaw Pact
D. the blockade of Berlin

26. How did U.S. foreign policy differ between the ends of WWI and WWII?

A. It became isolationist.
B. It became willing to intervene in European affairs.
C. It supported the Soviet Union.
D. It did not pledge defense for Western Europe.

27. Why is the Warsaw Pact no longer in force?

A. Communism and the U.S.S.R. fell.
B. The Warsaw Pact countries joined NATO.
C. The U.S.S.R. nullified the Pact.
D. Czechoslovakia was invaded.

DIRECTIONS: Read the passage and the questions, then choose the **best** answer to each question.

President Ronald Reagan delivered the following speech at Germany's Berlin Wall in June of 1987. The Berlin Wall divided democratic West Berlin from Communist-controlled East Berlin and the rest of East Germany. In this speech, President Reagan addresses Soviet leader Mikhail Gorbachev:

"And now the Soviets may, in a limited way, be coming to understand the importance of freedom. We hear much from Moscow about a new policy of reform and openness. ...

Are these the beginnings of profound changes in the Soviet state? Or are they token gestures, intended to raise false hopes in the West, or to strengthen the Soviet system without changing it? ... There is one sign the Soviets can make that would be unmistakable, that would advance dramatically the cause of freedom and peace.

General Secretary Gorbachev, if you seek peace, if you seek prosperity for the Soviet Union and Eastern Europe, if you seek liberalization: Come here to this gate! Mr. Gorbachev, open this gate! Mr. Gorbachev, tear down this wall!"

28. Which of the following best summarizes President Reagan's purpose for delivering this speech?

    A. to encourage Soviet leadership to acknowledge the importance of freedom
    B. to propose a treaty between the United States and the Soviet Union
    C. to criticize communist policies in Eastern Europe
    D. to proclaim American support for West Germany

29. What symbolic action does President Reagan want General Secretary Gorbachev to take?

    A. raise false hopes in the West
    B. perform token gestures
    C. adopt a new policy of reform
    D. destroy the Berlin Wall

DIRECTIONS: Read the passage and the questions, then choose the **best** answer to each question.

In 1989, as nations across Eastern Europe began to transition from communism to democratic forms of government, Mikhail Gorbachev and the Soviet Union chose not to intervene. This allowed democratic reforms to take place in nations such as Hungary, Poland, and Bulgaria. Gorbachev's many reforms also allowed opposition to communism to develop within the Soviet Union. In 1990, individual Soviet republics started to assert their sovereignty over Soviet rule. By August 1991, a failed coup by conservative communist leaders led to increased support for democratic reforms. By November 1991, the Communist Party had been dissolved. Boris Yeltsin, a pro-democracy leader, negotiated the formation of the Commonwealth of Independent States. Gorbachev resigned on December 25, 1991, and one day later, the Soviet Union officially dissolved.

30. Which evidence best supports the idea that not all Eastern Europeans supported democratic reform?

    A. Conservative leaders staged a coup against the Soviet government.
    B. Gorbachev's reforms allowed growing opposition.
    C. Democratic governments rose to power in nations such as Hungary and Poland.
    D. The Soviet Union chose not to intervene in outside conflicts.

31. Prior to this time, how did the Soviet Union most likely handle political unrest in Eastern Europe?

    A. by avoiding involvement in the internal affairs of other Eastern European countries
    B. by using military force to stop uprisings
    C. by mediating peaceful resolutions
    D. by seeking the assistance of the United States

UNIT 3

Michael J. Fox

Just as he was adamant about earning his GED® certificate, Michael J. Fox believes that a concentrated effort from our elected representatives can help find the cause of Parkinson's disease.

Michael J. Fox dreamed of becoming an actor. He also struggled as a student. Finding some success in film and television in his native Edmonton, Canada, Fox dropped out of high school his senior year to pursue an acting career in the United States. However, his educational journey was far from over.

During the 1980s, Fox earned stardom and awards for his role as "Alex P. Keaton" on television's *Family Ties*. Fox also gained acclaim in films such as the *Back To The Future* movies. Still, thoughts of continuing his education lingered. At the insistence of his four-year-old child, Fox earned his GED® certificate in 1995.

Three years later, Fox announced to the world that he had been diagnosed with Parkinson's disease, a disorder that affects the nervous system and for which there is no known cure. Instead of retreating from the public eye, Fox optimized his challenge as an opportunity to raise awareness about and funding for the disease. In 1999, Fox testified before Congress for more federal money for Parkinson's research. In 2000, he left his popular *Spin City* television show and started the Michael J. Fox Foundation for Parkinson's Research. Soon the Foundation announced its partnership with the National Institute of Health to identify physical traits indicating the presence of Parkinson's.

"We have no *Department of Cures* **in government; it's us. I wanted to create an entity that does something about it."**

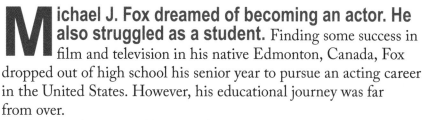

CAREER HIGHLIGHTS: *Michael J. Fox*

- Earned 3 Emmy Awards and a Golden Globe Award
- Bestselling author of 3 books
- Started the Michael J. Fox Foundation for Parkinson's Research, raising more that $250 million by 2012

- Received an Honorary Degree of Medicine in 2010 from the Karolinska Institute in Sweden
- Received numerous humanitarian awards for his work and was appointed an Officer of the Order of Canada in 2010

Civics and Government

Unit 3:
Civics and Government

The United States embraces to its fullest extent a democratic form of government. In a democracy, leaders represent the interests of the citizens who elect them. As U.S. citizens, we have various rights and responsibilities. Every time you vote for representatives, leaders, and issues, you are exercising one of those rights. Similarly, as citizens we also have certain responsibilities. One such responsibility involves staying informed about current events.

The importance of civics and government extends to the GED® Social Studies Test, where this section makes up 50 percent of all questions. As with other areas of the GED® Tests, the civics and government section will test your ability to interpret information at various Depth of Knowledge levels through the use of complex reading skills and thinking skills. In Unit 3, the introduction of various critical-thinking skills, along with specialized instruction about text, charts, and graphs, will help you prepare for the GED® Social Studies Test.

Table of Contents

UNIT 3

Written in 1787, ratified in 1788, and in operation since 1789, the United States Constitution is the world's longest surviving written charter of government. Its first three words – "We The People" – affirm that the government of the United States exists to serve its citizens.

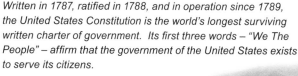

Interpret Diagrams

SS CONTENT TOPICS: I.CG.a.1, I.CG.b.1, I.CG.b.5, I.CG.b.8
SS PRACTICES: SSP.1.a, SSP.6.b

UNIT 3

1 Learn the Skill

Diagrams are different from other types of graphics, such as charts or graphs, because they can show the relationships that exist between pieces of information. For instance, diagrams can show sequence, similarities, differences, and other comparisons. Authors often use diagrams to present or summarize social studies information concisely. By learning how to **interpret diagrams**, you can maximize your understanding of the information presented in these visuals.

As with other areas of the GED® test, questions about interpreting diagrams will test your ability to interpret information at various Depth of Knowledge levels through the use of complex reading skills and thinking skills.

2 Practice the Skill

By practicing the skill of interpreting diagrams, you will improve your study and test-taking abilities, especially as they relate to the GED® Social Studies Test. Study the diagram below. Then answer the question that follows.

12TH AND 13TH CENTURY MONARCHIES

a The format of a diagram provides clues to its purpose and the type of information that it includes. A Venn diagram shows how two subjects are similar and how they are different.

a

England **b** **b** **France** **b**

England
- Instituted new justice system that established common law in England
- Magna Carta forced king to grant more authority to barons in 1215
- Parliament established in 1264

Both
- Centralized government
- Made rule over vassals more official
- Increased wealth from new tax systems

France
- In prior years, king only had authority of area near Paris
- Under Philip II, claimed lands from England
- Philip II established capable administration to facilitate tax collection

b Pay attention to the titles and headings of diagrams. What information can you learn from these items? Here, the headings above and inside the two main circles identify the subjects that will be compared and contrasted.

TEST-TAKING TIPS

When asked to use a diagram in a testing situation, first preview the questions related to the diagram. Determine what information you will need to locate in the diagram to answer these questions correctly.

1. In which of the following ways did France strengthen its monarchy that England did not?

A. France centralized its national government.
B. France established a new system of justice.
C. France increased wealth from a new tax system.
D. France claimed new territories for the nation.

⭐ Spotlighted Item: **DROP-DOWN**

DIRECTIONS: The passage below is incomplete. Use information from the diagram to complete the passage. For each drop-down item, choose the option that correctly completes the sentence.

Thomas Hobbes
People are born with natural rights, but are ruled by destructive passions and self-interest. To ensure security and decrease conflict, people must make a social contract in which they submit totally to a strong government with a wise, powerful leader.

John Locke
People are born with natural rights to life, liberty, and property that can neither be taken nor given away. People make a social contract with government to serve the will of the majority. If government attempts to take away rights, it can be removed.

Contributors to American Political Thought

Charles-Louis Montesquieu
The power of the king must be balanced by a strong legislature. However, the best government is one in which the executive, legislative, and judicial powers are separated so that no government body or leader can become too powerful.

Jean-Jacques Rousseau
People have natural rights but create governments to protect life, liberty, and property. The majority does not always make wise decisions, but the best government is one in which people make laws to govern themselves.

2. In the 17th and 18th centuries centuries, writers and philosophers such as John Locke and Jean-Jacques Rousseau developed new ways to think about government and individual rights. Their ideas influenced the events that led to the American Revolution. They also influenced several important documents in the early history of our country. These documents include the Declaration of Independence and the Constitution of the United States.

Known as Enlightenment thinkers, Locke and Rousseau believed that people were born free and with natural ⌈ 2. Drop-down 1 ⌉ . They also believed that the power of government came from the ⌈ 2. Drop-down 2 ⌉ . The agreement between the government and the governed was called the ⌈ 2. Drop-down 3 ⌉ . If a government tried to take away the rights of the people, this agreement was broken. In that case, Locke believed that the people had the right to ⌈ 2. Drop-down 4 ⌉ . Although all of the Enlightenment thinkers believed in individual rights, the governmental ideas presented by ⌈ 2. Drop-down 5 ⌉ differed most from those of the other three men.

Drop-Down Answer Options

2.1 A. intelligence
    B. government
    C. rights
    D. duties

2.2 A. leaders
    B. people
    C. executive
    D. clergy

2.3 A. natural right
    B. social study
    C. central power
    D. social contract

2.4 A. rebel
    B. vote
    C. submit
    D. complain

2.5 A. Hobbes
    B. Locke
    C. Montesquieu
    D. Rousseau

UNIT 3

Interpret the Constitution

SS CONTENT TOPICS: I.CG.b.2, I.CG.b.3, I.CG.b.5, I.CG.b.8, I.CG.c.1, I.CG.c.2, I.CG.c.3, I.CG.c.4, I.CG.d.1, I.CG.d.2, I.USH.a.1
SS PRACTICES: SSP.1.a, SSP.2.a, SSP.4.a

1 Learn the Skill

The **Constitution of the United States** includes a Preamble and seven Articles along with 27 amendments that have been added since the Constitution was first written. The Constitution describes the basic structure of the federal government and the principles under which it operates. Because the Constitution describes these principles in a general manner, it becomes important to **interpret the Constitution** in order to understand how its principles apply to the everyday workings of our national government.

As with other areas of the GED® test, questions about interpreting the Constitution will test your ability to interpret information at various Depth of Knowledge levels through the use of complex reading skills and thinking skills.

2 Practice the Skill

By practicing the skill of interpreting the Constitution, you will improve your study and test-taking abilities, especially as they relate to the GED® Social Studies Test. Read the excerpt and strategies below. Then answer the question that follows.

The following excerpt is from the Preamble to the United States Constitution. A *preamble* is an introduction to a longer piece of writing.

Because the original Articles of the U.S. Constitution were written in the late 1700s, the language includes words that may seem confusing or unfamiliar.

a The initial words of the Preamble identify the perspective from which the Constitution is written. With this phrase, the authors of the Constitution indicate that they have written this document on behalf of all of the people in the United States.

a We the people of the United States, in order to form a more perfect union, **b** establish justice, insure domestic tranquility, provide for the common defense, promote the general welfare, and secure the blessings of liberty to ourselves and our posterity, do ordain and establish this Constitution for the United States of America.

b These phrases represent examples of the general principles discussed in the U.S. Constitution.

TEST-TAKING TIPS

When interpreting information from the Constitution, look for familiar words and phrases that can provide clues to the meanings of any unfamiliar concepts.

1. Which of the following best describes the meaning of the phrase "insure domestic tranquility"?

A. establish a fair court system
B. protect the rights of all people
C. maintain peace within the nation
D. help all citizens achieve success

★ Spotlighted Item: **DROP-DOWN**

DIRECTIONS: The passage below is incomplete. Use information from the excerpt to complete the passage. For each drop-down item, choose the option that correctly completes the sentence.

From Article I of the U.S. Constitution:

Section 7. All bills for raising revenue shall originate in the House of Representatives; but the Senate may propose or concur with amendments as on other bills.

Every bill which shall have passed the House of Representatives and the Senate, shall, before it becomes a law, be presented to the President of the United States; if he approve he shall sign it, but if not he shall return it, with his objections to that house in which it shall have originated, who shall enter the objections at large on their journal, and proceed to reconsider it. If after such reconsideration two thirds of that house shall agree to pass the bill, it shall be sent, together with the objections, to the other house, by which it shall likewise be reconsidered, and if approved by two thirds of that house, it shall become a law.

2. Section 7 of Article I of the Constitution of the United States explains how both houses of [2. Drop-down 1] can [2. Drop-down 2]. This section states that certain types of proposed laws may originate only from the House of Representatives. For example, the Senate could not propose a law that [2. Drop-down 3]. Section 7 also explains how Congress can override the President's veto through [2. Drop-down 4].

Drop-Down Answer Options

2.1 A. Congress
 B. the House of Representatives
 C. the Senate
 D. the President

2.2 A. raise revenue
 B. veto bills
 C. pass bills
 D. add amendments

2.3 A. changes the nation's health care system
 B. establishes new federal education standards
 C. provides financial aid to college students
 D. institutes a tax on gasoline

2.4 A. approval by two-thirds of both houses
 B. unanimous approval by the originating house
 C. approval by two-thirds of the originating house
 D. approval by the Speaker of the House and the Vice President

UNIT 3

DIRECTIONS: Study the excerpt, read the question, then choose the **best** answer.

AMENDMENT IX

The enumeration in the Constitution, of certain rights, shall not be construed to deny or disparage others retained by the people.

3. Which of the following offers the best interpretation of Amendment IX?

A. The Constitution lists all of the rights granted to citizens.
B. The United States government has inherent powers that are not described in the Constitution.
C. Each state has the authority to delegate rights to its citizens.
D. The fact that the Constitution describes certain rights does not mean that citizens do not have additional rights.

Summarize

SS CONTENT TOPICS: I.CG.a.1, I.CG.b.2, I.CG.b.3, I.CG.b.4, I.CG.b.7, I.CG.b.8, I.CG.b.9, I.CG.d.1
SS PRACTICES: SSP.1.a, SSP.1.b, SSP.2.a, SSP.2.b, SSP.3.c, SSP.9.b, SSP.9.c

1 Learn the Skill

To **summarize** means to restate briefly in your own words the main points of a passage or a visual element. When reading about historical events, you will often be presented with a great deal of detailed information. By summarizing, you can determine which details are important and which are unimportant for understanding events and their relationships to one another.

As with other areas of the GED® test, questions about summarizing will test your ability to interpret information at various Depth of Knowledge levels through the use of complex reading skills and thinking skills.

2 Practice the Skill

By practicing the skill of summarizing, you will improve your study and test-taking abilities, especially as they relate to the GED® Social Studies Test. Read the passage and strategies below. Then answer the question that follows.

a Look for the main points in a passage and think of ways to restate them in your own words.

b When summarizing, leave out details that lack significance or importance. Instead, concentrate on details that are important for understanding the main point of a passage.

The *Magna Carta* is a political document written in 1215, in which the relationship between the English king and his feudal lords is clarified. The document was written almost 1,000 years ago, but it is still important today. The *Magna Carta* is the foundation of many important rights held by the people of Great Britain and the United States. **b** The English feudal lords had several grievances against their king concerning the way justice was administered and the abuse of his power over them. Facing a revolt by the lords, the king agreed to limits on his power. For example, the king agreed that:

No free man shall be seized or imprisoned, or stripped of his rights or possessions, or outlawed or exiled … except by the lawful judgement [*sic*] of his equals or by the law of the land. To no one will we … deny or delay right or justice.

Within this section of *Magna Carta*, scholars see the roots of the right to trial by jury and a statement on individual freedom and rights. It also contains the idea—unusual for its time—that even a ruler is subject to the law.

USING LOGIC

Use logic to classify information as a main idea or as a detail. Think about whether each piece of information is the dominant theme of the passage or a specific fact that supports a larger point.

1. Which of the following statements provides the **best** summary of the passage above?

A. With the *Magna Carta*, a group of feudal lords forced a tyrannical king to meet their demands.
B. The *Magna Carta* was an important step in developing the concept of individual rights.
C. The *Magna Carta* ensured the rights of kings over their feudal subjects.
D. The *Magna Carta* was the first constitution to guarantee representative government.

UNIT 3

★ Spotlighted Item: EXTENDED RESPONSE

DIRECTIONS: Read the information and the question, then write your answer on the lines below. Please refer to Unit 3 and Unit 4 in the Reasoning Through Language Arts Student Edition and Workbook for detailed information about reading, writing, and editing Extended Response answers.

In the summer of 1787, delegates from 12 states met in Philadelphia to try to correct problems with the Articles of Confederation, making them more workable for the new nation. The delegates decided that the Articles were too weak and imperfect to be fixed, so they created a new plan, one with a much stronger federal government. That September, the new Constitution they had written was submitted to each of the states for ratification. Only 9 of the 13 states had to ratify the new Constitution for it to go into effect.

Many people opposed the Constitution, however, citing the fact that it did not protect individual rights against a now more powerful federal government. A few states, such as Delaware, New Jersey, and Pennsylvania, ratified the Constitution within a few months. However, several states refused to ratify the document without protections for individual rights. Several other states did approve, but with the understanding that a "Bill of Rights" would be added. The Constitution went into effect when New Hampshire became the ninth state to ratify it on June 21, 1788. Even so, several large states were still holdouts, including Virginia, New York, and North Carolina. They eventually approved the Constitution, but with very close votes. The last holdout, Rhode Island, did not ratify the Constitution until May 1790, after all other states had done so.

2. Write a summary of the information presented in the passage above. In your response, analyze the arguments about how all of the states eventually ratified the new Constitution. Incorporate relevant and specific evidence from the passage, as well as your own knowledge of the circumstances surrounding the ratification of the new Constitution, to support your analysis. This task may require 25 minutes to complete. You may use another sheet of paper to complete your answer.

_____

_____

_____

_____

_____

_____

_____

_____

_____

_____

_____

UNIT 3

Compare and Contrast

SS CONTENT TOPICS: I.CG.b.7, I.CG.c.1, I.USH.c.3, I.USH.c.4
SS PRACTICES: SSP.1.a, SSP.1.b, SSP.2.a, SSP.2.b, SSP.3.d

1 Learn the Skill

When you **compare** two or more items, you consider both the similarities and the differences between them. The study of history, geography, civics, government, and other social studies subjects often requires you to compare details about people, places, and events.

To **contrast** means to focus only on the differences between items. By focusing on the ways in which things are alike and how they are different, you gain a deeper understanding of the material you read.

As with other areas of the GED® test, questions about comparing and contrasting will test your ability to interpret information at various Depth of Knowledge levels through the use of complex reading skills and thinking skills.

2 Practice the Skill

By practicing the skill of comparing and contrasting, you will improve your study and test-taking abilities, especially as they relate to the GED® Social Studies Test. Read the passage and strategies below. Then answer the question that follows.

a You may find information to compare and contrast in both text and visuals, such as tables, charts, and graphs. You may assume that most parallel items described in a text or visual can be compared and contrasted, such as two plans, or two belief systems.

a As the Civil War came to a close, President Abraham Lincoln began to consider how the United States should be rebuilt. His plan for reconstructing the South called for generous terms that would allow the nation to heal with as little animosity as possible between the North and the South. **b** On the other hand, the Radical Republicans in Congress strongly opposed this plan. They believed that the Confederacy should receive harsh penalties for the difficulties of the Civil War.

b Words and phrases such as *similarly, likewise, on the other hand,* and *however* often signal that an author is comparing or contrasting information.

CONTENT PRACTICES

Practicing compare and contrast will prepare you to describe people, places, and events and the connections among them, a key element of the GED® Social Studies Test.

1. When comparing or contrasting the plans of President Lincoln and the Radical Republicans, which of the following statements is accurate?

   A. They both aimed to rebuild the nation as quickly as possible.
   B. Both plans imposed similarly harsh penalties on the Confederacy.
   C. They featured different objectives for how to move forward after the Civil War.
   D. The two plans delegated much of the responsibility for Reconstruction to state governments.

DIRECTIONS: Study the information, read the questions, then choose the **best** answer.

No time in the history of the United States was more tumultuous than the dozen years following the Civil War, the period known as Reconstruction. The reasons for this are obvious, in retrospect. Some people wanted the South to pay for its actions; they had a punitive attitude. Others, however, wanted a gentler "healing" hand to reunite the country. The new President, Andrew Johnson, exemplified this latter group. President Johnson supported the views of the recently assassinated Abraham Lincoln.

The North, and the group of politicians from the South known as the Radical Republicans, wanted to give full rights to recently freed enslaved people (Freedmen), whereas much of the South remained committed to preserving its social and economic way of life. The Radical Republicans disapproved of President Johnson's lenient approach. Eventually, they impeached him. Their actions fell just one Senatorial vote short of having President Johnson removed from office.

The war devastated the South, with many cities such as Atlanta, Georgia, and Columbia, South Carolina, burned to the ground. A significant percentage of Southern men had been killed or wounded in the war, leaving the South less able to rebuild itself. It would take years to restore the cities and repair the damage to industry and the economy, but these desperate needs created opportunities for extraordinary profits and exploitation of those weakened by the war. Northerners moving to the South to take advantage of those opportunities were known as carpetbaggers, owing to the type of luggage they carried. Protections against such exploitation were not nearly so numerous or effective as they are today.

A serious economic depression in the United States in 1873 significantly hampered the **resolve** of the more economically powerful North to provide Reconstruction assistance to the South. The former Northern general Ulysses S. Grant was President at this time. He withdrew the troops protecting the South from various abuses, leaving Southerners to fend for themselves. This situation led to the rise of powerful Southern political and economic interests, including some radical groups such as the Ku Klux Klan. The South became a racially divided society, which continued until the Civil Rights Movement of the 1960s.

Reconstruction was a critical time for the United States. The decisions made and actions taken at the time have had lasting effects. As a result, this postwar period presents ample opportunities for comparing and contrasting.

2. Whose interests appear to be the most aligned?

   A. Radical Republicans and the Freedmen
   B. Andrew Johnson and the Radical Republicans
   C. Freedmen and the carpetbaggers
   D. President Grant and the Freedmen

3. Whose interests appear to differ most?

   A. Carpetbaggers and Freedmen
   B. Radical Republicans and President Johnson
   C. Northerners, in general, and President Grant
   D. President Johnson and President Lincoln

4. Which of the following can be substituted for *resolve* in order to provide the most accurate interpretation of the text?

   A. *attempt*
   B. *solution*
   C. *determination*
   D. *hesitation*

DIRECTIONS: Study the information, read the question, then choose the **best** answer.

In June 1863, Confederate General Robert E. Lee led his troops into Pennsylvania, with the aim of capturing the railroad hub at Harrisburg. While marching through Pennsylvania, Lee forbade his troops from looting farms or destroying homes. Instead, his troops paid for the food they took with useless Confederate money. In May 1864, Union General William T. Sherman began his march through Georgia. Sherman encouraged his men to take food and livestock from the farms they passed.

5. In which of the following ways were the actions of both generals similar?

   A. both required troops to take loyalty oaths
   B. both ordered troops to take over railroad lines
   C. both had troops collect supplies from local people
   D. both assigned troops to build roads

Charts, Graphs, and Flowcharts

SS CONTENT TOPICS: I.CG.b.7, I.CG.b.8, I.CG.c.1, I.CG.c.2, I.CG.c.6, I.CG.d.2, II.E.c.7, II.G.b.3, I.USH.d.4
SS PRACTICES: SSP.1.a, SSP.1.b, SSP.2.a, SSP.2.b, SSP.3.a, SSP.3.b, SSP.3.c, SSP.6.b, SSP.6.c, SSP.10.a, SSP.10.b

UNIT 3

➊ Learn the Skill

Charts, graphs, and flowcharts are ways to present information visually. Like tables, charts and graphs can present a great deal of numerical information in a relatively small amount of space. In social studies, authors often use these elements to show information that would be too lengthy to describe in a narrative passage. A flowchart is a graphic that describes a sequence. It communicates the steps of a process quickly by using concise explanatory text.

As with other areas of the GED® test, questions about charts, graphs, and flowcharts will test your ability to interpret information at various Depth of Knowledge levels through the use of complex reading skills and thinking skills.

➋ Practice the Skill

By practicing the skill of interpreting charts, graphs, and flowcharts, you will improve your study and test-taking abilities, especially as they relate to the GED® Social Studies Test. Study the information below. Then answer the question that follows.

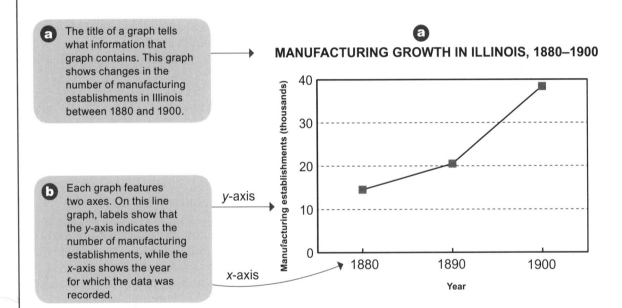

a The title of a graph tells what information that graph contains. This graph shows changes in the number of manufacturing establishments in Illinois between 1880 and 1900.

b Each graph features two axes. On this line graph, labels show that the *y*-axis indicates the number of manufacturing establishments, while the *x*-axis shows the year for which the data was recorded.

a
MANUFACTURING GROWTH IN ILLINOIS, 1880–1900

y-axis

x-axis

Manufacturing establishments (thousands)

Year

USING LOGIC

To interpret a graph, find how both axes relate to one another at certain points. To find manufacturing establishments in 1890, scan up from 1890 on the x-axis and find the number on the y-axis.

1. During the 1890s, what happened to the number of manufacturing establishments in Illinois?

A. They increased slightly.
B. They decreased slightly.
C. They remained nearly the same.
D. They increased dramatically.

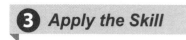

DIRECTIONS: Study the flowchart, read the questions, then choose the **best** answers.

**EVENTS LEADING TO PASSAGE
OF THE PENDLETON CIVIL SERVICE ACT**

Charles Guiteau writes to President James A. Garfield, asking for a high-level job in his new administration.

↓

President Garfield does not respond, angering Mr. Guiteau.

↓

Mr. Guiteau shoots President Garfield, partly as the result of the snub.

↓

When President Garfield dies, Chester A. Arthur becomes President.

↓

President Garfield's assassination helps focus attention on the need to reform the process by which people obtain federal jobs.

↓

Congress passes the Pendleton Civil Service Reform Act, which creates the Civil Service Commission.

↓

Many federal jobs become obtainable only by merit, rather than through political connections.

2. Based on the information presented in the flowchart, which of the following events resulted in the presidency of Chester A. Arthur?

   A. the passage of the Pendleton Civil Service Reform Act
   B. the election of Chester A. Arthur
   C. the assassination of President James Garfield
   D. the application of Charles Guiteau for a government job

3. How did President Garfield's death affect civil service reform?

   A. Congress passed a law that replaced many patronage jobs with jobs obtained through merit.
   B. Jobs could no longer be obtained through the Civil Service Commission.
   C. The Pendleton Civil Service Reform Act was rejected by a very narrow margin.
   D. All federal jobs were obtained only through political connections from that point forward.

4. Which of the following gives the best reason for displaying the information here on a flowchart rather than on a graph?

   A. Text cannot be used with graphs.
   B. The *x*-axis and *y*-axis on a flowchart are difficult to display.
   C. There is too much information to fit on a graph.
   D. Graphs usually display numbers, while flowcharts usually display text.

DIRECTIONS: Study the flowchart, read the questions, then choose the **best** answers.

THE EVENT	THE CASE	FIRST DECISION	SECOND DECISION
In 1890, an African American man named James Plessy sat in a railroad car designated only for white people. Told to move, he refused and was arrested.	Plessy's case reached the U.S. Supreme Court. His attorneys argued that the "whites-only" car was a violation of the Fourteenth Amendment.	In a seven-to-one decision in *Plessy* v. *Ferguson* (1896), the Court ruled that separate but equal facilities for African Americans and white people did not violate the Fourteenth Amendment.	In a unanimous decision in *Brown* v. *Board of Education* (1954), the U.S. Supreme Court ruled that separate but equal facilities violated the Fourteenth Amendment, overturning the *Plessy* decision.

5. What led to the court case *Plessy* v. *Ferguson*?

   A. James Plessy sat in a railroad car reserved for white passengers.
   B. There were railroad cars for each ethnic group.
   C. There was a ruling in the case of *Brown* v. *Board of Education*.
   D. The U.S. Congress passed the Fourteenth Amendment to the U.S. Constitution.

6. Which two levels of government were in possible conflict in the *Plessy* decision?

   A. federal and state governments
   B. state and local governments
   C. county and state governments
   D. two parts of the federal government

UNIT 3

Make Inferences

SS CONTENT TOPICS: I.CG.b.8, I.CG.c.2, I.CG.c.5, I.CG.d.2, II.CG.e.2, I.USH.d.2, II.USH.f.4, II.USH.f.7
SS PRACTICES: SSP.1.b, SSP.2.a, SSP.2.b, SSP.6.b

1 Learn the Skill

An **inference** is a logical guess based on facts or evidence. When you **make an inference**, you put two or more pieces of information together, along with your own knowledge, to determine a possible meaning. In this way, making an inference is similar to putting together the pieces of a puzzle.

Even before you have assembled the complete puzzle, you can begin to determine what it will look like. As you study historical information, making inferences will help you better understand the connections among people, places, and events that might not initially be obvious.

As with other areas of the GED® test, questions about making inferences will test your ability to interpret information at various Depth of Knowledge levels through the use of complex reading skills and thinking skills.

2 Practice the Skill

By practicing the skill of making inferences, you will improve your study and test-taking abilities, especially as they relate to the GED® Social Studies Test. Study the information below. Then answer the question that follows.

a This sentence states President Wilson's intentions about U.S. involvement in World War I. This fact can be combined with another to make an inference.

After becoming President in 1913, Woodrow Wilson's first term was dominated by the outbreak of World War I in Europe. **a** Throughout his first term, President Wilson aimed to keep the United States neutral. Tensions grew when German submarines attacked American ships. Britain also interfered with American ships in an attempt to blockade Germany. Despite these incidents, President Wilson worked to keep the United States out of the war. **b** For his re-election campaign in 1916, President Wilson ran under the slogan, "He kept us out of war." President Wilson won the election and began his second term in 1917.

b This information can be combined with the other information to make a logical guess about the way the American public felt about the war.

USING LOGIC

When making an inference, be sure your a logical guess is supported by available facts. Even though an inference is a guess, it should have a strong chance of turning out to be true.

1. What can you infer about the American public's feelings toward involvement in World War I during President Wilson's first term?

   A. Most Americans believed that the United States should support Britain's blockade.
   B. Many Americans supported President Wilson's policy of neutrality.
   C. Americans were angered by President Wilson's diplomatic approach to foreign policy.
   D. Most Americans hoped that the United States would avenge the loss of U.S. ships.

DIRECTIONS: Study the information, read the questions, then choose the **best** answers.

Two courageous women became early leaders in the women's suffrage movement at a time when "women's rights" was a startling idea to many Americans. Elizabeth Cady Stanton (1815–1902) was already active in the antislavery movement when, in 1840, she and other women delegates were barred from attending an antislavery convention. As a result, she began campaigning for women's rights and was a key organizer of the first Seneca Falls Convention in 1848. After she met Susan B. Anthony (1820–1906), the two women formed the National Woman Suffrage Association and worked to gain the right to vote through amendments to state and national constitutions.

In her effort to challenge the lack of suffrage for women, Susan B. Anthony voted in the 1872 presidential election. She was arrested and put on trial. The judge ordered the jury to find her guilty and imposed a $100 fine. When she refused to pay, the judge did not sentence Ms. Anthony to prison, which effectively ended her chance of an appeal. A prison sentence would have allowed the suffrage movement to appeal the decision and take the question of women's voting rights to the U.S. Supreme Court.

By 1900, women could vote in only four states, but the campaign for a national constitutional amendment continued. When the Nineteenth Amendment was ratified in 1920, women throughout the United States finally gained the right to vote.

2. Which of the following inferences can you make about Elizabeth Cady Stanton?

   A. She opposed the antislavery movement.
   B. She made speeches on women's suffrage.
   C. She worked for prison reform.
   D. She had difficulty working with others.

3. What can you infer about women's suffrage in the United States before 1920?

   A. Women were prohibited from voting in any election throughout the United States.
   B. Only white women had the right to vote throughout the United States.
   C. Women in some states could vote for governor, but women in other states could not.
   D. Women who were part of the suffrage movement could vote because of their political activism.

DIRECTIONS: Study the table, read the questions, then choose the **best** anwers.

LEADERS OF THE WOMEN'S SUFFRAGE MOVEMENT

LEADER	ACCOMPLISHMENTS
Lucretia Mott (1793–1880)	She was active in both the antislavery and women's rights movements. With others, including Elizabeth Cady Stanton, Lucretia Mott organized the Seneca Falls Convention in 1848. In 1866, she became the first president of the American Equal Rights Association, which worked for equality for women and African Americans.
Elizabeth Cady Stanton (1815–1902)	A founder of the women's rights movement in the United States, she helped plan the first Seneca Falls Convention. With Matilda Joslyn Gage, Elizabeth Cady Stanton wrote the Declaration of Rights of the Women of the United States in 1876.
Lucy Stone (1818–1893)	An early activist in both the women's rights and antislavery movements, her speech at the Seneca Falls Convention in 1852 influenced Susan B. Anthony. Later in her career, Lucy Stone worked with Frederick Douglass to support passage of the Fifteenth Amendment.
Susan B. Anthony (1820–1906)	She became part of the antislavery movement, and then was introduced to the women's rights movement by Elizabeth Cady Stanton. With Stanton, Susan B. Anthony formed the National Woman Suffrage Association in 1869.

4. What information can you infer from the table?

   A. Many leaders who fought for women's rights also supported rights for African Americans.
   B. Men and women did not work together to expand rights within the United States.
   C. Elizabeth Cady Stanton and Lucy Stone never actually met.
   D. All supporters of women's suffrage were in the North after the Civil War.

5. What inference can you make about the voting records of these women's suffrage leaders?

   A. All of the women were arrested for attempting to vote at some time in their lives.
   B. Although they could not vote nationally, all of the women could vote in their own states.
   C. The women only supported the right of white women to vote nationally.
   D. None of the women ever voted in a Presidential election.

Interpret Political Cartoons

SS CONTENT TOPICS: I.CG.c.1, I.CG.c.3, I.CG.d.2, II.CG.e.2, II.CG.e.3
SS PRACTICES: SSP.1.a, SSP.1.b, SSP.2.a, SSP.2.b, SSP.5.a, SSP.5.b, SSP.6.b

❶ Learn the Skill

Political cartoons are drawings that are intended to make political or social statements. These cartoons communicate the opinions of the artists who draw them. These individuals, known as **political cartoonists**, often use their editorial skills and humor or satire to make their points. Political cartoonists may also use a **caricature,** or an exaggerated representation of a thing or a person's physical features, to present a point of view. By **interpreting political cartoons**, you can gain valuable first-hand knowledge of the different ways that people viewed historical events during the time in which they were happening.

As with other areas of the GED® test, the skill of interpreting political cartoons will test your ability to interpret information at various Depth of Knowledge levels through the use of complex reading skills and thinking skills.

❷ Practice the Skill

By practicing the skill of interpreting political cartoons, you will improve your study and test-taking abilities, especially as they relate to the GED® Social Studies Test. Study the information below. Then answer the question that follows.

a Symbols often help convey meaning in political cartoons through the use of images and words, such as the axe blade (vote) chopping into the tree (saloon).

b Political cartoons often include labels that identify items shown in the cartoon. Captions that may appear below a cartoon help clarify the cartoon's meaning.

c The man to the right of the tree is a caricature of a politician. He is the one saying the words at the bottom of the cartoon.

The Prohibition Party formed in the mid-1800s and campaigned for several years to outlaw the production, sale, and transportation of alcoholic beverages. It is the oldest minor U.S. political party still in existence. From time to time it has nominated candidates for state and local office in nearly every state.

"Woodman, spare that Tree, Touch not a single bough; In youth it sheltered ME, And I'll protect it now."

MAKING ASSUMPTIONS

Political cartoons express editorial commentary or opinion. As you examine the words, pictures, or symbols in political cartoons, consider how these items express the artist's viewpoint.

1. Which of the following do the depictions of the two figures in the cartoon suggest about the cartoonist's viewpoint on Prohibition?

   A. The cartoonist believes that politicians are rightfully concerned about Prohibition.
   B. The cartoonist believes that the Prohibition Party is right in trying to outlaw alcohol.
   C. The cartoonist fears that the Prohibition Party is pursuing their goals recklessly.
   D. The cartoonist suggests that many politicians support the work of the Prohibition Party.

UNIT 3

DIRECTIONS: Study the information and the cartoon, read the questions, then choose the **best** answers.

Following the stock market crash of 1929, President Herbert Hoover sought to minimize the effects of the crash on the economy of the United States. American farmers were earning much less than before, and they could not pay their mortgages and bills. Without these payments, rural banks failed. After 1932, drought conditions plagued the Midwest, adding to existing agricultural problems. Industries failed, and factories and stores closed.

Between 1929 and 1933, 5,000 American banks collapsed, one in four farms went into foreclosure, and an average of 100,000 jobs vanished each week. By 1932, more than 12 million Americans were unemployed. Part of President Hoover's plan to improve the nation's economy involved working with business and labor leaders.

2. Which of the following statements best describes the cartoon's depiction of President Hoover?

   A. He is shown as a weak and ineffective leader.
   B. He is shown as guiding the country's economy back to stability.
   C. He is shown as unsure of the correct course of action to improve the economy.
   D. He is shown as wary of supporting big business during this crisis.

3. Which of the following does the cartoonist identify as the cause of the economic crash?

   A. The cartoonist blames President Hoover.
   B. The cartoonist thinks labor is the source of the problem.
   C. The cartoonist points to speculation as the cause.
   D. The cartoonist states that detours from regular business practices are to blame.

DIRECTIONS: Study the information and the cartoon, read the questions, then choose the **best** answers.

In February 1937, President Franklin Delano Roosevelt proposed legislation that would increase the number of U.S. Supreme Court justices from 9 to 15. For each justice over the age of 70 (a total of six at the time), he would be empowered to appoint a new justice. This would have altered a court that had struck down some of the proposed New Deal programs. After six months of hearings and debates in Congress, the President's plan failed.

"O, death! O, change! O, time!" A 1937 Herblock Cartoon, ©The Herb Block Foundation

4. How does the artist characterize President Roosevelt's demeanor in this political cartoon?

   A. His demeanor is portrayed as hopeful.
   B. His demeanor is portrayed as angry.
   C. His demeanor is somewhat sad and dismayed.
   D. His demeanor is cold and calculating.

5. Why does the cartoonist show pages from a calendar with wings attached?

   A. Six months' time was wasted while Congress considered the President's proposed plan.
   B. The six justices who were 70 years old had passed away.
   C. The wings represent the fleeting nature of service on the U.S. Supreme Court.
   D. The pages and wings represent President Roosevelt's strained relationship with Congress.

Draw Conclusions

SS CONTENT TOPICS: I.CG.c.1, I.CG.c.2, I.CG.c.3, II.CG.e.2
SS PRACTICES: SSP.1.a, SSP.1.b, SSP.2.a, SSP.2.b, SSP.3.c, SSP.9.a, SSP.9.b, SSP.9.c

1 Learn the Skill

You have already learned that an inference is a logical guess based on facts or evidence. By combining several inferences to make a judgment, you can **draw conclusions**. The ability to draw conclusions enables you to develop new ideas about social studies material. In this way, you can gain a deeper understanding of the information you need. You can also call upon your prior knowledge to help you draw conclusions.

As with other areas of the GED® test, questions about drawing conclusions will test your ability to interpret information at various Depth of Knowledge levels through the use of complex reading skills and thinking skills.

2 Practice the Skill

By practicing the skill of drawing conclusions, you will improve your study and test-taking abilities, especially as they relate to the GED® Social Studies Test. Study the passage below. Then answer the question that follows.

a As you read, look for pieces of information about which you can ask questions, such as: How do the people in the line of succession get their positions?

When the Constitution was written, its authors left much of the responsibility for how the new government would be structured to Congress to decide. **a** One of the most pressing issues of business was determining the order of succession in the unfortunate event that anything should happen to the President. The Second Congress acted by passing the Presidential Succession Act, which places the Vice President in charge if the President cannot serve. In its original form, the act placed the President pro tempore of the Senate first in line after the Vice President, with the Speaker of the House second. Both of these are elected positions.

b Remember that an inference is like a puzzle that must be put together using two or more pieces of information. These logical guesses can then be combined to form a larger conclusion.

The line of succession has been changed twice since then. First, in 1866, it was changed so that the President's cabinet members, who are <u>appointed by the President</u>, were to serve in order of rank, after the Vice President. The House Speaker and President pro tempore were no longer in line. The logic was that no President pro tempore had ever served as President, whereas six former Secretaries of State had. In 1947, the line of succession was changed to its current form—if the President dies, the Vice President is next in line, followed by the Speaker of the House and Senate President pro tempore, and then the Cabinet members.

MAKING ASSUMPTIONS

To answer this question, make assumptions based on the information given. Look for information about how the Cabinet members, President pro tempore, and House Speaker differ.

1. What conclusion can you draw as to the reason the line of succession was most likely changed in 1947, placing Cabinet members behind the Speaker of the House and President pro tempore?

   A. The Cabinet members are not all equally qualified to become President.
   B. The House Speaker is more qualified than members of the Cabinet to become President.
   C. The President pro tempore is more qualified than members of the Cabinet to become President.
   D. The Speaker of the House and the President pro tempore are elected officials, and the Cabinet members are appointed by the President.

★ Spotlighted Item: **EXTENDED RESPONSE**

DIRECTIONS: Read the information and the question, then write your answer on the lines below. Please refer to Unit 3 and Unit 4 in the Reasoning Through Language Arts Student Edition and Workbook for detailed information about reading, writing, and editing Extended Response answers. You may use another sheet of paper to complete your answer.

Attempting to avoid a nationwide strike of steel workers that he believed would jeopardize national defense, President Harry S. Truman issued an Executive Order in April 1952 to seize and operate most of the nation's steel mills. This order was not based upon any specific statutory authority, but rather upon powers vested in the President by the U.S. Constitution and laws of the United States. The Secretary of Commerce issued the order and the President promptly reported these events to Congress. However, Congress took no action, stating that the order was neither sanctioned by the Constitution nor by U.S. laws, since no statute expressly or implicitly authorized the President to take possession of steel mills. Congress correctly stated that the power that President Truman sought to exercise was the lawmaking power, which the U.S. Constitution grants only to Congress. The steel companies sued in U.S. District Court, which ruled that Truman's actions were unconstitutional. It issued a preliminary injunction restraining the order from being carried out. Shortly thereafter, the U.S. Supreme Court upheld the decision.

2. What can you conclude about Presidential power to seize private property prior to 1952? In your response, develop an argument about President Truman's actions and the subsequent rulings made by the U.S. Supreme Court. Incorporate relevant and specific evidence from the passage and from your own knowledge of the enduring issue. This task may require 25 minutes to complete.

Determine Point of View

SS CONTENT TOPICS: I.CG.b.1, I.CG.b.6, I.CG.b.8, I.CG.c.2, II.CG.e.1, II.CG.e.3 , II.CG.f
SS PRACTICES: SSP.1.a, SSP.1.b, SSP.4.a, SSP.5.a, SSP.5.b, SSP.7.a

❶ Learn the Skill

An author's **point of view** is the perspective from which he or she writes about a topic. When you **determine point of view**, you gain a better understanding of the text. Identify the subject or main idea of the writing, and consider the author's purpose. Then think of the different perspectives that the author may have on the topic. These steps will help you clarify the author's point of view.

As with other areas of the GED® test, questions about determining point of view will test your ability to interpret information at various Depth of Knowledge levels through the use of complex reading skills and thinking skills.

❷ Practice the Skill

By practicing the skill of determining point of view, you will improve your study and test-taking abilities, especially as they relate to the GED® Social Studies Test. Study the information below. Then answer the question that follows.

The Apollo-Soyuz Test Project was the first international human space flight. In 1975, an Apollo spacecraft from the United States docked with a Soyuz spacecraft from the Soviet Union. Until this time, the two nations had competed for success in space, but during this test, the crews cooperated on joint experiments. This milestone in space exploration marked the beginning of many international partnerships in space.

The following is from a letter written by President Gerald Ford to Soviet General Secretary Leonid Brezhnev soon after the astronauts returned to Earth:

ⓐ As you read a passage, consider the author's purpose for writing, and think about how that purpose relates to his or her point of view.

The members of the Apollo-Soyuz crew have travelled together above our planet for thousands of miles. … These courageous men shook hands and worked together as they orbited our earth. Now, travelling together in the Soviet Union and soon in the United States, they demonstrate in very human terms the fruits of our cooperation.

ⓑ To help determine an author's point of view, look for statements or passages that express opinions. When considered collectively, these opinions will help you identify the author's point of view.

I am confident you will agree that we should not rest content with these important achievements, but should continue working together to widen man's horizons and knowledge in space and to ensure peace and better understanding among nations on earth.

Once again, my greetings and sincere best wishes for the continued development of mutually beneficial cooperation and good relations between our two countries.

TEST-TAKING TIPS

When determining point of view, look for "loaded language" in the text. "Loaded" words or phrases create emotional responses in the reader and can be clues to the author's point of view.

1. Which of the following **best** describes President Ford's point of view?

   A. The Apollo-Soyuz crews should go on a worldwide tour.
   B. Cooperative space projects can benefit future generations.
   C. The leaders of both nations deserve congratulations.
   D. Competition is a way to ensure better understanding.

UNIT 3

DIRECTIONS: Study the information, read each question, then choose the **best** answer.

From Report of the Secretary-General on the Rule of Law and Transitional Justice in Conflict and Post-Conflict Societies:

The United Nations was founded in 1945, after World War II ended, by a group of 51 nations. Today it has 193 member states. Through its founding charter, the United Nations provides a forum for its member states to express their views and take action on a range of global issues. The United Nations is best known for its peacekeeping, conflict prevention, and humanitarian assistance work, but it is also heavily involved in other efforts to make the world safer.

For the United Nations, the rule of law refers to a principle of governance in which all persons, institutions and entities, public and private, including the State itself, are accountable to laws that are publicly promulgated, equally enforced and independently **adjudicated**, and which are consistent with international human rights norms and standards. It requires, as well, measures to ensure adherence to the principles of supremacy of law, equality before the law, accountability to the law, fairness in the application of the law, separation of powers, participation in decision making, legal certainty, avoidance of arbitrariness and procedural and legal transparency.

2. The excerpt best describes the point of view of the United Nations on which of the following?

   A. legal transparency
   B. separation of powers
   C. human rights
   D. rule of law

3. For which of the following purposes is this passage written?

   A. to persuade
   B. to educate and inform
   C. to offer an opinion
   D. as an editorial or commentary

4. The writer's use of the word *adjudicated* in this passage can **best** be substituted with which of the following?

   A. *negotiated*
   B. *administered*
   C. *legally decided*
   D. *enforced*

DIRECTIONS: Study the information, read each question, then choose the **best** answer.

From "John Kerry for President," *The New York Times,* October 17, 2004:

Mr. Kerry has an aggressive and in some cases innovative package of ideas about energy, aimed at addressing global warming and oil dependency. He is a longtime advocate of deficit reduction. In the Senate, he worked with John McCain in restoring relations between the United States and Vietnam, and led investigations of the way the international financial system has been gamed to permit the laundering of drug and terror money. He has always understood that America's appropriate role in world affairs is as leader of a willing community of nations, not in my-way-or-the-highway domination.

We look back on the past four years with hearts nearly breaking, both for the lives unnecessarily lost and for the opportunities so casually wasted. Time and again, history invited George W. Bush to play a heroic role, and time and again he chose the wrong course. We believe that with John Kerry as President, the nation will do better.

Voting for President is a leap of faith. A candidate can explain his positions in minute detail and wind up governing with a hostile Congress that refuses to let him deliver. A disaster can upend the best-laid plans. All citizens can do is mix guesswork and hope, examining what the candidates have done in the past, their apparent priorities and their general character. It's on those three grounds that we enthusiastically endorse John Kerry for President.

5. In which section of *The New York Times* would you expect to find this article?

   A. in the Education section
   B. in the World News section
   C. on the Opinion pages
   D. on the Local News pages

6. Which of the following **best** expresses the writer's point of view?

   A. George W. Bush made heroic choices.
   B. George W. Bush can lead the nation to a better future.
   C. John Kerry makes his positions known.
   D. John Kerry's past record and his character make him a good candidate.

Analyze Information Sources

SS CONTENT TOPICS: I.CG.b.5, I.CG.c.1, I.CG.c.2, I.CG.c.3, I.CG.c.6
SS PRACTICES: SSP.1.a, SSP.1.b, SSP.2.a, SSP.5.a, SSP.6.b

① Learn the Skill

When learning about social studies, you will often be required to **analyze** many different types of **information sources**. **Primary sources** are original accounts of events written by people who actually experienced them at the time, such as eyewitnesses. These sources may include speeches, documents, journal entries, and letters. **Secondary sources** interpret primary sources. Encyclopedias, newspaper articles, and history books are secondary sources. It is important to distinguish between primary and secondary sources to understand an author's purpose and point of view. Remember that all sources have a degree of **bias**, or partiality. Be sure to evaluate sources critically.

As with other areas of the GED® test, questions about analyzing information sources will test your ability to interpret information at various Depth of Knowledge levels through the use of complex reading skills and thinking skills.

② Practice the Skill

By practicing the skill of analyzing information sources, you will improve your study and test-taking abilities, especially as they relate to the GED® Social Studies Test. Study the information below. Then answer the question that follows.

ⓐ If people are trying to promote something, they have a bias in favor of it. If people are against something, then they are biased against it.

ⓑ Titles, labels, captions, and so on, can provide clues about reliability and bias. Information from a website ending with *.gov* is usually reliable, but it may still express bias.

On November 17, 2010—his 61st birthday—[John] Boehner was elected by his colleagues to serve as Speaker-designate, and on January 5, 2011 he swore in the 112th Congress as the 53rd Speaker of the House. John was re-elected by the House on January 3, 2013, to serve a second term as Speaker for the 113th Congress.

Under his leadership, the House majority has worked to make the legislative process more open and to ensure the priorities of the American people are reflected in the priorities of lawmakers. John led the drive for an aggressive set of reforms that require bills to be posted online at least three days before a vote, make it easier to cut spending, require legislation to cite its authority in the Constitution, and more.

John also led House Republicans in adopting the first ban on 'earmarks'—the secretive, pork-barrel spending he has opposed since his first days in Congress. Today, Speaker Boehner is focused on removing government barriers to private-sector job creation and economic growth, cutting government spending, reforming Congress, and rebuilding the bonds of trust between the American people and their representatives in Washington.

From speaker.gov, accessed 2013

TEST-TAKING TIPS

All sources have a degree of bias. Most scholarly works (secondary sources) attempt to prove a historical thesis, and have to acknowledge the bias in the primary sources they use.

1. In which of the following ways does this excerpt show bias?

   A. The author is biased toward the position of Speaker of the House.
   B. The author is biased against Republicans.
   C. The author is biased toward Speaker Boehner.
   D. The author is biased against John Boehner's record.

UNIT 3

DIRECTIONS: Study the information, read each question, then choose the **best** answer.

From *Encyclopædia Britannica Online,* Supreme Court of the United States:

The federal judicial system originally comprised only trial courts of original jurisdiction and the Supreme Court. As the country grew in size, and in the absence of intermediate appellate courts, the volume of cases awaiting review increased, and fidelity to Supreme Court precedents varied significantly among the lower courts. To remedy this problem, Congress passed the Circuit Court of Appeals Act (1891), which established nine intermediate courts with final authority over appeals from federal district courts, except when the case in question was of exceptional public importance. The Judiciary Act of 1925 (popularly known as the Judges' Bill), which was sponsored by the court itself, carried the reforms farther, greatly limiting obligatory jurisdiction (which required the Supreme Court to review a case) and expanding the classes of cases that the court could accept at its own discretion through the issue of a writ of certiorari. Further changes were enacted in 1988, when Congress passed legislation that required the Supreme Court to hear appeals of cases involving legislative reapportionment and federal civil rights and antitrust laws. Currently, there are 12 geographic judicial circuits and a court of appeals for the federal circuit, located in Washington, D.C. Roughly 98 percent of federal cases end with a decision by one of the lower appellate courts.

From britannica.com, accessed 2013

2. In which of the following ways would you describe the information found in this source?

   A. The information is impartial.
   B. The information is dated.
   C. The information is impassioned.
   D. The information is biased.

3. To confirm the information found in this source, which of the following organizations' websites would likely be the **best** to use?

   A. *The Washington Post*
   B. Georgetown University
   C. American Judges Association
   D. U.S. Supreme Court

DIRECTIONS: Study the graph, read each question, then choose the **best** answer.

POPULATION OF CHICAGO, 1970–2010

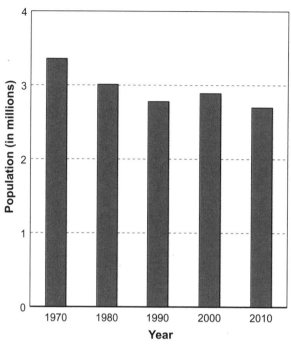

Source: U.S. Bureau of the Census

4. What is the source of information presented in this graph?

   A. the city of Chicago
   B. a federal government agency
   C. an encyclopedia
   D. a national magazine

5. Which of the following can be considered an example of a biased interpretation of this graph?

   A. The population of Chicago has declined over time.
   B. Chicago's population was higher in 1970 than it was in 2010.
   C. The decline in population was caused by an increase in violence by people with very low incomes.
   D. The population of Chicago has been declining over several decades for many reasons.

Generalize

SS CONTENT TOPICS: I.CG.b.5, I.CG.c.1, I.CG.c.2, I.CG.c.3, I.CG.c.6
SS PRACTICES: SSP.1.a, SSP.1.b, SSP.2.a, SSP.7.a, SSP.7.b

1 Learn the Skill

When you **generalize**, you make a broad statement that applies to entire groups of people, places, events, and so on. These statements typically contain words such as *usually, all, everyone, many, few, often,* or *overall.* Generalizing is useful when drawing a conclusion about something. For example, one might make the following generalization: *most Americans believe in the principles of democracy.* However, before you make a **generalization**, be sure that the information you use to support it is valid.

As with other areas of the GED® test, questions about generalizing will test your ability to interpret information at various Depth of Knowledge levels through the use of complex reading skills and thinking skills.

2 Practice the Skill

By practicing the skill of generalizing, you will improve your study and test-taking abilities, especially as they relate to the GED® Social Studies Test. Study the information below. Then answer the question that follows.

a Look closely at ideas to see how they are connected. Here, the writer connects access to electricity to poverty.

b Examine the text to find facts or evidence an author includes that will support a generalization or generalizations.

From "Shaping America's Global Energy Policy," Bureau of Energy Resources, U.S. Department of State:

Why a Bureau of Energy Resources?

The world runs on energy and people need affordable, reliable, and sustainable energy supplies. Energy provides for our most basic needs and fuels the technologies that can secure our futures. But over one billion of the world's people still do not have access to electricity. If we ignore their needs, we entrench their poverty. **a** If we expand their access to energy without making it sustainable, we accelerate environmental impacts and the competition for scarce resources.

The Department is charged with shaping U.S. international energy engagement, influencing how nations move to a cleaner energy future, and protecting our energy infrastructure and transit routes. This effort requires strong diplomatic relationships with major consumers and suppliers. We must anticipate changes in energy markets, and work with international organizations to stabilize markets and build capacity to manage them. Investments in secure, expanding, and ever-cleaner sources of energy will translate into improved health, greater economic sustainability, safer living environments, and enhanced U.S. national security. **b**

From state.gov, accessed 2013

USING LOGIC

As you encounter generalizations, you can classify them as either valid or invalid. A valid generalization is supported by facts and examples. An invalid generalization is one that is not supported.

1. Which of the following generalizations is supported by the excerpt?

   A. Most countries usually produce cleaner energy than the United States.
   B. Safe living environments are only available to those with electricity.
   C. People without access to electricity typically live in poverty.
   D. The Bureau of Energy Resources works mainly in fossil fuel energy.

UNIT 3

DIRECTIONS: Study the information, read the question, then choose the **best** answer.

From "Who Can Declare War?", the *New York Times*, December 15, 1990:

According to the Bush Administration, the fact that the Constitution gives Congress, and only Congress, the power "to declare war" doesn't stop the President from starting a war on his own. Congress might have interesting opinions, and its support is desirable, the argument goes. But its approval is not required should the President decide to attack Iraq, even if the attack is, in the Administration's phrase, sudden, massive and decisive.

... The President as Commander in Chief is authorized to conduct war. Aggressive Presidents have managed to wage executive wars, often because Congress has been unwilling to assert its power. But those failures do not change the Constitution.

Assistant Attorney General Stuart Gerson made the baldest, boldest argument for executive power. Under the war power clause, he told Judge Harold Greene in the suit by the members of Congress, either branch can initiate war: "Each branch might advance its conduct in support of belligerency ahead of the other: the President undertaking it, Congress in declaring it."

The President isn't denying Congress its war-declaring power, Mr. Gerson argued, going on to focus on its timing. "The Constitution does not say war must be declared in advance of hostilities." Congress could thus exercise its right to declare war—after the President had started it."

2. Which of the following generalizations does the author make in this passage?

   A. Congressional approval is not necessary for the President to declare war.
   B. Aggressive Presidents often take greater advantage of executive power.
   C. Congress is usually willing to declare war.
   D. The President may only start a war after Congress has authorized it.

DIRECTIONS: Study the information, read each question, and choose the **best** answer.

All 50 states have legislatures made up of elected representatives who consider matters brought forth by the governor or introduced by their members to create legislation that becomes law. The legislature also approves a state's budget and initiates tax legislation and articles of impeachment. The latter is part of a system of checks and balances among the three branches of government that mirrors the federal system and prevents any branch from abusing its power.

Except for one state, Nebraska, all states have a bicameral legislature made up of two chambers: a smaller upper house and a larger lower house. Together the two chambers make state laws and fulfill other governing responsibilities. (Nebraska is the lone state that has just one chamber in its legislature.) The smaller upper chamber is always called the Senate, and its members generally serve longer terms, usually four years. The larger lower chamber is most often called the House of Representatives, but some states call it the Assembly or the House of Delegates. Its members usually serve shorter terms, often two years.

From whitehouse.gov, accessed 2013

3. Which of the following generalizations can be made about the states?

   A. The states all have different systems for checks and balances.
   B. The states all have one-chamber legislatures.
   C. The states all have bicameral legislatures.
   D. The states have governments that operate similarly to the federal government.

4. "All 50 states have legislatures made up of elected representatives, who consider matters brought forth by the governor or introduced by its members to create legislation that becomes law."

   Which of the following words indicates that this is a generalization?

   A. all
   B. consider
   C. introduced
   D. create

UNIT 3

Identify Problem and Solution

UNIT 3

SS CONTENT TOPICS: I.CG.b.1, I.CG.b.3, I.CG.b.5, I.CG.c.1, I.CG.c.2, I.CG.c.3, I.CG.c.6
SS PRACTICES: SSP.1.a, SSP.1.b, SSP.2.a, SSP.5.a

❶ Learn the Skill

Each day, people work to solve **problems** in their homes, schools, workplaces, and communities. The first step in solving a problem is to **identify the problem** correctly in order to determine the best way to solve it. When determining a **solution**, it is important to identify a number of potential alternatives and evaluate the advantages and disadvantages of each.

As with other areas of the GED® test, identifying problems and solutions will test your ability to interpret information at various Depth of Knowledge levels through the use of complex reading skills and thinking skills.

❷ Practice the Skill

By practicing the skill of identifying problem and solution, you will improve your study and test-taking abilities, especially as they relate to the GED® Social Studies Test. Study the passage below. Then answer the question that follows.

From a statement by Treasury Secretary Henry M. Paulson, September 19, 2008:

ⓐ In this passage, Treasury Secretary Henry Paulson describes an economic problem. Examine the details and examples Paulson gives in order explain the problem clearly.

ⓐ The underlying weakness in our financial system today is the illiquid mortgage assets that have lost value as the housing correction has proceeded. These illiquid assets are choking off the flow of credit that is so vitally important to our economy. When the financial system works as it should, money and capital flow to and from households and businesses to pay for home loans, school loans, and investments that create jobs. As illiquid mortgage assets block the system, the clogging of our financial markets has the potential to have significant effects on our financial system and our economy.

ⓑ In this section, Paulson describes a solution to this problem. Not all solutions are simple. Difficult problems may require complex solutions.

ⓑ … The federal government must implement a program to remove these illiquid assets that are weighing down our financial institutions and threatening our economy. … First, to provide critical additional funding to our mortgage markets … Second, to increase the availability of capital for new home loans … These two steps will provide some initial support to mortgage assets, but they are not enough.

1. Which of the following is the main problem being addressed in this excerpt?

   A. home loans
   B. illiquid assets
   C. mortgage markets
   D. school loans

USING LOGIC

When reading about social studies, the text may not specifically state both the problem and the solution. You may need to use the information given to make inferences about possible solutions.

DIRECTIONS: Study the information, read each question, then choose the **best** answer.

From the Wilderness Act of 1964:

In order to assure that an increasing population, accompanied by expanding settlement and growing mechanization, does not occupy and modify all areas within the United States and its possessions, having no lands designated for preservation and protection in their natural condition, it is hereby declared to be the policy of the Congress to secure for the American people of present and future generations the benefit of an enduring resource of wilderness. For this purpose, there is hereby established a National Wilderness Preservation System to be composed of federally owned areas designated by Congress as 'wilderness areas', and these shall be administered for the use and enjoyment of the American people in such manner as will leave them **unimpaired** for future use and enjoyment as wilderness … .

2. Which of the following problems is outlined in this excerpt?

   A. deforestation by the lumber industry
   B. habitat loss for endangered wildlife
   C. financial complications from logging regulations
   D. loss of wilderness due to increasing growth and development

3. How does this legislation propose to solve the problem?

   A. by creating new national parks
   B. by establishing protected wilderness areas
   C. by protecting several species of wildlife
   D. by building small communities in wilderness areas

4. Which of the following can be substituted for the term *unimpaired* in order to provide the most accurate interpretation of the text?

   A. *unrestricted*
   B. *sober*
   C. *unspoiled*
   D. *accessible*

DIRECTIONS: Study the information, read each question, then choose the **best** answer.

From Amendment XXII of the U.S. Constitution (1951):

Section 1. No person shall be elected to the office of the President more than twice, and no person who has held the office of President, or acted as President, for more than two years of a term to which some other person was elected President shall be elected to the office of the President more than once. But this article shall not apply to any person holding the office of President when this article was proposed by the Congress, and shall not prevent any person who may be holding the office of President or acting as President, during the term within which this article becomes **operative** from holding the office of President or acting as President during the remainder of such term.

5. What problem is this amendment designed to address?

   A. an unclear order of succession to the Presidency
   B. the increasing power of the executive branch
   C. the lack of term limits for the presidency
   D. disputes between the President and Congress

6. Which historical event most likely prompted the creation of this amendment?

   A. Franklin D. Roosevelt's presidency
   B. President Richard M. Nixon's resignation
   C. the assassination of President John F. Kennedy
   D. the election of Lyndon B. Johnson

7. Which of the following can be substituted for the term *operative* in order to provide the most accurate interpretation of the text?

   A. *completed*
   B. *operatic*
   C. *public*
   D. *enacted*

Special-Purpose Maps

SS CONTENT TOPICS: I.CG.c.1, I.CG.c.3, II.G.c.1, II.G.c.3, II.G.d.1, II.G.d.3
SS PRACTICES: SSP.1.a, SSP.2.a, SSP.4.a, SSP.6.b, SSP.6.c, SSP.8.a

UNIT 3

1 Learn the Skill

Special-purpose maps share many similarities with political maps. Both types of maps show political boundaries such as cities, states, regions, and countries. However, special-purpose maps show additional features that do not appear on political maps. These features may include items such as congressional districts, products and resources, and population. Special-purpose maps often use symbols to represent key elements.

As with other areas of the GED® test, questions about special-purpose maps will test your ability to interpret information at various Depth of Knowledge levels through the use of complex reading skills and thinking skills.

2 Practice the Skill

By practicing the skill of interpreting special-purpose maps, you will improve your study and test-taking abilities, especially as they relate to the GED® Social Studies Test. Study the map and information below. Then answer the question that follows.

a This map shows political features associated with a political map. These features include the boundaries of the United States, as well as the locations of cities where the branches of the Federal Reserve are located.

U.S. FEDERAL RESERVE DISTRICTS

Alaska and Hawaii
are part of the
San Francisco District

b In addition to political features, the map shows the boundaries of the 12 Federal Reserve districts. The addition of this extra layer of information makes this visual a special-purpose map.

TEST-TAKING TIPS

When interpreting a special-purpose map in a test-taking situation, study the map's title and contents to identify the purpose of the map. Try to summarize this purpose in a sentence or two.

1. In which Federal Reserve district is the state of California located?

A. 5th District
B. 8th District
C. 10th District
D. 12th District

DIRECTIONS: Study the map, read the questions, then choose the **best** answer to each question.

DIRECTIONS: Study the map, read the questions, then choose the **best** answer to each question.

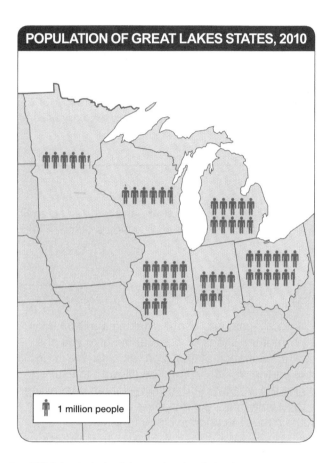

POPULATION OF GREAT LAKES STATES, 2010

1 million people

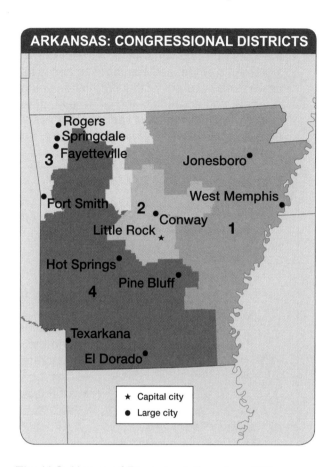

ARKANSAS: CONGRESSIONAL DISTRICTS

★ Capital city
● Large city

2. Which state in this region had the largest population in 2010?

A. Ohio
B. Illinois
C. Michigan
D. Wisconsin

3. Which state shares the northern border of the state with the largest population?

A. Wisconsin
B. Michigan
C. Minnesota
D. Indiana

4. Which of the following statements is correct based on the information on the map?

A. Minnesota had less than 5 million people.
B. Wisconsin had a larger population than Indiana.
C. Ohio and Michigan had a combined population of more than 20 million people.
D. The two most populous states share a border.

The U.S. House of Representatives has 435 seats. The number of seats assigned to each state is based on its population, which is determined every 10 years by a national census. Based on the 2010 Census, each Congressional district now contains 710,767 people. In 2000, each Congressional district contained 647,000 people.

5. How are the Congressional districts shown on this map alike?

A. They are alike in area.
B. They have the same number of large cities.
C. They have approximately the same population.
D. They have the same types of industries.

6. What information could you learn from the passage that you could not find on the map?

A. the number of large cities in the state
B. the basis for the census in districts
C. the number of districts in the state
D. the basis for the number of districts

Fact and Opinion

SS CONTENT TOPICS: I.CG.a.1, II.CG.e.1, II.CG.e.3, II.CG.f
SS PRACTICES: SSP.2.a, SSP.5.b, SSP.7.a

1 Learn the Skill

A **fact** is a statement that can be proven true or untrue, while an **opinion** is a viewpoint or a belief that cannot be proven true or untrue. When reading about social studies, you will frequently encounter statements of fact and opinion. The ability to distinguish between **fact and opinion** will enable you to assess the accuracy of the information you read and to determine the author's point of view or bias.

As with other areas of the GED® test, questions about distinguishing fact from opinion will test your ability to interpret information at various Depth of Knowledge levels through the use of complex reading skills and thinking skills.

2 Practice the Skill

By practicing the skill of recognizing fact and opinion, you will improve your study and test-taking abilities, especially as they relate to the GED® Social Studies Test. Read the passage and strategies below. Then answer the question that follows.

a In this example, the speaker uses statistical evidence that can be proven true or untrue. In social studies, facts are often used to support or discredit arguments.

b Strongly worded or emotional sentiments such as these provide clues to the reader that the speaker or author is expressing an opinion.

From a Vice-Presidential Debate, Joe Biden, 2012:

The middle class will pay less, and people making a million dollars or more will begin to contribute slightly more. Let me give you one concrete example: the continuation of the Bush tax cuts. We're arguing that the Bush tax cuts for the wealthy should be allowed to expire. Of the Bush tax cuts for the wealthy, 800 million—[about one] billion dollars of that goes to people making a minimum of a million dollars. We see no justification in these economic times for those.

And on top of that, they got another tax cut coming that's $5 trillion that all of the studies point out will, in fact, … $250 million—yeah, $250,000 a year to those 120,000 families and raise taxes for people who are middle-income with a child by $2,000 a year. This is unconscionable. There is no need for this. The middle class got knocked on their heels. The Great Recession crushed them. They need some help now. The last people who need help are 120,000 families for another—another $500 billion tax cut over the next 10 years.

From Joe Biden's remarks vice-presidential debate, October 11, 2012

USING LOGIC

If a piece of evidence can logically prove a statement true, it is likely a fact. If you cannot think of pieces of evidence that prove a statement true or false, that statement is likely an opinion.

1. Which of the following ideas in Biden's remarks expresses an opinion rather than statement of a fact that can be checked?

   A. The Bush tax cuts for the wealthy should be allowed to expire.
   B. Of the Bush tax cuts, almost one billion goes to people making a minimum of one million dollars.
   C. Another tax cut of $5 trillion is proposed.
   D. A cut in taxes for the most wealthy will result in a tax increase for middle-income people.

DIRECTIONS: Study the information, read each question, then choose the **best** answer.

A debate has grown in the United States between defenders and critics of the Electoral College system. Some critics contend that this system has become outdated due to changes in the U.S. government over time. Originally, the founders planned for the nation's government to take the form of a republic, in which citizens elected officials to govern for them. Over time, however, the government has evolved into a democracy, in which elected officials are expected to govern according to the wishes of the people.

Additionally, critics argue that the Electoral College system can result in a candidate's winning the presidency while losing the popular vote. This has occurred in three presidential elections. Critics believe that this thwarts the will of the majority.

2. Which of the following is a fact that a defender of the Electoral College might cite to support his or her position?

   A. The Electoral College has only failed to select the winner of the popular vote three times.
   B. The Electoral College makes wider state-by-state campaigning necessary so more voters see and hear candidates.
   C. The Electoral College was established many years ago.
   D. The Electoral College is necessary to preserve a two-party system.

3. Which of the following is one of the main opinions of Electoral College critics?

   A. The Electoral College system is biased.
   B. The Electoral College is controlled by a single party.
   C. The Electoral College is no longer needed.
   D. The Electoral College is too expensive.

4. Based on this excerpt, what can you determine about the author's opinion on the issue?

   A. The author presents the opinions of critics of the Electoral College but does not take a stance on the issue.
   B. The author believes that the President should be chosen by votes in state legislatures.
   C. The author believes that a revamped Electoral College should choose the President.
   D. The author believes that the President should be chosen by Congressional hearings.

DIRECTIONS: Study the poster, read each question, then choose the **best** answer.

5. Why would campaign posters like this one be likely to feature opinions?

   A. They aim to publicize the beliefs of experts.
   B. They are intended to appeal to the emotions of voters.
   C. They are made to confuse Electoral College members.
   D. They are meant to promote candidates' party platforms.

6. Which fact might an opponent use to refute the opinions on this poster?

   A. Roosevelt had taken the country into World War II.
   B. Roosevelt was 62 years old when he ran for reelection in 1944.
   C. Roosevelt had already served three terms as President.
   D. Truman had replaced Roosevelt's previous vice president.

7. Which would be the **best** source for truthful, unbiased information on the Roosevelt-Truman ticket, to counter opinions expressed by the poster?

   A. The League of War Resisters
   B. The National Museum of American History
   C. The Young Democrats Club
   D. The Republican National Committee

UNIT 3

LESSON 15

Faulty Logic or Reasoning

SS CONTENT TOPICS: I.CG.b.7, I.CG.b.8, I.CG.c.1, I.CG.c.2, I.CG.d.2
SS PRACTICES: SSP.5.a, SSP.6.b, SSP.7.a, SSP.7.b

① Learn the Skill

Generalizations are broad statements that apply to an entire group of people, things, or events. A generalization is considered invalid if it is not supported by facts. Such a generalization is also known as a **hasty generalization** and is an example of **faulty logic or reasoning**.

As with other areas of the GED® test, questions about identifying faulty logic or reasoning will test your ability to interpret information at various Depth of Knowledge levels thorough the use of complex reading skills and thinking skills.

② Practice the Skill

By practicing the skill of recognizing faulty logic and reasoning, you will improve your study and test-taking abilities, especially as they relate to the GED® Social Studies Test. Study the information below. Then answer the question that follows.

Lilly Ledbetter worked for Goodyear Tire and Rubber Company for 19 years. Near her time of retirement, she discovered that for years the company had paid her much less than men with the same job. She sued Goodyear for gender discrimination and won, but Goodyear appealed. The appeals court overturned Ledbetter's victory. It agreed that there had been discrimination, but the court stated that Ledbetter had not filed suit in time. According to the court, the suit had to have been filed within 180 days of the discriminatory action—or the first time Ledbetter had received lower pay. Ledbetter stated that she could not have done that because for many years, she did not know that she was being paid less.

a You can find faulty logic in the statements of professionals, public officials—even court decisions. This five-to-four decision shows that four justices disagreed with the logic of the majority.

Still hoping for justice, Ledbetter appealed to the U.S. Supreme Court. In *Ledbetter v. Goodyear Tire and Rubber Company,* the Court also sided with Goodyear in a five-to-four decision. To right this wrong, Congress changed the law. It passed the Lilly Ledbetter Fair Pay Act in early 2009. It allows victims of discrimination to sue regardless of how long it takes to discover the discrimination. On January 29, 2009, it became the first legislation that newly elected President Barack Obama signed into law.

 In this case, faulty logic in a court decision was corrected by changing the law.

MAKING ASSUMPTIONS

You can usually assume that an official decision uses reasoning and logic. When looking for faulty reasoning, look for flaws in the arguments used to support the decision.

1. Which of the following statements summarizes the problem with the faulty reasoning of the court decision?

A. A person cannot report pay discrimination within 180 days of its start if she does not know that it is happening.

B. No one can ever report pay discrimination, because employers always keep comparative salaries secret.

C. If the complaint was made too late, there was no pay discrimination.

D. The court should have recognized that 180 days is not enough time to make a complaint about discrimination.

UNIT 3

3 *Apply the Skill*

★ Spotlighted Item: **FILL-IN-THE-BLANK**

DIRECTIONS: Study the information and the political cartoon. Then read the questions and write your answers in the boxes below.

Solutions to the problem of gun violence have been hotly debated in the United States in recent years in the wake of several mass shootings. Many people believe that there should be stricter gun control laws. Other people believe that our laws need to have stricter enforcement. Many people who do not want stronger gun control laws believe that their right to have guns is protected by the Second Amendment to the U.S. Constitution, which states: *A well regulated Militia, being necessary to the security of a free State, the right of the people to keep and bear Arms, shall not be infringed.*

© Tribune Media Services, Inc. All rights reserved. Reprinted with permission.

2. In the cartoon, James Holmes is the person charged in 2012 with killing several people in Aurora, Colorado. The man with the striped pants and the stars and stripes hat represents

[   ] .

3. The cartoon presents an example of faulty reasoning because

[   ] .

4. A hasty generalization about people who wish to own guns would be

[   ] .

DIRECTIONS: Study the information, read each question, then choose the **best** answer.

From Executive Order 9066, 1942:

Whereas the successful prosecution of the war requires every possible protection against espionage and against sabotage to national-defense material, national-defense premises, and national-defense utilities … I hereby authorize and direct the Secretary of War … to prescribe military areas … from which any or all persons may be excluded, and within such respect to which, the right of any person to enter, remain in, or leave shall be subject to whatever restrictions the Secretary of War or the appropriate Military Commander may impose in his discretion.

From Executive Order 9066, issued by President Franklin D. Roosevelt after the bombing of Pearl Harbor, February 19, 1942

5. Which of the following **best** expresses the hasty generalization made in this executive order?

A. War makes citizens give up personal freedoms.
B. All military commanders should receive absolute authority during times of war.
C. Governments can never establish military areas.
D. All people whose ancestry traces to an enemy nation are worthy of suspicion.

6. Which of the following is an example of faulty logic that could be used to support the order?

A. A majority of voters select their elected officials.
B. All rules are meant to be broken.
C. Every action has an equal and opposite reaction.
D. The Articles of Incorporation preceded the U.S. Constitution.

UNIT 3

Evaluate Information

SS CONTENT TOPICS: II.CG.e.1, II.CG.e.3, II.CG.f
SS PRACTICES: SSP.1.a, SSP.1.b, SSP.2.a, SSP.3.d, SSP.5.a, SSP.5.b, SSP.7.a, SSP.7.b

1 Learn the Skill

Just as you have learned to analyze information sources, you will also need to evaluate the information that you find in these various sources. **Evaluating information** requires you to examine it carefully and to look for purpose, bias, faulty logic or reasoning, and facts or opinions in order to make judgments about the information's quality. This skill combines many of the skills you have learned previously.

As with other areas of the GED® test, questions about evaluating information will test your ability to interpret information at various Depth of Knowledge levels through the use of complex reading skills and thinking skills.

2 Practice the Skill

By practicing the skill of evaluating information, you will improve your study and test-taking abilities, especially as they relate to the GED® Social Studies Test. Study the passage below. Then answer the question that follows.

a The text lays out the problem using (1) actions of a popular past President to set a tone for change, and (2) a fact that underscores the problem.

b Then the text lists several general actions that Democrats would take that score well with the voting public.

From the Democratic Party Platform of 2008:

a A century ago, Teddy Roosevelt called together leaders from business and government to develop a plan for the next century's infrastructure. It falls to us to do the same. Right now, we are spending less than at any time in recent history and far less than our international competitors on this critical component of our nation's strength. We will start a National Infrastructure Reinvestment Bank that can leverage private investment in infrastructure improvement, and create nearly two million new good jobs. **b** We will undertake projects that maximize our safety and security and ability to compete …

In this time of economic transformation and crisis, we must be stewards of this economy more than ever before. We will maintain fiscal responsibility, so that we do not mortgage our children's future on a mountain of debt. We can do this at the same time that we invest in our future. We will restore fairness and responsibility to our tax code. We will bring balance back to the housing markets, so that people do not have to lose their homes. And we will encourage personal savings, so that our economy remains strong and Americans can live well in their retirements.

TEST-TAKING TIPS

Evaluating information requires you to assess a text for many characteristics. Preview the questions first. Then you can narrow your focus as you read and evaluate the text.

1. Which of the following tactics do the Democrats use here to persuade the public?

   A. They offer specific changes they will make.
   B. They promise to consult the public on what is important.
   C. They ensure that successful past practices will continue.
   D. They list general changes without specifying them.

UNIT 3

DIRECTIONS: Study the information, read each question, then choose the **best** answer.

From: "George W. Bush for President," the *Chicago Tribune,* 2004:

On domestic issues, the choice is also clear. In critical areas such as public education and health care, Bush's emphasis is on greater competition. His "No Child Left Behind" Act has flaws, but its requirements have created a new climate of expectation and accountability. On both of these important fronts, but especially with his expensive health-care plan, Kerry primarily sees a need to raise and spend more money. ...

John Kerry has been a discerning critic of where Bush has erred. But Kerry's message—a more restrained assault on global threats, earnest comfort with the international community's noble inaction—suggests what many voters sense: After 20 years in the Senate, the moral certitude Kerry once displayed has evaporated. There is no landmark Kennedy-Kerry Education Act, no Kerry-Frist Health Bill. Today's Kerry is more about plans and process than solutions. He is better suited to analysis than to action. He has not delivered a compelling blueprint for change.

2. Which of the following does the author cite in order to validate an endorsement of one candidate's domestic policies?

   A. Mr. Bush's landmark health care plan
   B. the "No Child Left Behind" Act
   C. the Kennedy-Kerry Education Act
   D. Mr. Bush's assault on global threats

3. What is the main purpose of this editorial?

   A. It is designed to explain why the writer voted for John Kerry.
   B. It is supposed to explain why the writer voted for George W. Bush.
   C. It is meant to persuade voters that John Kerry's policies were failures.
   D. It is intended to persuade people to vote for George W. Bush.

4. What evidence does the author cite to support his claim of Mr. Kerry's unfitness to be President?

   A. Mr. Kerry's discerning criticism of Mr. Bush
   B. the flaws in the "No Child Left Behind" Act
   C. Mr. Kerry's inability to get legislation passed
   D. Mr. Bush's competitive stand on health care

DIRECTIONS: Study the information, read each question, then choose the **best** answer.

From a campaign speech by Barack Obama, 2008:

Years of pain on Main Street have finally trickled up to Wall Street and sent us hurtling toward recession, reminding us that we're all connected—that we can't prosper as a nation where a few people are doing well and everyone else is struggling.

John McCain is an American hero and a worthy opponent, but he's proven time and time again that he just doesn't understand this. ...

I'm betting on the American people. ... We may come from different places and have different stories, but we share common hopes, and one very American dream.

That is the dream I am running to help restore in this election. ... That is the choice that I'll offer the American people—four more years of what we had for the last eight, or fundamental change in Washington.

People may be bitter about their leaders and the state of our politics, but beneath that, they are hopeful about what's possible in America. ... Because they believe that we can change things. Because they believe in that dream.

5. How would you evaluate the information presented in this speech excerpt?

   A. all facts and little opinion
   B. mostly opinion with some facts
   C. about half facts and half opinion
   D. all opinion and no facts

6. What tactic does the excerpt use to garner support for Mr. Obama?

   A. It explains Mr. Obama's program.
   B. It emphasizes Mr. Obama's goal of restoring the American dream.
   C. It explains unpopular parts of Mr. McCain's plan.
   D. It links Mr. Obama's opponent to an unpopular President.

UNIT 3

Analyze Effectiveness of Arguments

SS CONTENT TOPICS: I.CG.c.1, I.CG.c.2, II.CG.e.1, II.CG.e.3, II.CG.f
SS PRACTICES: SSP.1.a, SSP.1.b, SSP.2.a, SSP.5.a, SSP.5.d, SSP.7.b, SSP.9.a, SSP.9.b, SSP.9.c

1 Learn the Skill

When learning about social studies, you may need to **identify strong and weak arguments.** A strong argument is persuasive and is backed by accurate sources. On the other hand, a weak argument lacks the factual support needed to make it convincing.

In order to **analyze the effectiveness of an argument,** notice any supporting evidence that the author or speaker provides, and consider whether it is reliable and convincing.

As with other areas of the GED® test, questions about learning how to analyze the effectiveness of arguments will test your ability to interpret information at various Depth of Knowledge levels through the use of complex reading skills and thinking skills.

2 Practice the Skill

By practicing the skill of analyzing effectiveness of arguments, you will improve your study and test-taking abilities, especially as they relate to the GED® Social Studies Test. Study the information below. Then answer the question that follows.

(a) To be effective, a spoken argument often has features that a written argument does not. Here, Mr. Clinton uses language that is more casual and conversational than he would if this speech were written.

(b) While conversational language and humor engage the audience, the speaker's arguments still rely on facts and other supporting evidence.

From Bill Clinton's Democratic National Convention speech, 2012:

He [President Barack Obama] has laid the foundation for a new, modern, successful economy of shared prosperity. … **(a)** Folks, whether the American people believe what I just said or not may be the whole election. I just want you to know that I believe it. With all my heart, I believe it.

(a) Now, why do I believe it? I'm fixing to tell you why. I believe it because President Obama's approach embodies the values, the ideas and the direction America has to take to build the twenty-first century version of the American Dream: a nation of shared opportunities, shared responsibilities, shared prosperity, a shared sense of community.

(a) So let's get back to the story. In 2010, as the President's recovery program kicked in, the job losses stopped, and things began to turn around. **(b)** The Recovery Act saved or created millions of jobs and cut taxes—let me say this again—cut taxes for 95 percent of the American people. And, in the last 29 months, our economy has produced about 4 ½ million private-sector jobs. We could have done better, but last year the Republicans blocked the President's job plan, costing the economy more than a million new jobs.

TEST-TAKING TIPS

When analyzing an argument's effectiveness, first summarize the argument. Then determine whether the supporting details are facts or only anecdotes or opinions.

1. Which of the following would strengthen Mr. Clinton's argument for Mr. Obama's presidential campaign?

A. Add more details about how Mr. Obama's program has increased jobs.
B. Give more personal anecdotes about his personal relationship with Mr. Obama.
C. Talk more about the successes of the Clinton administration and tie that to Mr. Obama's presidency.
D. Ridicule Mr. Obama's opponent and the opponent's campaign.

UNIT 3

Apply the Skill

★ Spotlighted Item: **EXTENDED RESPONSE**

DIRECTIONS: Read the excerpts and the question, then write your answer on the lines below. Please refer to Unit 3 and Unit 4 in the Reasoning Through Language Arts Student Edition and Workbook for detailed information about reading, writing, and editing Extended Response answers. You may use another sheet of paper to complete your answer.

From Debates in the U.S. Senate on the Tonkin Gulf Resolution, 1964:

Senator William Fulbright: As I stated, section I is intended to deal primarily with aggression against our forces. ... I do not know what the limits are. I do not think this resolution can be determinative of that fact. I think it would indicate that he [President Johnson] would take reasonable means first to prevent any further aggression, or repel further aggression against our own forces. ... I do not know how to answer the Senator's question and give him an absolute assurance that large numbers of troops would not be put ashore. I would deplore it. ...

Senator Ernest Gruening: Regrettably, I find myself in disagreement with the President's Southeast Asian policy ... . The serious events of the past few days, the attack by North Vietnamese vessels on American warships and our reprisal, strikes me as the inevitable ... consequence of U.S. unilateral military aggressive policy in Southeast Asia. ... We now are about to authorize the President ... to move our Armed Forces ... not only into South Vietnam, but also into North Vietnam, Laos, Cambodia, Thailand, and, of course, the authorization includes all the rest of the SEATO nations. ... This resolution is a further authorization for escalation unlimited. I am opposed to sacrificing a single American boy in this venture. We have lost far too many already ... .

2. Senator Fulbright supports the Resolution, while Senator Gruening does not. In your response, develop an argument about how each senator's argument for or against the President's policy is effective. Incorporate relevant and specific evidence from the texts, and your own knowledge of the enduring issue and the circumstances surrounding the topic. This task may require 25 minutes to complete.

_____

_____

_____

_____

_____

_____

_____

_____

_____

_____

UNIT 3

DIRECTIONS: Read the passage and the questions, then choose the **best** answers.

Senator Joseph McCarthy gained notoriety after a 1950 speech in which he claimed to have evidence of more than 200 Communist Party members working in the U.S. State Department.

Senator McCarthy used his position as Chairman of the Committee on Government Operations and its Permanent Subcommittee on Investigations to launch investigations designed to document charges of communists in government.

From his powerful post, Senator McCarthy held hearings in which he accused many government officials of communist ties. McCarthy was not able to substantiate his accusations and they became increasingly reckless and unpopular over time. His attacks on members of the U.S. Army were particularly divisive.

For more than two years, he relentlessly questioned numerous government departments. The resultant alarm and panic arising from Senator McCarthy's "witch hunts" and fear of Communism became known as *McCarthyism.* The McCarthy hearings ended when the Senate **censured** him on December 2, 1954, for behavior deemed "contrary to senatorial traditions."

1. Which type of information below would **not** be included in a summary of this passage?

    A. the event that caused Senator McCarthy's downfall
    B. a description of "senatorial traditions"
    C. a mention of Senator McCarthy's position as chair of a powerful Senate committee
    D. an overview of Senator McCarthy's accusations

2. It is likely that the word *censured* would appear in a summary of this passage. What does the word mean here?

    A. Senator McCarthy was honored.
    B. Senator McCarthy was questioned.
    C. Senator McCarthy was condemned.
    D. Senator McCarthy was ignored.

DIRECTIONS: Study the information, read the question, then choose the **best** answer.

RECONSTRUCTION PLANS

Lincoln	Radical Republicans
Aimed for reconciliation	Hoped to institute harsh punishments for Confederates
Offered pardons to former Confederates who agreed to support the Constitution and the United States	Refused to seat any former Confederates in Congress
Allowed Southern states to elect former Confederates to Congress	Placed Southern states under military rule
Allowed Confederate states to rejoin the Union if they established antislavery governments	Established the Freedmen's Bureau to assist former slaves

3. Which of the following **best** summarizes the Reconstruction plan presented by President Lincoln?

    A. The plan made rejoining the nation simple for former Confederate states.
    B. The plan ultimately hoped to successfully rebuild the Union.
    C. The plan established the Freedmen's Bureau.
    D. The plan sought to punish Confederates.

DIRECTIONS: Read the passage and the question, then choose the **best** answer.

The Democratic Party, at more than 200 years old, is the oldest political party in the United States. While the party supported slavery during the 19th century, by the mid-20th century, it had reinvented itself as a progressive party supporting civil rights and health-care reform.

Sources: *Encyclopedia Britannica* and democrats.org

4. Which of the following would you **not** find in the remainder of this article?

    A. names of major Democratic Party leaders
    B. information about how the Party was formed
    C. details about where the Party stands on issues
    D. opinions about the Party's effectiveness

DIRECTIONS: Read the passage and the question, then choose the **best** answer.

By August 1918, more than one million U.S. soldiers had been deployed to France. Their French and British allies, who had been fighting Germany and its allies for four years, were not impressed with the military skills of the conscripted "doughboys" of the American Expeditionary Force. They believed that the Americans should be used only as replacements in French or British divisions. However, American commander General John J. Pershing refused to allow this. He insisted that the U.S. Army fight together as one unit.

5. Which of the following can you infer, based on the passage?

    A. British commanders respected American doughboys, but French commanders did not.
    B. The British and French commanders had little respect for American troops, but needed their help.
    C. General Pershing was a much better commanding officer than any of the British or French commanders.
    D. American troops had to fight against British and French soldiers as well as German ones.

DIRECTIONS: Read the passage and the question, then choose the **best** answer.

From Article II of the U.S. Constitution:

No person except a national-born citizen, or a citizen of the United States at the time of the adoption of this Constitution shall be eligible to the office of President; neither shall any person be eligible to that office who shall not have attained the age of thirty-five years, and fourteen years a resident within the United States.

6. Which of the following does the Constitution list as qualifications to be President of the United States?

    A. a citizen who has lived in the United States for at least 14 years
    B. a person born in the United States, who is at least 35 years old, and has lived in the United States for at least 14 years
    C. anyone who is a citizen of the United States
    D. a person who has lived in the United States for at least 35 years

DIRECTIONS: Study the information in the graph, read the question, then choose the **best** answer.

CHANGES IN EMPLOYMENT OF SELECTED SECTORS, 2000 AND 2010

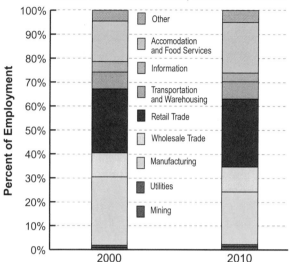

7. Which of the following employment sectors saw the largest increase between 2000 and 2010?

    A. Transportation and Warehousing
    B. Wholesale Trade
    C. Manufacturing
    D. Accomodation and Food Services

DIRECTIONS: Read the passage and the question, then choose the **best** answer.

The Russian term *glasnost,* meaning "openness," refers to a key component of Soviet leader Mikhail Gorbachev's plan to reform the Soviet way of life by encouraging more free and open discussions of politics and culture. Under this policy, Soviet citizens were allowed to voice their concerns and take part in activities that had long been prohibited. Cultural works that had been banned were published. Scholars could discuss their ideas. Glasnost allowed more freedom in the national government-run media, as well.

8. Which of the following groups of Soviet citizens would generally have opposed glasnost?

    A. artists
    B. scientists
    C. journalists
    D. Communists

DIRECTIONS: Study the information, read the questions, then choose the **best** answers.

After more than a decade of having American blood spilled in Afghanistan … it is time for United States forces to leave … It should not take more than a year [because] … prolonging the war will only do more harm. Vice President Joseph Biden Jr. said … that "we are leaving Afghanistan in 2014, period. There is no ifs, ands or buts." Mr. Obama indicated earlier this year this could mean the end of 2014 … two more years of sending the one percent of Americans serving in uniform to die and be wounded, is too long … the only final mission we know of, to provide security for a 2014 Afghan election, seems dubious at best and more likely will only lend American approval to a thoroughly corrupt political system.

… Some experts say a secure withdrawal would take at least six months, and possibly a year. But one year is a huge improvement over two. It would be one less year of having soldiers die or come home with wounds that are terrifying, physically and mentally.

From the nytimes.com editorial "Time to Pack Up," October 13, 2012

9. Which of the following is the purpose of this editorial?

   A. to speak out against Afghan corruption
   B. to argue for bringing U.S. troops home from Afghanistan soon
   C. to say that President Obama does not keep his promises
   D. to insist that U.S. troops should not be used to provide security for elections

10. Which of the following does the writer use to support his statements about the war?

   A. quotations from important military leaders
   B. anecdotes from his travels in Afghanistan
   C. assertions of the likely harm to soldiers
   D. polls showing that the American public is against the war

DIRECTIONS: Study the political cartoon, read the question, then choose the **best** answer.

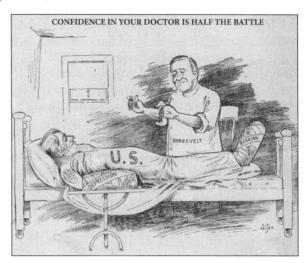

11. Why does the artist depict Franklin D. Roosevelt in doctor's clothing?

   A. to show how Roosevelt's policies affect health care
   B. to show Roosevelt as trying to help other countries during the Depression
   C. to show that Roosevelt's policies have made the country ill
   D. to show Roosevelt as healing the nation

DIRECTIONS: Study the poster, read the question, then choose the **best** answer.

12. To what does "REMEMBER DEC. 7th!" refer?

   A. the D-Day invasion
   B. the Japanese attack on Pearl Harbor
   C. the end of World War II
   D. the dropping of the atomic bomb

DIRECTIONS: Read the passages and the questions, then choose the **best** answer.

From The Declaration of Independence, Thomas Jefferson, 1776:

We hold these truths to be self-evident, that all men are created equal; that they are endowed by their Creator with certain unalienable rights; that among these, are life, liberty, and the pursuit of happiness. That, to secure these rights, governments are instituted among men, deriving their just powers from the consent of the governed.

From *Two Treatises of Government,* John Locke, 1690:

To understand political power right, and derive it from its original, we must consider, what state all men are naturally in, and that is, a state of perfect freedom to order their actions, and dispose of their possessions and persons, as they think fit, within the bounds of law of nature, without asking leave, or depending upon the will of any other man …

13. With which statement would Thomas Jefferson and John Locke likely agree?

   A. All powers of government flow from a naturally free people.
   B. If elected, governments can determine the actions of their people.
   C. Only some people chosen by God are fit to rule over others.
   D. To keep order in society, there must be a strong central government.

14. Which of the following words is a good description of both men's point of view concerning the role of government?

   A. strong
   B. militaristic
   C. limited
   D. religious

15. In *Two Treatises of Government*, what does John Locke mean by the words, "without asking leave"?

   A. One need not have to be excused.
   B. One need not ask permission.
   C. One may go outside the country freely.
   D. One may choose his or her own government.

DIRECTIONS: Study the information, read the questions, then choose the **best** answers.

From presidential candidate Al Gore's speech in which he insists on a recount in Florida in the disputed 2000 election (November 15, 2000):

This is a time to respect every voter and every vote. This is a time to honor the true will of the people. So our goal must be what is right for America.

There is a simple reason that Florida law and the law in many other states calls for a careful check by real people of the machine results in elections like this one.

The reason? Machines can sometimes misread or fail to detect the way ballots are cast, and when there are serious doubts, checking the machine count with a careful hand count is accepted far and wide as the best way to know the true intentions of the voters ...

We need a resolution that is fair and final. We need to move expeditiously to the most complete and accurate count that is possible.

16. Which of the following **best** describes Mr. Gore's opinion?

   A. We must wait to make sure all votes are counted correctly.
   B. It is important to count all the votes, but only if the count can proceed quickly.
   C. The present election results are fair and show the true intentions of the voters of Florida.
   D. Regardless of the number of recounts, there will always be mistakes.

17. Which of the following statements is a fact?

   A. "This is a time to respect every voter and every vote."
   B. "So our goal must be what's right for America."
   C. "Checking the machine count with a careful hand count is accepted … as the best way to know the true intentions of votes … "
   D. "We need to move expeditiously to the most complete and accurate count that is possible."

DIRECTIONS: The passage below is incomplete. Use information from the map to complete the passage. For each drop-down item, choose the option that correctly completes the sentence.

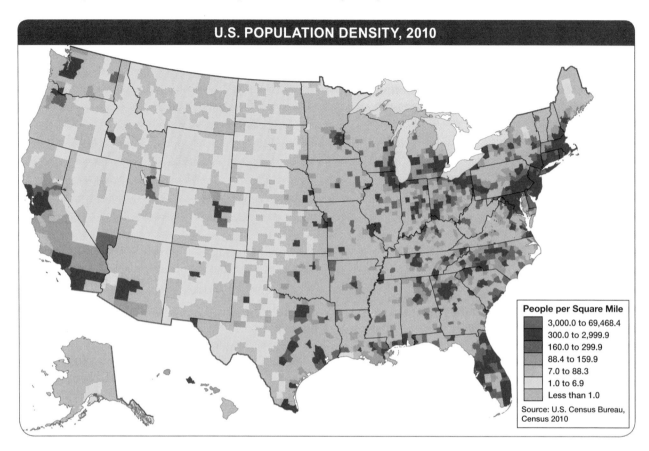

U.S. POPULATION DENSITY, 2010

People per Square Mile
- 3,000.0 to 69,468.4
- 300.0 to 2,999.9
- 160.0 to 299.9
- 88.4 to 159.9
- 7.0 to 88.3
- 1.0 to 6.9
- Less than 1.0

Source: U.S. Census Bureau, Census 2010

18. According to the 2010 Census, the United States had more than 308 million people. Most of the population was concentrated in the [18. Drop-down 1] area of the country.

The areas with the lowest population densities in the United States were in the [18. Drop-down 2], and also in the state of [18. Drop-down 3]. The state of South Dakota was home to fewer people than the state of [18. Drop-down 4].

Drop-Down Answer Options

18.1 A. eastern
B. central
C. Canadian border
D. Mexican border

18.2 A. northeast
B. central plains
C. northwest
D. Hawaiian Islands

18.3 A. Hawaii
B. Texas
C. Alaska
D. Florida

18.4 A. Alaska
B. Montana
C. Idaho
D. Wyoming

DIRECTIONS: Read the passage and the question, then choose the **best** answer.

From the minority opinion of Justice Ruth Bader Ginsburg in *Ledbetter v. Goodyear Tire and Rubber Company*, 2007:

Ledbetter's evidence demonstrated that her current pay was discriminatorily low due to a long series of decisions reflecting Goodyear's pervasive discrimination against women managers in general and Ledbetter in particular. … Yet, under the Court's decision, the discrimination Ledbetter proved is not redressable under Title VII. … Once again, the ball is in Congress' court. As in 1991, the Legislature may act to correct this Court's parsimonious reading of Title VII …

19. Which of the following describes Justice Ginsburg's solution to the problem of Lilly Ledbetter's failure to get justice from the Court?

    A. She urges a change in the Court justices.
    B. She suggests that Congress change the law.
    C. She states that Ledbetter should sue Goodyear again.
    D. She insists that Title VII does not allow suits for discrimination.

DIRECTIONS: Read the passage and the question, then choose the **best** answer.

From Amendment V of the U.S. Constitution:

No person shall be held to answer for a capital, or otherwise infamous crime, unless on a presentment or indictment of a grand jury … nor shall any person be subject for the same offence to be twice put in jeopardy of life or limb; nor shall be compelled in any criminal case to be a witness against himself, nor be deprived of life, liberty, or property, without due process of law; nor shall private property be taken for public use without just compensation.

20. Which of the following rights is not covered by Amendment V?

    A. the right to a grand jury hearing before being charged with a serious crime
    B. the right to refuse to testify against oneself
    C. the right to trial by jury
    D. the right to not have property taken by the government without just compensation

DIRECTIONS: Read the passage and the questions, then choose the **best** answer.

From the resignation speech of President Richard M. Nixon, August 8, 1974:

In all the decisions I have made in my public life, I have always tried to do what was best for the Nation. Throughout the long and difficult period of Watergate, I have felt it was my duty to persevere, to make every possible effort to complete the term of office to which you elected me.

From the discussions I have had with Congressional and other leaders, I have concluded that because of the Watergate matter I might not have had the support of the Congress that I would consider necessary to … carry out the duties of this office.

I have never been a quitter … But as President, I must put the interest of America first. America needs a full-time President and a full-time Congress …

To continue to fight through the months ahead for my personal vindication would almost totally absorb the time and attention of both the President and the Congress in a period when your entire focus should be on the great issues …

21. Which of the following statements best summarizes President Nixon's reason for leaving office?

    A. Congress has made it impossible for him to continue to serve as President.
    B. Because of the Watergate matter, he can no longer carry out his duties effectively.
    C. He must resign because he no longer wishes to serve as President full time.
    D. Because public sentiment has turned against him, he can no longer stay in office.

22. Which of the following best describes the tone of President Nixon's speech?

    A. defiant
    B. joyful
    C. stubborn
    D. remorseful

DIRECTIONS: Study the information presented in the table, read the questions, then choose the **best** answers.

TEN U.S. CITIES WITH THE HIGHEST PERCENTAGE OF POPULATION AGE 85 YEARS AND OLDER: 2010

Place	Total Population	Population 85 Years and Older	
		Number	Percent
Urban Honolulu CDP*, HI	337,256	11,781	3.5
Clearwater, FL	107,685	3,725	3.5
Santa Rosa, CA	167,815	4,654	2.8
Warren, MI	134,056	3,636	2.7
Scottsdale, AZ	217,385	5,821	2.7
Metairie CDP*, LA	138,481	3,665	2.6
Pueblo, CO	106,595	2,818	2.6
Billings, MT	104,170	2,749	2.6
Springfield, MO	159,498	4,209	2.6
Rockford, IL	152,871	3,970	2.6
* CDP = Census Designated Place			

DIRECTIONS: Study the cartoon, read the questions, then choose the **best** answers.

"BY TH' WAY, WHAT'S THAT BIG WORD?" by Bill Mauldin

23. According to information presented in the table, in which region of the United States do most people age 85 years or older live?

  A. the Southeast
  B. the Northeast
  C. the West
  D. the Midwest

24. Based on the information in the chart, which of the following reasons do you infer may be a factor for where many people age 85 years or older live?

  A. the number of major cultural institutions
  B. favorable climate
  C. high population density
  D. proximity to the East Coast

25. How do the figures shown in this cartoon demonstrate faulty logic?

  A. They cannot agree on the best method for testing voters.
  B. They have oversimplified the qualifications for voting.
  C. They made a hasty generalization that only opposing party members would be affected by the literacy tests.
  D. An honest literacy test would prevent them from voting.

26. Under which of the following headings could this cartoon best be categorized?

  A. civil rights
  B. government spending
  C. presidential elections
  D. democratic reforms

DIRECTIONS: Study the flowchart, read the questions, then choose the **best** answers.

1763	Proclamation of 1763 forbids settlement west of Appalachians
1765	Parliament passes Stamp Act, putting a tax on documents
1767	Parliament passes Townshend duties, which tax tea, glass, and other items
1770	Boston Massacre occurs; Townshend duties repealed
1772	Committees of Correspondence form to keep colonists aware of fast-moving events
1773	Parliament passes Tea Act; Boston Tea Party occurs
1774	As punishment for Tea Party, Parliament passes a number of coercive acts and closes the port of Boston
1775	The battles of Lexington and Concord occur

27. Which of the following two events likely influenced each other?

A. The Proclamation of 1763 was passed in response to the Boston Tea Party.
B. The Boston Massacre was a response to the Boston Tea Party.
C. The Committees of Correspondence were a partial response to the Boston Massacre.
D. The Boston Tea Party was revenge for the battles of Lexington and Concord.

28. In which year of the flowchart would you likely find the most people involved in actions against the British?

A. 1763
B. 1770
C. 1772
D. 1773

29. After the final event shown on this flowchart, which of the following events likely occurred in 1776?

A. the Treaty of Paris that ended the war with Britain
B. the surrender at Yorktown of the British forces to General Washington
C. the writing of the U.S. Constitution
D. the signing of the Declaration of Independence

DIRECTIONS: Read the passage and the question, then choose the **best** answer.

In 1989, as Eastern European nations moved from Communist forms of government to democratic ones, Mikhail Gorbachev and the Soviet Union did not intervene. Mr. Gorbachev also allowed opposition to Communism within the Soviet Union, and in 1990, individual Soviet republics began to assert their sovereignty.

In August 1991, a failed coup led by Communist conservatives increased support for democracy. By November, the Communist Party was gone, and pro-democracy leader Boris Yeltsin had begun to negotiate formation of a new Commonwealth of Independent States. Gorbachev resigned on December 25, and one day later, the Soviet Union officially dissolved.

30. Use the information in the passage to generalize about what caused the fall of the Soviet Union.

A. Mr. Gorbachev's decision to allow democracy and dissent unleashed forces that caused the fall of the Soviet Union.
B. Mr. Yeltsin caused Mr. Gorbachev to resign, causing the Soviet Union to fall.
C. Democracy in Eastern Europe led the Soviet Union to adopt democracy, too.
D. Communist leaders in the Soviet Union dissolved the government to resist Mr. Yeltsin.

UNIT 3

GED® JOURNEYS

Wally Amos

Wally Amos's recipe for success included obtaining his GED® certificate.

Wally Amos, founder of the Famous Amos line of cookies, learned his craft from his aunt who loved to bake chocolate chip cookies for him.

Amos left high school before graduation and joined the U.S. Air Force. While enlisted, Amos earned his GED® certificate, which led to his hiring by the William Morris Talent Agency. Amos rose through the ranks and became the company's first African American talent agent, eventually leaving to form his own theatrical management agency in California. He learned to unwind on weekends by taking up a new hobby—baking chocolate chip cookies.

In time, Amos decided to bake and sell cookies under his own name. He opened the Famous Amos Chocolate Chip Cookie Store on Sunset Boulevard in Hollywood, California. Other stores quickly followed. In 1995, Amos founded another successful company, Uncle Wally's Muffins. Today, Famous Amos Cookies and Uncle Wally's Muffins are sold in thousands of grocery stores across the United States.

Wally Amos has worked tirelessly for the cause of literacy, serving as national spokesperson for Literacy Volunteers of America for more than 20 years. He has became a renowned author and motivational speaker whose books and lectures convey his positive attitude.

> "Everyone who has achieved greatness or fulfillment in life started out with a dream."

CAREER HIGHLIGHTS: *Wally Amos*

- Earned his GED® certificate while serving in the Air Force
- Opened his own theatrical management agency in California
- Started the Famous Amos Chocolate Chip Cookie Store in 1975
- Started Uncle Wally's Muffins in 1995
- In 2005, created the Chip & Cookie Read-Aloud Foundation, promoting childhood literacy
- Received various honors for business and literacy efforts

Unit 4: Economics

Many of the choices we make each day revolve around economics. For example, we earn paychecks, make bank deposits and withdrawals, shop, and pay bills and taxes. Economics is the study of the decisions involved in the production, distribution, and consumption of goods and services. By understanding economics, we become better consumers about when and how we use our time and money.

Economics plays an important part in the GED® Social Studies Test, making up 15 percent of all questions. As with other parts of the GED® Tests, economics will test your ability to interpret text and graphics at various Depth of Knowledge levels through the use of complex reading skills and thinking skills. In Unit 4, the continuation of core skills and the introduction of others will help you prepare for the GED® Social Studies Test.

Table of Contents

UNIT 4

Economics is an integral part of everyday life. Whenever you calculate your grocery budget, plan for a special purchase, or manage your bank account, understanding how economics works helps your decision making.

Understand Economics

SS CONTENT TOPICS: II.E.c.1, II.E.c.3, II.E.d.1, II.E.d.6, II.E.d.9, II.E.d.10
SS PRACTICES: SSP.1.a, SSP.1.b, SSP.2.a, SSP.2.b, SSP.4.a, SSP.6.b

1 Learn the Skill

Economics is the study of the way in which goods and services are exchanged. It includes exchanges between people, groups, businesses, and governments. The study of economics borrows from human psychology, ethics, and history in its attempts to explain and predict behaviors related to buying and selling. Learning to **understand economics** is essential for making sense of societal behaviors and world events.

As with other areas of the GED® test, understanding economics and how economics can relate to your everyday life will test your ability to interpret information at various Depth of Knowledge levels through the use of complex reading skills and thinking skills.

2 Practice the Skill

By practicing the skill of understanding economics, you will improve your study and test-taking abilities, especially as they relate to the GED® Social Studies Test. Study the information below. Then answer the question that follows.

Economics is divided into two main categories—microeconomics and macroeconomics. Microeconomics involves economic decision making at an individual level or company level. This includes individuals, households, businesses, and industries. Macroeconomics studies the behavior of the entire economy.

The table illustrates some of the differences between microeconomics and macroeconomics.

a The table highlights some of the main economic indicators and how they apply to microeconomics versus macroeconomics.

b To help you remember the difference between micro- and macroeconomics, remember that *micro* means "small" and *macro* means "large."

	a Production	Prices	Income	Employment
Microeconomics	How many bottles of juice does Company A produce?	What is the price of a bottle of juice from Company A?	What are the wages of the employees at Company A?	How many people are employed at Company A?
b Macroeconomics	How many goods and services does the United States produce?	What is the Gross Domestic Product (GDP) of the United States?	What are the total wages and salaries of employees in the United States?	What is the unemployment rate in the United States?

TEST-TAKING TIPS

Try to think of an example that illustrates any unfamiliar term or concept. To differentiate between micro- and macroeconomics, think about your own spending habits versus U.S. economic policies.

1. Which of the following is an example of microeconomics?

   A. The United States produced more oranges this year than last year.
   B. A can of frozen orange juice costs $2.09 at the supermarket.
   C. Oranges are one of the primary crops in Florida.
   D. Millions of gallons of orange juice are exported each year.

DIRECTIONS: Study the information, read the questions, then choose the **best** answer.

A market is a place or infrastructure in which the exchange of goods and services takes place. In the most literal sense, a market is a physical place in which things are bought and sold, like a farmer's market, for example. To economists, a market is not necessarily a specific place, but a structure in which buyers and sellers are free to trade with one another. This freedom for buyers and sellers leads to similar prices for the same goods.

Sellers that sell cucumbers at a farmer's market, for example, will tend to have their cucumbers priced similarly. Competition between sellers keeps the price of cucumbers from going too high. Sellers know that if they raise their price too high, their buyers will move to other sellers that have lower prices. Some sellers may add incentives to persuade buyers to purchase their produce or product. In this case, a seller with a higher-priced cucumber might incentivize customers by giving them a free tomato with each cucumber purchase.

Some markets are not competitive, but have monopolies. If there were only one seller of cucumbers at the farmer's market and no other sellers of cucumbers could get a spot at the market, this seller could form a monopoly. Without any government regulation, this seller could set the price of the cucumbers wherever he or she wanted.

2. Which of the following holds prices for the same goods at about the same level in a market?

    A. competition between sellers
    B. high demand for the goods
    C. incentives for consumers
    D. quantity of goods available

3. Which of the following describes when a monopoly can occur?

    A. A small number of companies control the market for a good or product.
    B. Each company in a market produces goods that are slightly different and appeal to different customers.
    C. One company sells a good or product that has no good substitutes and other companies are blocked from entering the market.
    D. There are many companies producing the same product, leading to low prices that cannot sustain companies.

DIRECTIONS: Study the information, read the questions, then choose the **best** answer.

Businesses rely on economic indicators to guide their decision making. An economic indicator is an economic statistic. The unemployment rate, or percentage of people unemployed, is an economic indicator. The purpose of an economic indicator is to indicate how well an economy is currently doing and will do in the future.

Some indicators are leading, meaning they change before the economy changes, so they are helpful in making predictions. The stock market, for example, often begins to decline or improve before the larger economy. Leading economic indicators are helpful to investors as they make decisions about where to invest their money.

Other indicators are lagging, meaning they change after the economy changes. The unemployment rate, for example, may continue to increase for several months after the economy has started to improve.

4. Gross domestic product, or GDP, represents the total value of a country's production. Which of the following is an investor most likely to do if the GDP of the United States is consistently increasing?

    A. invest in foreign-manufactured goods
    B. sell investments in foreign companies
    C. sell investments in U.S. businesses
    D. invest in U.S.-based companies

5. Leading indicators are used to predict economic trends, while lagging indicators confirm long-term trends. Which of the following is a lagging indicator?

    A. the stock market
    B. unemployment
    C. money supply
    D. building permits

UNIT 4

Multiple Causes and Effects

SS CONTENT TOPICS: II.E.d.1, II.E.d.2, II.E.d.8
SS PRACTICES: SSP.3.c, SSP.6.a, SSP.6.b, SSP.6.c, SSP.10.a

1 Learn the Skill

Not every cause-and-effect relationship is simple. Many causes can contribute to a single result, and a single event or situation may result in multiple effects. Knowing how to identify **multiple causes and effects** will help you form a better understanding of economics and the complex factors that affect the economy.

As with other areas of the GED® test, questions about multiple causes and effects will test your ability to interpret information at various Depth of Knowledge levels through the use of complex reading skills and thinking skills.

2 Practice the Skill

By practicing the skill of identifying multiple causes and effects, you will improve your study and test-taking abilities, especially as they relate to the GED® Social Studies Test. Study the information below. Then answer the question that follows.

a Inflation causes a chain reaction of events, such as rising prices and fewer purchases.

b Inflation is the cause. Wars, problems with the food supply, and political unrest are some of the effects.

Two important areas of the study of macroeconomics are inflation and deflation. **a** Inflation occurs when the supply of money exceeds the goods and services available. This causes the value of the money to fall and prices to rise. This, in turn, discourages people from making purchases. Inflation's effects are felt in all sectors of the economy and all segments of society. Deflation occurs when prices fall and the value of money rises. Negative inflation is the same as deflation.

b Inflation and the economic instability it spawns have been known to cause wars, problems in the food supply, and political unrest. Developing nations are in the most danger from inflation.

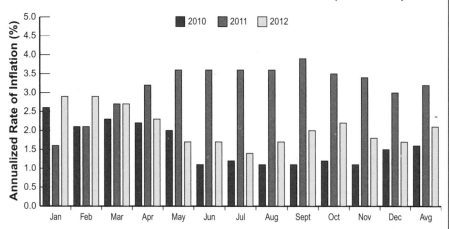

U.S. INFLATION RATES BY MONTH AND YEAR (2010–2012)

MAKING ASSUMPTIONS

You might assume that having more money than can be spent is good for an economy. The information on this page explains why this is not true.

1. Which of the following was most likely true in mid-to-late 2011?

   A. higher prices, reduced consumer spending, and increased value of money

   B. higher prices, reduced consumer spending, and political unrest

   C. increased demand for goods, higher prices, and political unrest

   D. reduced consumer spending, deflation, and political unrest

Apply the Skill

⭐ Spotlighted Item: **DRAG-AND-DROP**

DIRECTIONS: Read the passage on supply and demand below the drag-and-drop. Then, read the drag-and-drop question and complete the diagram by placing the drag-and-drop options into the appropriate boxes.

2. Drag and drop the effects on supply and demand when prices rise above or fall below the equilibrium point, or the point at which supply and demand are equal, into the correct places in the diagram above and below the equilibrium point.

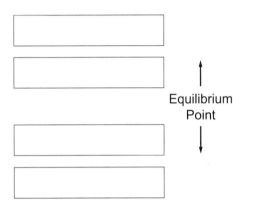

Drag-and-Drop Options

| Demand goes down |
| Demand goes up |
| Supply goes down |
| Supply goes up |

DIRECTIONS: Study the graph and information, read the questions, then choose the **best** answer to each question.

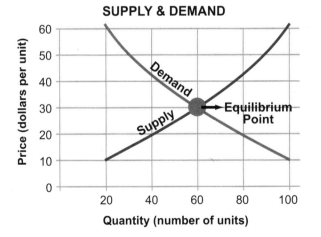

SUPPLY & DEMAND

The cause-and-effect relationship between supply and demand is a strong determining factor of prices. According to the economic laws of supply and demand, people will pay more for something they want when less of it is available. Alternatively, if there is more of a supply of a good or service than people demand, the supplier will lower the price to coax people into buying more of it. The point at which the supply of an item is set in response to an equality of supply and demand is called the equilibrium point. At prices above the equilibrium point, demand drops.

If the price becomes too high, demand may disappear completely. However, if the price becomes too low, the seller will be unable to make a profit and will stop producing the item.

Supply and demand are themselves the effects of other causes. For example, the effects of inflation can decrease demand and force down an item's price. Inflation can also raise the cost of producing an item, resulting in a higher price, which can also lead to a decrease in demand.

3. Which of the following statements is true?

   Supply, demand, and inflation

   A. are each basic causes of economic activity.
   B. do not influence the economy.
   C. operate independently of one another.
   D. are each influenced by many causes.

4. Based on the information, which of the following needs to exist for the law of supply and demand to function freely?

   A. competition
   B. government regulation of prices
   C. inflation
   D. a growing economy

UNIT 4

Compare and Contrast Visuals

SS CONTENT TOPICS: II.E.c.5, II.E.e.1, II.E.e.2
SS PRACTICES: SSP.6.a, SSP.6.c, SSP.10.a, SSP.10.b

1 Learn the Skill

When you **compare** two or more **visual elements**, you consider the similarities between them. Details about each item are used to gain insight into the other items.

Once you have compared the items, you can **contrast** them. To contrast is to focus only on the differences. As you contrast items, you prepare yourself to analyze why the differences exist.

As with other areas of the GED® test, questions about **comparing and contrasting visuals** will test your ability to interpret information at various Depth of Knowledge levels through the use of complex reading skills and thinking skills.

2 Practice the Skill

By practicing the skill of comparing and contrasting visuals, you will improve your study and test-taking abilities, especially as they relate to the GED® Social Studies Test. Study the visuals and the information below. Then answer the question that follows.

a When analyzing two visuals, look for similarities and differences. These graphs both show consumer credit—but two different types of consumer credit.

b Look for ways to connect the information in order to answer the question. In this case, study the trends beginning in 2009 and decide what they both support.

REVOLVING CONSUMER CREDIT 2008–2012 **a**

NONREVOLVING CONSUMER CREDIT 2008–2012

There are two main types of credit—revolving and nonrevolving. Revolving credit is a line of credit with a pre-approved limit, such as a credit card. As you make charges, less credit is available to you. You can pay the balance off at any time, or over time, but you also must pay finance charges on any unpaid balance.

Nonrevolving credit is a loan paid back on a schedule with interest, such as a car loan or a home loan.

1. Which of the following does the shift in each graph most likely indicate??

   A. an upswing in the economy
   B. increased fear of an economic downturn
   C. the beginning of a recession
   D. a decrease in the amount of credit available

MAKING ASSUMPTIONS

You can assume that two visuals presented together on the GED® Test will have a connection. Ensure that you understand the information before trying to answer the questions.

DIRECTIONS: Study the graphs, read the question, then choose the **best** answer.

PERSONAL INCOME

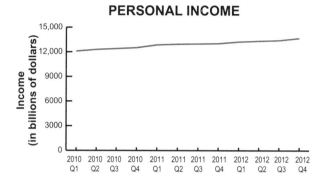

SAVINGS AS A PERCENTAGE OF DISPOSABLE PERSONAL INCOME

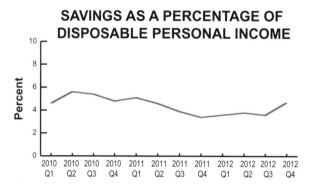

2. According to the graphs, there is a slow increase in income, while savings as a percentage of *disposable* income are more volatile and trending downward. Which of the following could be reasons for this trend difference?

    A. Savings are not dependent on income.
    B. People always spend whatever they make.
    C. People are paying down debt, not saving.
    D. Personal income and disposable personal income are unrelated.

DIRECTIONS: Study the information and the graphs, read the questions, then choose the **best** answers.

Countries often specialize in goods and services depending on the resources available to them. They will most often choose to produce goods and services that provide them with a comparative advantage over other producers in a market. A country has a comparative advantage when it is better at producing a product (more efficiently and cheaply) than another country.

To analyze comparative advantage, compare opportunity costs. The opportunity cost of producing a good or service is the value of the next best choice. For example, if Country A is capable of producing

4 tons of wheat and 1 ton of corn, but decides to produce only wheat, the opportunity cost of producing 1 ton of wheat is 1/4 ton of corn. When using comparative advantage to determine who should produce what, a country should specialize in goods and services that have a lower opportunity cost. Opportunity cost and comparative advantage can be shown using graphs.

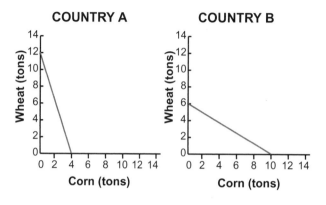

3. What is the opportunity cost for Country B to produce 10 tons of corn?

    A. 2 tons of wheat
    B. 4 tons of wheat
    C. 6 tons of wheat
    D. 8 tons of wheat

4. If each country specializes to the benefit of both countries, which of the following best describes what each country should produce, and why?

    A. Country A should produce corn and Country B should produce wheat because Country A has the highest opportunity cost for wheat and Country B has the highest opportunity cost for corn.
    B. Country A should produce corn and Country B should produce wheat because Country A has the lowest opportunity cost for wheat and Country B has the lowest opportunity cost for corn.
    C. Country A should produce wheat and Country B should produce corn because Country A has the highest opportunity cost for wheat and Country B has the highest opportunity cost for corn.
    D. Country A should produce wheat and Country B should produce corn because Country A has the lowest opportunity cost for wheat and Country B has the lowest opportunity cost for corn.

UNIT 4

LESSON 4

Interpret Pictographs

SS CONTENT TOPICS: II.E.c.8, II.E.c.9, II.E.c.10, II.E.c.11
SS PRACTICES: SSP.6.a, SSP.6.b, SSP.10.a, SSP.11.a

UNIT 4

1 Learn the Skill

Pictographs are visuals that use symbols to illustrate data in chart form. Pictographs are very versatile because their symbols can represent any type of item. These symbols also can represent any quantity of the featured item. A single symbol could represent one dollar of income or one million members of a population group. Pictographs are not used to identify an exact measure of something, but can show how the value has changed over time, or how it compares to other similar items.

As with other areas of the GED® test, questions about **interpreting pictographs** will test your ability to interpret information at various Depth of Knowledge levels through the use of complex reading skills and thinking skills.

2 Practice the Skill

By practicing the skill of interpreting pictographs, you will improve your study and test-taking abilities, especially as they relate to the GED® Social Studies Test. Study the information and pictograph below. Then answer the question that follows.

Countries and economies are interdependent, meaning that they rely on each other for goods and services. The amount of trade between two countries can be a measure of their interdependence.

a Similar to a map key, a key to a pictograph identifies the symbol used in the pictograph, and also gives its value so you can then calculate the values represented on the chart itself.

b At times, the symbol will appear in partial or incomplete form. In these instances, the incomplete symbols represent some portion of the quantity indicated by the full symbol.

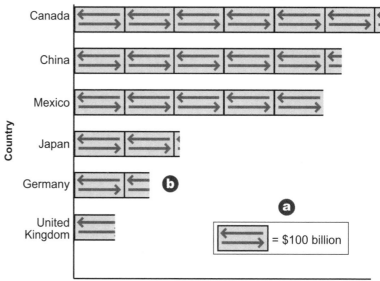

**TOP U.S. TRADE PARTNERS:
TOTAL TRADE VALUE OF GOODS, 2012**

MAKING ASSUMPTIONS

You can make the assumption that when you are interpreting a pictograph, you will probably be asked to estimate the values represented by the symbols on the chart.

1. Which of the following is the approximate total value of goods traded between the United States and Japan?

   A. $100 billion
   B. $150 billion
   C. $200 billion
   D. $250 billion

★ Spotlighted Item: **DROP-DOWN**

DIRECTIONS: The passage below is incomplete. Use information from the passage and the pictograph to complete the passage. For each drop-down item, choose the option that correctly completes the sentence.

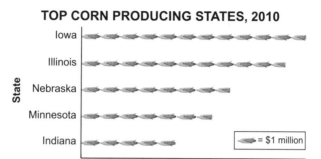

TOP CORN PRODUCING STATES, 2010

Specialization, in an economic sense, refers to individuals and organizations focusing on a limited range of production tasks they perform best. It requires workers, organizations, or even countries to give up performing other tasks at which they are not as skilled, leaving those jobs to others who are better suited for them. An assembly line, for example, where individual workers perform specific tasks in the production process, is the best example of specialization. Specialization is related to another economic concept, division of labor.

Specialization occurs within the United States. For example, citrus goods naturally occur in the warmer climates of the South and West, while maple syrup comes from the maple trees of Vermont and New Hampshire. In the area of agriculture, for example, the Midwest region of the United States is well known to specialize in corn production.

The top corn-producing state in 2010 was Iowa. Its value of production was more than twice that of
[2. Drop-down 1] , which ranked fifth of the top five states in U.S. corn production. Kansas, South Dakota, Ohio, Wisconsin, and Missouri rounded out the top 10 states in terms of U.S. corn production. The median value of production for the top five states is [2. Drop-down 2] . From this information, you can assume that the value of the corn produced in [2. Drop-down 3] was less in 2010 than that produced in Ohio.

Drop-Down Answer Options

2.1 A. Minnesota
 B. Iowa
 C. Indiana
 D. Nebraska

2.2 A. $11,735 million
 B. $10,707 million
 C. $7,860 million
 D. $6,719 million

2.3 A. Iowa
 B. Illinois
 C. Indiana
 D. Wisconsin

UNIT 4

Interpret Multi-Bar and Line Graphs

SS CONTENT TOPICS: II.E.c.4, II.E.d.4, II.E.d.5, II.E.e.1, II.E.e.3
SS PRACTICES: SSP.1.a, SSP.6.a, SSP.6.b, SSP.6.c, SSP.10.a, SSP.10.c

1 Learn the Skill

When studying economics, you will often encounter data presented in **multi-bar and line graphs**. Like single-bar and line graphs, these visuals can be used to compare values and to show changes over time. However, because they use more than one bar or line, they also allow for the comparison of varied, but connected, data over time.

As with other areas of the GED® test, learning to **interpret multi-bar and line graphs** will test your ability to interpret information at various Depth of Knowledge levels through the use of complex reading skills and thinking skills.

2 Practice the Skill

By practicing the skill of interpreting multi-bar and line graphs, you will improve your study and test-taking abilities, especially as they relate to the GED® Social Studies Test. Study the information below. Then answer the question that follows.

a By studying the bars of a double-bar graph, you can compare two quantities at a given time, as well as the ways in which these quantities change over time.

b The key of a double-bar graph will typically use color or shading to identify what each bar represents. In this graph, one bar represents the average annual mortgage rate, while the other represents the average annual prime interest rate.

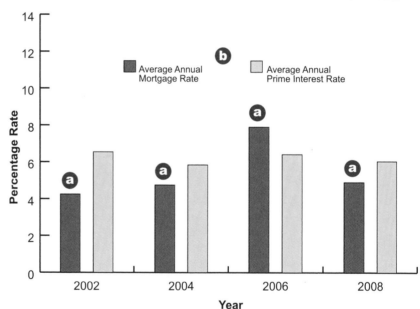

AVERAGE ANNUAL MORTGAGE & PRIME INTEREST RATE

MAKING ASSUMPTIONS

You can typically assume that an author includes information in a multi-bar or line graph to convey a relationship, such as compare-contrast or cause-effect between or among the data.

1. Based on the double-bar graph above, which of the following statements is true?

   A. In 2002, the average mortgage rate was higher than the average prime interest rate.
   B. The average prime interest rate in 2008 was about 6 percent.
   C. The average mortgage rate in 2006 was about 10 percent.
   D. The average mortgage rate dropped by about 2 percent between 2004 and 2006.

DIRECTIONS: Study the information and the graph, read the questions, then choose the **best** answer.

The Federal Reserve, or "The Fed," as it is popularly known, is the central bank of both the United States government and the nation's banking system. The Fed regulates banks, in addition to issuing currency and carrying out monetary policy for the nation. One of the Fed's most notable functions is its control of the nation's money supply. To increase the nation's money supply, the Fed can buy U.S. Treasury securities from banks and the American public, injecting new cash into the economy. It also can increase the money supply by lowering the interest rate at which it lends to commercial banks. This will encourage banks to borrow more money from the Fed, thereby raising the money supply.

In the United States, money supply is evaluated in different categories, or measures. Items are placed into these categories according to their liquidity, or how easily they can be turned into cash. The first category, M1, includes the coins and paper money held by the public and checking deposits at public banks. The second category, M2, includes all of M1 plus savings deposits, interest-earning deposits less than $100,000, and money market deposits and mutual funds.

U.S. MONETARY SUPPLY, M1 & M2

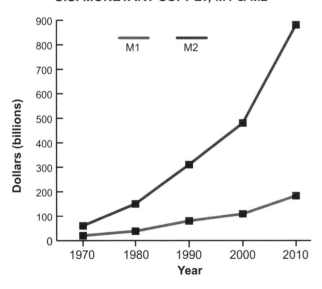

2. Which of the following statements will always be true?

   A. The value of M1 exceeds $300 billion.
   B. The value of M2 is increasing steadily.
   C. The value of M2 is greater than that of M1.
   D. The value of M1 is approximately one-half the value of M2.

3. Which of the following was the approximate value of M1 in 2010?

   A. about $100 billion
   B. about $200 billion
   C. about $300 billion
   D. about $400 billion

4. Based on the information, in which of the following years did the economy probably have the most liquidity in total dollars?

   A. 1980
   B. 1990
   C. 2000
   D. 2010

DIRECTIONS: Study the information presented on the double-bar graph, read the question, then choose the **best** answer.

AGE DISTRIBUTION OF RESPONDENT TELEWORKERS

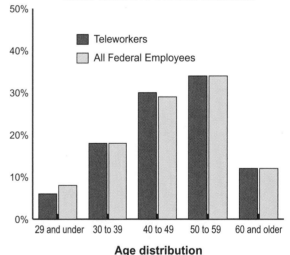

5. Which of the following is true of the federal labor force?

   A. Older employees are less likely to telecommute than younger employees.
   B. Age is not a factor in whether federal employees telecommute.
   C. More younger employees than older employees telecommute.
   D. The percentage of employees that telecommute decreases with age.

UNIT 4

DIRECTIONS: Study the information and the table, read the questions, then choose the **best** answer.

An economic depression, which lasts a number of years, is characterized by economic factors such as substantial increases in unemployment, a drop in available credit, diminishing output, bankruptcies, government debt defaults, reduced commerce and trade, and sustained **volatility** in currency values.

The output of an economy is based on the Gross Domestic Product (GDP). The table below shows the progression of the GDP from its high level in 1929 to its low point in 1933 and the recovery that followed. Although the recovery from The Great Depression of the 1930s, appears to happen fairly quickly, the U.S. was not meeting its capabilities in domestic products.

Depressions usually begin through a combination of decreases in demand and overproduction. These factors lead to decreased production, workforce reductions, and diminished wages for employees. As these changes weaken consumers' purchasing power, a depression can worsen and become more widespread.

Recovery from a depression typically requires either the existing overstock of goods to be depleted or the emergence of new markets. At times, government intervention might be necessary to **stimulate** an economic recovery.

REAL U.S. GROSS DOMESTIC PRODUCT, 1929–1939 (YEAR-2005 DOLLARS)

YEAR	REAL GDP IN BILLIONS
1929	976.1
1930	892.0
1931	834.2
1932	725.2
1933	715.8
1934	793.7
1935	864.2
1936	977.0
1937	1,027.1
1938	991.8
1939	1,071.9

1. Which of the following conclusions can be drawn based on the information and the table?

   A. The United States had been in a period of recession throughout the 1920s.
   B. The production of war supplies for World War II led to a depression in the United States.
   C. The purchasing power of U.S. consumers grew increasingly weak during the early 1930s.
   D. Government intervention in the U.S. economy during the 1920s created a depression during the 1930s.

2. Which of the following predictions could you have made about the years following 1939?

   A. Unemployment in the United States would gradually decrease.
   B. The United States would experience a growing number of bankruptcies.
   C. Decreases in demand would continue to drive prices down.
   D. Depression conditions would continue to drive prices down.

3. Which of the following explains why the table shows the U.S. GDP in year-2005 dollars?

   A. unemployment
   B. overproduction
   C. inflation
   D. supply and demand

4. Which of the following can be substituted for the term *volatility* in order to provide the most accurate interpretation of the text?

   A. fullness
   B. ambulatory
   C. loudness
   D. instability

5. Which of the following can be substituted for the term *stimulate* in order to provide the most accurate interpretation of the text?

   A. explode
   B. motivate or encourage
   C. inflate
   D. bring to an abrupt halt

DIRECTIONS: Study the graph, read the questions, then choose the **best** answer.

U.S. OUTSTANDING NATIONAL DEBT, 1975–2010

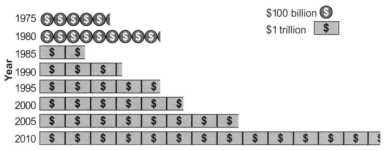

6. Which of the following actions would guarantee a reduction in the rising U.S. national debt as shown in the graph?

A. the continuation of many government programs

B. the approval of a federal budget that produces a surplus dedicated to paying money owed to other nations

C. an increase in tax benefits given to large corporations

D. the passage of new economic stimulus legislation

7. Which of the following statements can you determine to be true based on the pictograph?

A. The U.S. national debt had exceeded $600 billion by 1975.

B. The U.S. national debt decreased between the years 1980 and 1985.

C. The national debt level has continued to rise since 1975.

D. The U.S. national debt expanded more between 1995 and 2000 than it did between 2000 and 2005.

DIRECTIONS: Study the information, read the question, then choose the **best** answer.

The Telework Enhancement Act of 2010 was signed into law on December 9, 2010. The passage and signing of this legislation was a significant milestone in the history of federal telework [telecommuting]. The Act is a key factor in the federal government's ability to achieve greater flexibility in managing its workforce through the use of telework. Well-established and implemented telework programs provide agencies a valuable tool to meet mission objectives while helping employees enhance work/life effectiveness.

Federal agencies, including managers and supervisors, can benefit from telework because it:

- helps with recruiting and retaining the best possible workforce;
- ensures continuity of operations and maintains operations during emergency events—telework is a key component in ensuring the performance of essential government functions during national or local emergencies such as natural disasters or national security incidents, or other situations that may disrupt

normal operations;
- helps to reduce traffic congestion, emissions from vehicles … thereby improving the environment;
- promotes management effectiveness by targeting reductions in management costs related to employee turnover and absenteeism, and reduces real estate costs, transit costs, and environmental impact, and
- enhances work/life effectiveness and balance—telework allows employees to better manage their work and family obligations, thereby retaining a more resilient, results-oriented federal workforce …

From the telework.gov *Guide to Telework in the Federal Government,* 2011

8. Which can be expected based on the description of benefits to managers and supervisors?

A. large turnover in the workforce

B. higher overhead costs for the government

C. the need for higher level security clearances

D. increased productivity from teleworkers

FLOW OF MONEY, GOODS, AND SERVICES IN THE U.S. ECONOMY

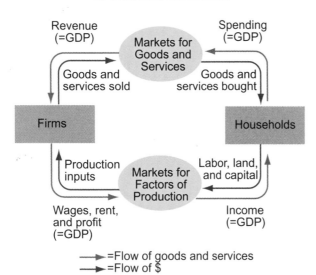

=Flow of goods and services
=Flow of $

Factors of production are the items used to complete a production process. These factors typically fall into three main categories—land, labor, and capital. At times, a fourth category, defined as entrepreneurship or management, also appears alongside these. In order for a business to achieve success, it must maintain a healthy balance of these factors of production.

The flowchart shows the flow of money, as well as goods and services, throughout the U.S. economy. In this flowchart, households own all of the factors of production. The people in these households sell their labor, land, and capital to firms. In exchange for these factors of production, the people receive wages, rent, and profits.

9. Suppose you own a company that manufactures lawnmowers. Which of the following factors of production would fall under the category of labor?

   A. money contributed to shareholders in your company
   B. your ability to manage your employees effectively
   C. the work of your employees
   D. the property on which your company is located

10. Which of the following factors of production is your willingness to start your own business and manufacture products?

   The willingness to start one's own business and manufacture products is an example of

   A. labor.
   B. capital.
   C. profit.
   D. entrepreneurship.

11. Which of the following actions generates income for firms?

   A. buying goods and services from people in households
   B. selling goods and services to people in households
   C. buying factors of production from households
   D. avoiding the markets for goods and services and factors of production

12. Based on the information and the flowchart, which of the following statements can you determine to be true?

   A. Money, goods, and services move in the same direction throughout this economic system.
   B. After receiving wages, rent, and profit, firms use these items to purchase factors of production.
   C. All transactions between firms and households contribute to the nation's GDP.
   D. Firms control all of the production inputs in this economic system.

DIRECTIONS: Study the passage and the graphs, read the questions, then choose the **best** answer.

Credit is a form of borrowing money. When you use revolving credit, you have a pre-approved limit and maintain a credit balance. When you use non-revolving credit, you borrow a set amount of money and make equal monthly payments to pay for it. The graphs show the billions of dollars Americans borrowed on credit between 2008 and 2012.

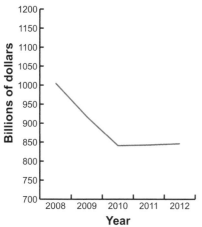

REVOLVING
CONSUMER CREDIT 2008–2012

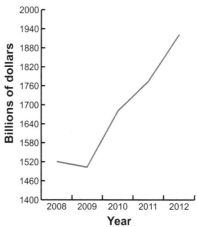

NON-REVOLVING
CONSUMER CREDIT 2008–2012

13. How did the recovery period between 2010 and 2012 differ in the areas of revolving and non-revolving credit?

   A. Revolving credit stayed lower and steadier than in previous years, and non-revolving credit spiked upward.
   B. Revolving credit dropped drastically, while non-revolving credit dropped slightly.
   C. Revolving credit stayed higher than in previous years, and non-revolving credit spiked downward.
   D. Revolving credit spiked drastically, while non-revolving credit dropped drastically.

14. Why does a lower level of non-revolving credit as shown in 2008 and 2009 indicate an economic recession?

   A. Consumer resources and confidence are down so fewer people are buying cars, homes, and businesses.
   B. Consumer resources and confidence are up so more people are buying cars, homes, and businesses.
   C. Fewer people are paying off credit card balances.
   D. More people are paying off credit card balances.

DIRECTIONS: Study the information and the table, read the question, then choose the **best** answer.

The Dow Jones Industrial Average is an indicator that measures changes in the performances of different groupings of stocks. Many people use the Dow Jones Industrial Average as an indicator for stock market growth and economic strength.

DOW JONES INDUSTRIAL AVERAGE, 1995–2010

YEAR	DOW AT START OF YEAR	DOW AT CLOSE OF YEAR	CHANGE
1995	3,838.48	5,117.12	+33.45
2000	11,357.51	10,786.85	-6.18%
2005	10,729.43	10,717.50	-0.61%
2010	11,577.51	12,217.56	+5.53%

15. Based on the information and the table, which of the following is most likely true?

   A. Many investors made money on their investments in 1995.
   B. Most people shied away from investing in 2005.
   C. There was a healthy return on investments in 2000.
   D. Investors invested heavily in technology in 2010.

DIRECTIONS: Study the graphs, read the questions, then choose the **best** answer.

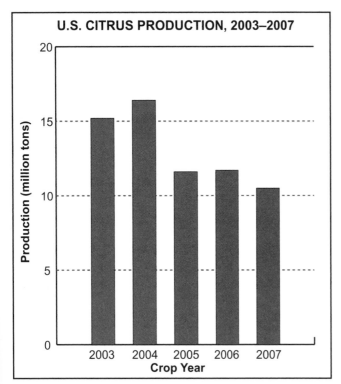

U.S. CITRUS PRODUCTION, 2003–2007

Production (million tons) vs. Crop Year

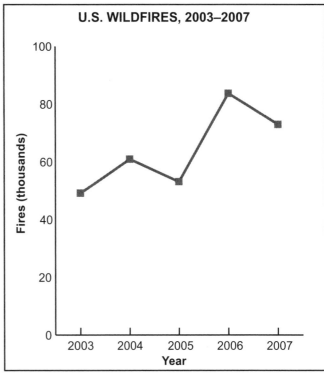

U.S. WILDFIRES, 2003–2007

Fires (thousands) vs. Year

16. Which of the following could have caused the changes shown on both graphs between 2005 and 2007?

    A. a greater demand for agricultural products
    B. a decrease in productivity per hour
    C. more farmers specializing in citrus
    D. a nationwide drought

17. Assuming that high production yields high profits, which of the following conclusions can be drawn about profits in the citrus industry during the years with the most wildfires?

    A. Profits doubled from previous years.
    B. Profits remained the same as in previous years.
    C. Profits declined from previous years.
    D. Profits increased from previous years.

18. How does the year 2004 compare with regard to citrus production and wildfires?

    While citrus production peaked in 2004, wildfires

    A. were the highest in a five-year span.
    B. were the second highest in a five-year span.
    C. were the third highest in a five-year span.
    D. were the fourth highest in a five-year span.

19. Between which periods did the number of wildfires in the United States increase the most?

    U.S. wildfires increased the most between

    A. 2006 and 2007.
    B. 2005 and 2006.
    C. 2004 and 2005.
    D. 2003 and 2004.

DIRECTIONS: Study the multi-bar and multi-line graphs, read the questions, then choose the **best** answer.

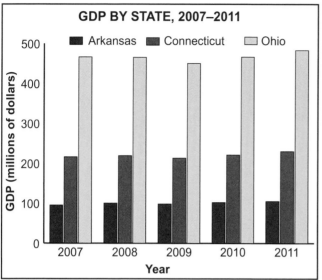

GDP BY STATE, 2007–2011

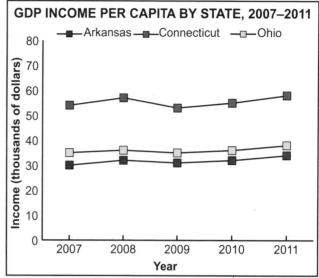

GDP INCOME PER CAPITA BY STATE, 2007–2011

20. Which of the following statements is true based on the two graphs?

   A. The GDP and per capita income of Arkansas remained at about 50% of those of Ohio for the period shown.
   B. For each state, the GDP and per capita income increased at similar rates.
   C. The period from 2011 to 2015 would likely feature little change in GDP and per capita income for each state.
   D. GDP and per capita income are not related.

21. Which conclusion are you able to reasonably draw based on a comparison of GDP and income by state as shown in the two graphs?

   A. Imports to Ohio have decreased each year since 2003.
   B. The population of Arkansas is expanding at a higher rate than that at which its wages are increasing.
   C. The GDP of Arkansas and Connecticut will eventually reach the same level.
   D. Connecticut has a smaller population than Ohio.

22. Unlike the multi-line graph, the multi-bar graph does not take into account which of the following items when measuring the data?

   A. the population of each state
   B. the number of businesses located in each state
   C. the variety of industries found in each state
   D. the national standard for its subject

DIRECTIONS: Study the information and the question, then choose the **best** answer.

   Economic incentives are used to encourage people to make certain choices. Most often, economic incentives involve money, but they may also involve goods or services. An economic incentive can be positive or negative. A positive incentive rewards you for making a certain choice or behaving in a certain way. A negative incentive does the opposite—it punishes you for making a certain choice or behaving in a certain way.

23. Which of the following is an example of a positive economic incentive?

   A. interest charged on your credit card for nonpayment of the entire debt
   B. fines for returning library books late
   C. a $50.00 refund for opening a new checking account
   D. an extra ten-cent charge per minute on your monthly cell phone statement

DIRECTIONS: Read the passage and the question. Then use the drag-and-drop options to complete the Venn diagram.

YOUR CREDIT RIGHTS: HOW THE LAW PROTECTS YOU

Credit is valuable and how you use it goes far beyond shopping. Whether you **manage your credit** well or poorly can affect where you live and even where you work, because your credit record may be considered by prospective employers. That is why you need to understand how credit is awarded or denied and what you can do if you are treated unfairly. The **Fair Credit Reporting Act** promotes the **accuracy** and **privacy** of information in consumer credit reports. It also controls the use of credit reports and requires consumer reporting agencies to maintain correct and complete files. According to this act, you have a right to review your credit report and to have incorrect information corrected.

Issuing Credit Reports
Credit bureaus are required to help you understand your report. Reports can be issued only to those with a legitimate business reason, including creditors, employers, insurers, and government agencies.

Credit Report Errors
If you find an **error** in your report, notify the credit bureau in writing immediately. The bureau is responsible for investigating and changing or removing any incorrect data. The source of the error must then notify all consumer reporting agencies where they sent information. If you are not satisfied with the correction, you have the right to add a brief statement about the issue to your credit report.

Denied Credit
If your application is denied due to report error, the **lender** must provide you with the name and address of the credit bureau that issued the report. Then, you have 30 days to request a free copy from the bureau. The bureaus must disclose to you all information in the report, its source, and who has recently received the report. You have the right to have the credit bureau re-issue corrected reports to lenders who received reports within the last six months, or to employers who received one in the past two years.

Disclosure
Consumer reporting agencies must provide you access to the information in your credit report, as well as identify those who have requested the information recently. You are entitled to one free report a year. You may be charged if you request additional reports within a twelve-month period.

Limiting Access
You may ask reporting agencies to not distribute your name on lists used by creditors and insurers to make unsolicited offers. Consumers have the right to sue consumer reporting agencies, users, and providers in state and federal court for violations of the Fair Credit Reporting Act.

---

24. Obligations to use and manage credit fall into one of these responsibility categories. Based on the passage, determine whether each drag-and-drop option is your obligation, the Credit Bureau's obligation, or the obligation of both.

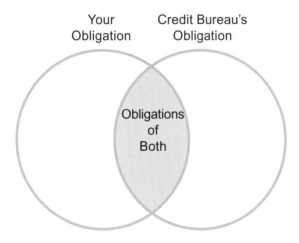

Your Obligation   Credit Bureau's Obligation

Obligations of Both

Drag-and-Drop Options

Accuracy
Compliance with the Act
Error Investigation
Managing Credit
Privacy
Working with Lenders

UNIT 4

DIRECTIONS: Study the information, read the questions, then choose the **best** answer.

COMPETITION COUNTS

HOW CONSUMERS WIN WHEN BUSINESSES COMPETE

The FTC's Bureau of Competition: Protecting Free Enterprise and American Consumers

What if there were only one grocery store in your community? What if you could buy a camera from only one supplier? What if only one dealer in your area sold cars?

Without competition, the grocer may have no incentive to lower prices. The camera shop may have no reason to offer a range of choices. The car dealer may have no motivation to offer a variety of car models and services.

Competition in America is about price, selection, and service. It benefits consumers by keeping prices low and the quality and choice of goods and services high.

Competition makes our economy work. By enforcing antitrust laws, the Federal Trade Commission helps to ensure that our markets are open and free. The FTC promotes healthy competition and challenges anticompetitive business practices to make sure that consumers have access to quality goods and services, and that businesses can compete on the merits of their work. The FTC does not choose winners and losers – you, as the consumer, do that. Rather, our job is to make sure that businesses are competing fairly within a set of rules …

Monopoly

A monopoly exists when one company controls a product or service in a market. If it's because it offers consumers a better product at a better price, that's not against the law. But a company that creates or maintains a monopoly by unreasonably excluding other companies, or by impairing other companies' ability to compete … raises antitrust concerns. For example, a newspaper with a monopoly in a small town could not refuse to run advertisements from businesses that also advertised on a local television station.

From ftc.gov, accessed 2013

25. Which of the following is necessary for a market to be competitive?

    A. international exchange
    B. government control over prices
    C. one company to sell each product
    D. more than a single seller and buyer

26. Which of the following best describes a monopolistic market?

    A. one in which multiple sellers help maintain lower prices
    B. one in which consumers only have one seller from which to purchase a product
    C. one in which only one type of good is exchanged
    D. one in which consumers are given more power than sellers

27. How do consumers select business "winners and losers" in a free market economy?

    A. Consumers choose which products to buy.
    B. Consumers support monopolies.
    C. Consumers pay higher prices for convenience.
    D. Consumers shop for the best values.

Answer Key

UNIT 1 GEOGRAPHY AND THE WORLD

LESSON 1, *pp. 2–3*

1. **B; DOK Level:** 1; **Content Topics:** II.G.c.1, II.G.c.3; **Practice:** SSP.6.b. Brazil is in South America and is the only choice that is on the equator. Mexico is north of the equator, in North America. Saudi Arabia is north of the equator, in Africa, and Italy is on the continent of Europe, far north of the equator.

2. **the Costa and the Galápagos; DOK Level:** 1; **Content Topics:** II.G.b.2, II.G.b.4, II.G.c.1; **Practices:** SSP.2.b, SSP.6.b. The Costa Region's western border is the Pacific Ocean. The Galápagos Islands are surrounded by the Pacific Ocean.

3. **the Costa and Sierra regions; DOK Level:** 2; **Content Topics:** II.G.b.2, II.G.b.3, II.G.b.4, II.G.b.5, II.G.c.2, II.G.d.1, II.G.d.2, II.G.d.3, II.E.g; **Practices:** SSP.2.b, SSP.6.b. Many people migrated to the Costa region in the 1950s when banana production increased in that area. The Sierra experienced a similar population boom when oil was discovered in that region in the 1970s.

4. **the Sierra and the Galápagos; DOK Level:** 2; **Content Topics:** II.G.b.4, II.G.b.5, II.G.c.2; **Practices:** SSP.2.b, SSP.6.b. Several volcanoes provide hiking opportunities on the Galápagos Islands, as do the Andes Mountains in the Sierra Region.

5. **the Sierra and the Oriente; DOK Level:** 2; **Content Topics:** II.G.b.2, II.G.b.3, II.G.b.4, II.G.b.5, II.G.d.3, II.E.h; **Practices:** SSP.2.b, SSP.3.c, SSP.6.b.

6. **the Sierra and the Galápagos; DOK Level:** 2; **Content Topics:** II.G.b.4, II.G.c.1, II.G.c.2; **Practices:** SSP.2.b, SSP.6.b. The Sierra Region features the world's highest active volcano, Cotopaxi, and the Galápagos Islands are themselves a collection of volcanic islands that continue to grow through eruptions.

LESSON 2, *pp. 4–5*

1. **C; DOK Level:** 1; **Content Topics:** II.G.d.3, II.G.d.4; **Practice:** SSP.6.b. There are six major cities in northeastern New Jersey, more than in any other area. The northwestern, western, and southern areas of the state do not have as many major cities as the northeastern area.

2. **C; DOK Level:** 2; **Content Topics:** II.G.c.1, II.G.c.3; **Practice:** SSP.6.b. Sydney is the only city east of 150°E longitude. Canberra, not Sydney, is the capital of Australia. Sydney is located on the east coast, not the west coast, of the country. Sydney is south, not north, of 30°S latitude.

3. **B; DOK Level:** 1; **Content Topics:** II.G.c.1, II.G.d.3, II.G.d.4; **Practice:** SSP.6.b. Looking at the map, you can see that most of the cities are located along the coast. Darwin is the only city that is located north of 15°S. Perth is the only city that is west of 120°E.

4. **D; DOK Level:** 2; **Content Topics:** II.G.c.1, II.G.c.3; **Practice:** SSP.6.b. Using the map scale, you can determine that the two cities farthest away from one another are Sydney and Darwin. The other answer choice options give cities that are closer together than Sydney and Darwin.

5. **D; DOK Level:** 1; **Content Topics:** II.G.b.1, II.G.b.5, II.G.c.3, II.G.d.3, II.G.d.4; **Practice:** SSP.6.b. The star symbol indicates that Atlanta is the capital. Interstate 75 goes through Atlanta. Highway 19 is north of Atlanta and does not pass through the city. Highway 16 is south of Atlanta and does not pass through the city. Interstate Highway 95 is far southeast of Atlanta and does not pass through the city.

6. **C; DOK Level:** 1; **Content Topics:** II.G.c.1, II.G.c.3; **Practice:** SSP.6.b. Highways 16 and 95 merge in Savannah. Atlanta is north of Interstate Highway 95 and Highway 16. Augusta also is north of 95 and 16. Highway 16 goes to Macon, but Interstate Highway 95 does not.

7. **A; DOK Level:** 1; **Content Topics:** II.G.c.1, II.G.c.3; **Practice:** SSP.6.b. Savannah is the closest city to those coordinates. Athens and Macon are located between 83°W and 84°W. Atlanta is located between 84°W and 85°W. Athens, Atlanta, and Macon are all located north of 32°N.

8. **B; DOK Level:** 1; **Content Topics:** II.G.c.1, II.G.d.3, II.G.d.4; **Practice:** SSP.6.b. Looking at the map, you can see that most of the cities are located in the north-central part of Georgia, not the north, south, or the east.

LESSON 3, *pp. 6–7*

1. **D; DOK Level:** 3; **Content Topics:** II.G.b.4, II.G.c.1, II.G.c.2, II.G.c.3; **Practices:** SSP.2.b, SSP.6.b, SSP.6.c. The shading on the map indicates that the elevation of California is varied and has lowland, hills, and mountains. The land in California is not mostly low with some hills because there are mountains in the state. The Coast Ranges lie along the coast of the state; thus the land on the coast is not very low. There are places along the coast, however, such as the San Francisco and Monterey Bay areas, where the land is not mountainous.

2. **Lake Michigan; DOK Level:** 2; **Content Topics:** II.G.c.1, II.G.c.2; **Practices:** SSP.2.b, SSP.6.b, SSP.6.c.

3. **the Au Sable River; DOK Level:** 1; **Content Topics:** II.G.b.4, II.G.c.1; **Practices:** SSP.2.b, SSP.4.a, SSP.6.b.

4. **C; DOK Level:** 2; **Content Topics:** II.G.b.4, II.G.c.1, II.G.c.2; **Practices:** SSP.2.b, SSP.6.b. The coastal area receives more than 60 inches of rain per year, making it the wettest area. The other answer options, the north, the southeast, and the west, all receive less rain than the coastal area.

5. **B; DOK Level:** 2; **Content Topics:** II.G.b.4, II.G.c.1, II.G.c.2, II.G.c.3; **Practices:** SSP.2.b, SSP.6.b, SSP.6.c. The shading on the map indicates that the lowest amount of precipitation along Alabama's Florida border is between 52 and 55 inches. There is no shading that indicates that this border area receives less than 52 inches, and the other shading along the border shows that it sometimes receives more than 60 inches of precipitation per year.

6. **C; DOK Level:** 2; **Content Topics:** II.G.b.2, II.G.b.3, II.G.b.4, II.G.b.5, II.G.c.1, II.G.c.2, II.E.c.7; **Practices:** SSP.2.b, SSP.6.b, SSP.6.c. Peanut farming would thrive the best in the southeastern part of Alabama due to its relative dryness compared to the coastal, northeastern, or central regions of the state.

ANSWER KEY

LESSON 4, *pp. 8–9*

1. **B; DOK Level:** 2; **Content Topics:** II.G.b.1, II.G.c.1, II.G.c.3; **Practices:** SSP.2.b, SSP.6.b. This map shows the counties in Wyoming and the states that border Wyoming. The map does not just show only the counties of Wyoming, nor does the map present the elevation of Wyoming.

2. **D; DOK Level:** 2; **Content Topics:** II.G.c.1, II.G.c.3, II.G.d.3, II.G.d.4; **Practices:** SSP.2.b, SSP.6.b. The shading on the map indicates that the highest population densities are near major cities. There are areas between Madrid and Saragossa where population is very sparse, as well as along the French border and between Madrid and Cordova.

3. **A; DOK Level:** 2; **Content Topics:** II.G.c.1, II.G.c.3, II.G.d.3, II.G.d.4; **Practices:** SSP.2.b, SSP.6.b. Madrid shows the largest area shaded hot pink, or more than 2,500 people per square mile. Seville has a population under one million, while Barcelona has a population over one million. There are between 250 and 1,250 people per square mile along the Mediterranean coast. Murcia has no more than 1,250 people per square mile.

4. **D; DOK Level:** 2; **Content Topics:** II.G.c.1, II.G.c.3, II.G.d.3, II.G.d.4; **Practices:** SSP.2.b, SSP.6.b. Of the towns listed, Cordova has the lowest population and least population density. Both Madrid and Barcelona are larger cities with dense populations. Although both Bilbao and Cordova have populations of less than 1 million, Bilbao has a denser population than does Cordova.

5. **B; DOK Level:** 3; **Content Topics:** II.G.c.1, II.G.c.3, II.G.d.3, II.G.d.4; **Practices:** SSP.2.b, SSP.6.b. The most logical option is that Tucson is both a large city and the county seat. The symbol for county seat alone is not what is represented by the symbol near Tucson, and Tucson is not the state capital.

6. **B; DOK Level:** 2; **Content Topics:** II.G.c.1, II.G.c.3, II.G.d.3, II.G.d.4; **Practices:** SSP.2.b,SSP.6.b. The map shows no small or large cities in the far northern portion of Arizona. Therefore, it can be assumed that this part of the state has a low population. Maricopa County has several large cities. Pima County includes Tucson. The southeast portion of the state includes several small cities, as well as Tucson.

7. **D; DOK Level:** 3; **Content Topics:** II.G.c.1, II.G.c.3, II.G.d.3, II.G.d.4; **Practices:** SSP.2.b, SSP.6.b. Even though Coconino County has a larger area, most of the large cities are in Maricopa County. Therefore, it can be assumed that Maricopa County has the largest population. There is just one city located on the map in Coconino County, and it is not a large city, but a county seat. The state's population is not evenly distributed across all counties, nor is most of the population located near the California border.

LESSON 5, *pp. 10–11*

1. **D; DOK Level:** 2; **Content Topics:** II.G.b.1, II.G.b.2, II.G.b.4, II.G.c.1, II.G.c.2, II.G.d.2, II.G.d.3, II.E.g; **Practices:** SSP.2.b, SSP.3.a, SSP.3.c, SSP.6.b. After the founding of Jamestown Colony, slave traders began taking enslaved people to North America. There is no indication on the map that shows that the areas of Africa where enslaved people were taken increased after the founding of Jamestown, nor is there any indication that areas with major concentrations of enslaved people moved from South America. Movement on the map shows just the opposite: that enslaved people moved from Africa to South America. There is no indication on the map that enslaved people were sent *from* South America, just *to* South America.

2. **D; DOK Level:** 2; **Content Topics:** II.G.b.1, II.G.b.2, II.G.b.4, II.G.c.1, II.G.c.2, II.G.d.2, II.G.d.3, II.E.g; **Practices:** SSP.2.b, SSP.3.a, SSP.3.c, SSP.6.b. It is logical to assume that both trade goods and ideas *were* exchanged among countries along the Silk Road, and not prevented from being exchanged. There is no mention of Africa's economy benefiting from the Silk Road. Silk was traded *from* Asians in the Far East, not *to* Asians in the Far East.

3. **B; DOK Level:** 2; **Content Topics:** II.G.b.1, II.G.b.2, II.G.b.4, II.G.c.1, II.G.c.2, II.G.d.2, II.G.d.3, II.E.g; **Practices:** SSP.2.b, SSP.3.a, SSP.3.c, SSP.6.b. The best route from Alexandria to Kabul is through Seleucia and Bactra. The other options are not logical routes for goods to travel from Alexandria to Kabul.

4. **C; DOK Level:** 2; **Content Topics:** II.G.b.1, II.G.b.2, II.G.b.4, II.G.c.1, II.G.c.2, II.G.d.2, II.G.d.3, II.E.g; **Practices:** SSP.2.b, SSP.3.a, SSP.3.c, SSP.6.b. Samarqand, Kashi, Kabul, and Bactra are all centrally located on the Silk Road. Kabul and Bactra are located on the main connecting route of the Silk Road. These cities are located south of the Great Wall of China, not north of it. Kashi and Kabul are located east, not west, of Samarqand and Bactra.

5. **D; DOK Level:** 2; **Content Topics:** II.G.b.4, II.G.c.1, II.G.c.2, II.G.c.3, II.G.d.1, II.G.d.2, II.G.d.3, II.E.g; **Practices:** SSP.2.b, SSP.3.a, SSP.3.c, SSP.6.b. According to the dotted lines, traders from Rome had to cross the Mediterranean, which was likely done by boat, not wagon, horse, or foot.

UNIT 1 REVIEW, *pp. 12–19*

1. **B; DOK Level:** 2; **Content Topics:** II.G.c.1, II.G.c.3; **Practices:** SSP.4.a, SSP.6.b. This general description best explains Beijing's relative location. Beijing is located east, not west, of Moscow. A city's relative location does not depend on its latitude or longitude.

2. **D; DOK Level:** 2; **Content Topics:** II.G.c.1, II.G.c.3; **Practices:** SSP.4.a, SSP.6.b. Latitude and longitude are map tools that can be used to determine a place's absolute location. A map scale, key, or symbols on a map do not in and of themselves provide an absolute location of a place.

3. **C; DOK Level:** 2; **Content Topics:** II.G.c.1, II.G.c.3; **Practices:** SSP.4.a, SSP.6.b. Australia is the only continent listed that falls fully within the Southern Hemisphere on the map. Part of Africa and a part of Asia are located in the Southern Hemisphere, but not all of those continents. Europe is located in the Northern Hemisphere.

ANSWER KEY

Answer Key

UNIT 1 *(continued)*

4. **D; DOK Level: 2; Content Topics:** II.G.c.1, II.G.c.2, II.G.c.3, II.G.d.3; **Practices:** SSP.4.a, SSP.6.b. Early settlements were built along waterways. Although Lake Erie is a waterway, many settlements were also built along rivers. Cincinnati was the westernmost settlement. Most of the settlements were not built in the interior of the territory, but in the east and along its borders.

5. **A; DOK Level: 3; Content Topics:** II.G.c.1, I.USH.b.1, I.USH.b.2, I.USH.c; **Practices:** SSP.2.b, SSP.6.b. The American Revolution ended in 1783. The settlements on the map were all founded soon after that date. The French and Indian War ended in 1763. The War of 1812 ended with the Treaty of Ghent, signed in 1814, and the Civil War ended in 1865.

6. **B; DOK Level: 1; Content Topics:** II.G.c.1, II.G.d.4; **Practices:** SSP.2.b, SSP.3.a, SSP.6.b. Portsmouth was founded in 1803, after the founding of Cleveland and Chillicothe in 1796, Marietta in 1788, Cincinnati in 1789, and Zanesville in 1800.

7. **D; DOK Level: 2; Content Topics:** II.G.c.1, II.G.c.3; **Practices:** SSP.2.b, SSP.4.a, SSP.6.b. All of the states that border the Gulf of Mexico are in the Southern region. There are states in the Southern region that are west of the Mississippi River. The Southern region includes both Virginia and West Virginia. There are several states in the Southern region that do not feature the Appalachian Mountains.

8. **A; DOK Level: 2; Content Topics:** II.G.c.1, II.G.c.3; **Practices:** SSP.2.b, SSP.4.a, SSP.6.b. Nashville is located in Tennessee and Tennessee is the only city located in a Southern region state.

9. **B; DOK Level: 2; Content Topics:** II.G.c.1, II.G.c.3; **Practices:** SSP.2.b, SSP.4.a, SSP.6.b. Pennsylvania borders the Southern region states of West Virginia, Maryland, and Delaware. None of the other answer choices are in a state that borders the Southern region.

10. **C; DOK Level: 3; Content Topics:** II.G.c.1, II.G.c.3; **Practices:** SSP.2.b, SSP.4.a, SSP.6.b. Using the map scale, you can measure the distance at around 700 miles. The other answer choices are incorrect.

11. **D; DOK Level: 3; Content Topics:** II.G.c.1, II.G.c.3; **Practices:** SSP.2.b SSP.4.a, , SSP.6.b. Tennessee is the only state that shares a border with seven other states in the Southern region: Tennessee borders Kentucky, Virginia, North Carolina, Georgia, Alabama, Mississippi, and Arkansas.

12. **C; DOK Level: 3; Content Topics:** II.G.b.1, II.G.c.1, II.G.c.2, II.G.c.3, II.G.d.2; **Practices:** SSP.2.a, SSP.2.b, SSP.3.a, SSP.4.a, SSP.6.b. The Southern region make up the states that eventually formed the Confederacy, or the Confederate States of America, during the Civil War. Delaware, not West Virginia, is the smallest state in the Southern region. Not all of the states border the Atlantic Ocean. Although some states in the region border the Mississippi River, not all border it. There is no evidence presented that the states in the Southern region make up half of the land of the United States. The New England states, the rest of the Midwest, the West, and the largest state, Alaska, are not shown in their entirety on the map, so it is not possible to make this assertion.

13. **The majority of the people live in the southeast, near Ottawa, the capital; DOK Level: 2; Content Topics:** II.G.c.1, II.G.d.3, II.G.d.4; **Practices:** SSP.2.b, SSP.4.a, SSP.6.b.

14. **Iqaluit; DOK Level: 2; Content Topic:** II.G.c.1; **Practices:** SSP.2.b, SSP.4.a, SSP.6.b.

15. **British Columbia, Alberta, Saskatchewan, Manitoba, Ontario, Quebec, New Brunswick; DOK Level: 2; Content Topic:** II.G.c.1; **Practices:** SSP.2.b, SSP.4.a, SSP.6.b.

16. **Yukon; DOK Level: 3; Content Topics:** II.G.c.1, II.G.d.3, II.G.d.4; **Practices:** SSP.2.b, SSP.4.a, SSP.6.b.

17. **Yellowknife; DOK Level: 3; Content Topics:** II.G.c.1, II.G.c.3; **Practices:** SSP.2.b, SSP.4.a, SSP.6.b.

18. **Hudson Bay; DOK Level: 2; Content Topics:** II.G.c.1, II.G.c.3; **Practices:** SSP.2.b, SSP.4.a, SSP.6.b.

19. **Manitoba and Prince Edward Island; DOK Level: 2; Content Topics:** II.G.c.1, II.G.c.3, II.G.d.3, II.G.d.4; **Practices:** SSP.2.b, SSP.4.a, SSP.6.b.

20. **B; DOK Level: 2; Content Topics:** II.G.b.4, II.G.c.1, II.G.c.2, II.G.c.3; **Practices:** SSP.2.b, SSP.4.a, SSP.6.b. Of the states listed as choices, Nevada is the state with the lowest amount of annual precipitation. Arizona is a close second.

21. **A; DOK Level: 3; Content Topics:** II.G.b.4, II.G.c.1, II.G.c.2, II.G.c.3; **Practices:** SSP.2.b, SSP.4.a, SSP.6.b. The Pacific Coast area has the greatest diversity in precipitation levels, so logically it has the most diverse climate. The Atlantic Coast, the Midwest, and the Northeast do not have such diversity.

22. **B; DOK Level: 2; Content Topics:** II.G.b.4, II.G.c.1, II.G.c.2, II.G.c.3; **Practices:** SSP.2.b, SSP.4.a, SSP.6.b. California receives between 0 and 128 inches in annual precipitation.

23. **A; DOK Level: 2; Content Topics:** II.G.b.4, II.G.c.1, II.G.c.2, II.G.c.3; **Practices:** SSP.2.b, SSP.4.a, SSP.6.b. Florida has the highest annual precipitation.

24. **A; DOK Level: 3; Content Topics:** II.G.b.1, II.G.b.2, II.G.b.3, II.G.b.4, II.G.b.5, II.G.c.1, II.G.c.2, II.G.d.2, II.G.d.3, II.G.d.4, II.E.g; **Practices:** SSP.1.a, SSP.1.b, SSP.2.a, SSP.2.b, SSP.4.a, SSP.6.b, SSP.7.a. It is logical to assume that most people do not live in the Kalahari Desert.

ANSWER KEY

25. **A; DOK Level:** 1; **Content Topics:** II.G.b.1, II.G.b.2, II.G.b.3, II.G.b.4, II.G.b.5, II.G.c.1, II.G.c.2, II.G.d.2, II.G.d.3, II.G.d.4, II.E.g; **Practices:** SSP.1.a, SSP.1.b, SSP.2.a, SSP.2.b, SSP.4.a, SSP.6.b, SSP.7.a. The passage specifically states that diamond mining and the tourism industry help Botswana's economy. There is not much farming in Botswana because the climate is very dry. The economy in Botswana is not failing, and there are tourist attractions, such as nature preserves, which help the economy.

26. **D; DOK Level:** 2; **Content Topic:** II.G.c.1; **Practices:** SSP.2.b, SSP.6.b. The capital is Gaborone.

27. **D; DOK Level:** 2; **Content Topic:** II.G.c.1; **Practices:** SSP.2.b, SSP.6.b. The African country of Namibia lies west of Mamuno. The country of Angola is northwest of Botswana; Zimbabwe lies to the northeast of Botswana, and South Africa is to the southeast of Botswana.

28. **C; DOK Level:** 2; **Content Topics:** II.G.b.5, II.G.c.1, II.G.c.3, II.G.d.3, II.G.d.4; **Practices:** SSP.2.a, SSP.2.b, SSP.4.a, SSP.6.b. Nashville is the capital city and is located near the central part of the state. Not all of Tennessee's major cities are located near the central part of the state. The Appalachian Mountains are located in the eastern part of the state and would not be a highly-populated area, and Chattanooga is not centrally located but is near the state's southeast border.

29. **A; DOK Level:** 2; **Content Topics:** II.G.b.5, II.G.c.1, II.G.c.3, II.G.d.3, II.G.d.4; **Practices:** SSP.2.a, SSP.2.b, SSP.4.a, SSP.6.b. Georgia borders both Tennessee and South Carolina. The other answer options do not.

30. **B; DOK Level:** 3; **Content Topics:** II.G.b.5, II.G.c.1, II.G.c.3, II.G.d.3, II.G.d.4; **Practices:** SSP.2.a, SSP.2.b, SSP.4.a, SSP.6.b. Of the answer choices, only the area between the counties west and southwest of Clarksville and northeast and southeast of Jackson has the lowest population density. The other answer options all show more population density.

31. **D; DOK Level:** 2; **Content Topics:** II.G.b.5, II.G.c.1, II.G.c.3, II.G.d.3, II.G.d.4; **Practices:** SSP.2.a, SSP.2.b, SSP.4.a, SSP.6.b. The Mississippi River borders Tennessee on the west, and Memphis is a large population center. The Tennessee River flows across eastern and southern Tennessee.

32. **Burgas; DOK Level:** 2; **Content Topics:** II.G.b.4, II.G.c.1; **Practices:** SSP.2.b, SSP.6.b.

33. **Slovenia; DOK Level:** 2; **Content Topics:** II.G.c.1, II.G.c.3; **Practices:** SSP.2.b, SSP.6.b.

34. **Kosovo, Serbia, Romania, Bosnia and Herzegovina, Bulgaria; DOK Level:** 2; **Content Topics:** II.E.d, II.G.b.3, II.G.b.4, II.G.b.5, II.G.c.1; **Practices:** SSP.2.b, SSP.6.b.

35. **Slovenia, Croatia, Bosnia and Herzegovina, Serbia, Macedonia, Montenegro, and Kosovo; DOK Level:** 3; **Content Topics:** I.G.a, II.G.b, II.G.c.1, II.G.c.2, II.G.c.3, II.G.d.1, II.G.d.2, II.G.d.3; **Practices:** SSP.2.b, SSP.4.a, SSP.6.b.

36. **C; DOK Level:** 2; **Content Topics:** II.G.b.4, II.G.c.1, II.G.c.2, II.G.c.3; **Practices:** SSP.2.b, SSP.6.b. Kahului's average annual precipitation is between 0 and 25 inches, according to the map and the map key. Honolulu's is between 25.1 and 65 inches. Hilo's is between 100.1 and 160 inches; and Lihue's is between 25.1 and 65 inches.

37. **A; DOK Level:** 2; **Content Topics:** II.G.b.4, II.G.c.1, II.G.c.2, II.G.c.3; **Practices:** SSP.2.b, SSP.6.b. Hilo's average annual precipitation is between 100.1 and 160 inches, according to the map and the map key. Kahului's is between 0 and 25 inches; Honolulu's is between 25.1 and 65 inches, and Lihu'e's is between 25.1 and 65 inches.

38. **D; DOK Level:** 2; **Content Topics:** II.G.b.4, II.G.c.1, II.G.c.2, II.G.c.3; **Practices:** SSP.2.b, SSP.6.b. According to the map and the key, Lana'i, Kaho'olawe, and Ni'ihau are the islands with the lowest annual average precipitation. The other answer options include islands with higher annual averages.

39. **B; DOK Level:** 2; **Content Topics:** II.G.c.1, II.G.c.3; **Practices:** SSP.2.b, SSP.6.b. The approximate distance between Honolulu and Haleakala National Park is 125 miles, according to the map scale. The other answer options are incorrect.

UNIT 2 UNITED STATES HISTORY

LESSON 1, *pp. 22–23*
1. **C; DOK Level:** 2; **Content Topics:** II.G.b.1, II.G.c.1, II.G.c.3, II.G.d.1, II.G.d.3, I.USH.a.1; **Practices:** SSP.1.a, SSP.1.b, SSP.2.a, SSP.2.b, SSP.3.a, SSP.3.b, SSP.3.c, SSP.4.a, SSP.6.a, SSP.6.b, SSP.6.c. The map shows five whole states and a small part of another. The text says that no more than five states would be formed.

2. **MA or Massachusetts; DOK Level:** 2; **Content Topics:** II.G.c.1, II.G.c.2 II.G.c.3, II.G.d.1, II.G.d.2, II.G.d.3; II.G.d.4; **Practices:** SSP.2.b, SSP.3.a, SSP.3.b, SSP.4.a, SSP.6.a, SSP.6.b.

3. **Santa Fe; Gila; DOK Level:** 2; **Content Topics:** I.USH.b.6, II.G.b.1, II.G.b.5, II.G.c.1, II.G.c.3, II.G.d.1, II.G.d.3; **Practices:** SSP.2.b, SSP.3.a, SSP.3.b, SSP.4.a, SSP.6.a, SSP.6.b.

LESSON 2, *pp. 24–25*
1. **D; DOK Level:** 3; **Content Topics:** II.G.b.1, II.G.b.2, II.G.b.4, II.G.b.5, II.G.d.2, II.G.d.3, II.USH.b.1; **Practices:** SSP.1.a, SSP.1.b, SSP.2.b, SSP.6.b. Virginia's population grew year to year, so choice D is the correct answer. Virginia's population grew, so many people probably did not leave Virginia for other colonies. Virginia's population was greater in 1750 that in the hundred years before, so the population did not peak before 1750. If the population doubled every twenty years, the population in 1650 would be 5,000, for example.

2. **Africa; DOK Level:** 1; **Content Topics:** II.G.d.1, II.G.d.2, II.G.d.3, II.USH.e; **Practices:** SSP.1.a, SSP.2.b, SSP.6.a. England, Wales, and Scotland are all part of Britain; the other countries on the table are Africa, Ireland, Germany, and Other. Of those countries, Africa had the largest number of immigrants to the American colonies.

3. **the slave trade; DOK Level:** 3; **Content Topics:** II.G.d.1, II.G.d.2, II.G.d.3, II.USH.e; **Practices:** SSP.1.a, SSP.2.b, SSP.6.a. The large number of people from Africa were brought to the colonies as enslaved workers.

Answer Key

UNIT 2 *(continued)*

4. **B; DOK Level:** 3; **Content Topic:** I.USH.b.1; **Practices:** SSP.1.a, SSP.1.b, SSP.2.b, SSP.6.b. Because the British are better prepared in every category, it appears that they will win the war. The colonies have fewer people, little money, an army with little equipment and few officers, which suggests they will not win even though they know the lay of the land. A truce could be declared, but no information in the table suggests that will happen. The Thirteen Colonies probably will expand if the colonists win the war, but no information in the table indicates that will happen.

5. **D; DOK Level:** 3; **Content Topics:** II.USH.b.1, II.G.c.1, II.G.c.3; **Practices:** SSP.1.a, SSP.1.b, SSP.2.b, SSP.6.b. The colonists are most prepared in the area of geography; they are familiar with their territory and know how to get to their supplies easily. The population of the colonies is smaller than the number of British fighting. The British have more money than the colonists. The British have more military officers than the Colonial Army.

LESSON 3, *pp. 26–27*

1. **C; DOK Level:** 2; **Content Topics:** I.CG.b.2, I.E.b, I.USH.a.1, I.USH.b.1; **Practices:** SSP.1.a, SSP.1.b, SSP.2.a, SSP.4.a, SSP.5.a, SSP.5.c, SSP.7.a. Paine clearly states that the bravest achievements occur when a nation is young, which supports the argument in favor of independence. The quotation regarding population is speculative. The quotations regarding trade and armies show cause-and-effect relationships between population and trade and population and military size, neither of which directly addresses the fight for independence.

2. **Middle and Southern Colonies; DOK Level:** 3; **Content Topic:** I.USH.a.1; **Practice:** SSP.6.b. The Middle and Southern Colonies each had 21 delegates, while the New England Colonies had 14.

3. **C; DOK Level:** 2; **Content Topics:** I.CG.a, I.CG.b.2, I.USH.a.1, I.USH.b.1, I.E.a; **Practices:** SSP.1.a, SSP.1.b, SSP.2.a, SSP.2.b, SSP.4.a. The main idea that colonists cautiously pursued independence is implied in the text as a main idea. Colonists did not want to gain independence from Britain when war broke out in 1775, and this is a detail, not a main idea. North Carolina's and Virginia's delegates agreed regarding independence. Virginia was not alone in leading the movement; Delegates from North Carolina and the writers of the Declaration were involved, too.

4. **D; DOK Level:** 2; **Content Topics:** I.CG.a, I.CG.b.2, I.USH.a.1, I.USH.b.1; **Practices:** SSP.1.a, SSP.1.b, SSP.2.a, SSP.2.b, SSP.4.a. That people have the right to end destructive governments and form new ones is a main idea offered in the *Declaration of Independence*. That men are endowed with unalienable rights is a detail that supports the main idea. Life, liberty, and the pursuit of happiness are important rights, but this statement is a detail that supports the main idea. King George III of Britain may have been a tyrant, but this claim is a detail that supports the main idea.

LESSON 4, *pp. 28–29*

1. **C; DOK Level:** 2; **Content Topics:** I.USH.a.1, I.USH.b.4, I.CG.a.1, I.CG.b.3, I.CG.b.9; **Practices:** SSP.3.d, SSP.6.b. The Anti-Federalists believed that the government should favor agriculture over commerce and industry. Therefore, you can categorize Answer "C" as expressing an Anti-Federalist viewpoint. Anti-Federalists opposed adoption of the Constitution, and they wanted to limit power of national government. There is no mention in the table about either group endorsing the raising of taxes.

2. **B; DOK Level:** 3; **Content Topics:** I.USH.a.1, I.CG.a.1, I.CG.b.8, I.CG.b.9, II.G.b.1; **Practice:** SSP.3.d. Jay describes people who wish to remain firmly united, a situation that would require a strong central government, and people who want a division of the states, which would result in strong state governments. Jay and Alexander Hamilton were both Federalists, so their followers would have been the same. Jay refers to the people of America and politicians, but not British politicians. Supporting state militias or a national army are categories into which people could be placed, but Jay does not identify these categories.

3. **D; DOK Level:** 2; **Content Topics:** I.USH.a.1, I.CG.a.1, II.CG.b.8, II.CG.b.9, II.G.b.1; **Practices:** SSP.2.b, SSP.3.d. The author explains that people will not give up their rights to those who govern and want government that has limits on its power. The author does say that the people are free and enlightened. The author also says that people have unalienable and fundamental rights. The author claims the people want a limited, not strong, national government.

4. **D; DOK Level:** 2; **Content Topics:** I.USH.b.1, II.G.b.1, II.G.d.1, II.G.d.2, II.G.d.3, II.G.d.4; **Practice:** SSP.1.a. Georgia was a southern colony so nearby Alabama and Mississippi would eventually become southern states. The Federalist states were generally anti-slavery, while the southern states supported slavery. The question references future states, which postdates the foreign colonies.

5. **D; DOK Level:** 2; **Content Topics:** I.USH.b.1, II.G.b.1, II.G.d.1, II.G.d.2, II.G.d.3, II.G.d.4; **Practices:** SSP.1.a, SSP.2.a, SSP.2.b. Georgia was the southernmost colony and bordered Florida, which was held by Spain. They had withstood a previous attack from the Spanish over land claims. The fact that Georgia was the least-populated colony at the time of the American Revolution, or that its land was mostly wilderness, was not a valid reason for Georgians to consider the Spanish a threat. British and Spanish forces were not at war over Georgia.

6. **A; DOK Level:** 3; **Content Topics:** I.USH.b.1, II.G.b.1, II.G.d.1, II.G.d.2, II.G.d.3, II.G.d.4; **Practices:** SSP.1.a, SSP.2.a, SSP.2.b. The passage focuses on a troubled relationship regarding land claims between the U.S. and Spain. Although English-Spanish and English-American relations are mentioned, they are minor points. Although Georgia-Florida relations are mentioned, they are set within a larger context.

LESSON 5, *pp. 30–31*

1. **C; DOK Level:** 1; **Content Topics:** I.USH.b.7, II.G.c.1, II.G.c.2, II.G.d.1, II.G.d.2, II.G.d.3, II.G.d.4; **Practices:** SSP.2.b, SSP.3.a. The passage explains that after Jackson took office in 1829, Congress passed the Indian Removal Act of 1830. Jackson negotiated the treaty with the Cherokee after 1832, and it was approved in 1835, which was not immediately after Jackson became President. The Cherokee disputed policies that limited their freedoms following the Congressional passage of the act. Troops did lead Native Americans on the Trail of Tears, but this event was almost 10 years after Jackson was elected in 1829.

2. **B; DOK Level:** 2; **Content Topics:** I.USH.b.2, I.USH.b.7, II.G.c.1; **Practices:** SSP.2.b, SSP.3.a, SSP.3.b, SSP.6.b. The Battle of Tippecanoe took place in 1811, so it preceded the War of 1812. The Battle of the Thames occurred after the War of 1812 began. The Capitol and White House were burned during the War of 1812. The Treaty of Ghent ended the War of 1812, so it could not have preceded the war.

3. **D; DOK Level:** 3; **Content Topics:** I.USH.b.2, I.USH.b.7, II.G.c.1; **Practices:** SSP.2.b, SSP.3.a, SSP.3.b, SSP.6.b. The correct assumption is that after defeating the British in the War of 1812, nationalism, or national pride, began to grow. The United States never controlled Canada. The Battle of New Orleans did occur after the Treaty of Ghent was signed, but Jackson defeated the British. The United States was just 30 years old, so it is not likely that it would have become the most powerful nation in the world.

4. **B; DOK Level:** 2; **Content Topics:** I.USH.b.6, II.G.c.1, II.G.d.1, II.G.d.2, II.G.d.3, II.G.d.4; **Practices:** SSP.1.a, SSP.1.b, SSP.3.b, SSP.3.c. B is the only sequence of events that is listed in chronological order. The American Revolution preceded the Louisiana Purchase (of 1803), followed by the War of 1812, then Americans' quest for Manifest Destiny. The other answer choices are not in chronological order.

5. **A; DOK Level:** 3; **Content Topics:** I.USH.b.6, II.G.c.1, II.G.d.1, II.G.d.2, II.G.d.3, II.G.d.4; **Practices:** SSP.1.a, SSP.1.b, SSP.3.b, SSP.3.c. Britain and the United States both claimed the Oregon Territory as early as 1818, following the belief in Manifest Destiny and nationalism in the United States. The French and Indian War took place in 1754–1763. There was no prolonged period of peace throughout the United States during this time. The Civil War was not fought to expand the territory of the U.S.

LESSON 6, *pp. 32–33*

1. **C; DOK Level:** 2; **Content Topics:** I.USH.c.1, I.USH.c.2, II.G.b.1, II.G.b.3, II.G.b.4, II.G.b.5, II.G.c.1, II.G.c.2, II.G.d.3, I.E.a; **Practices:** SSP.2.b, SSP.3.a, SSP.4.a. The information in the passage states that the Northern economy featured commercial and industrial sectors as well as agriculture. Therefore, one effect of sectional differences between the North and the South was that the Northern economy became increasingly diverse. There is no indication in the passage that Northern states strongly supported states' rights. The South had already been using the labor of enslaved people, and the passage does not state that Northern farmers began establishing plantations, just "agriculture." Plantations usually were quite large and required the labor of many workers, usually enslaved people, as in the South.

2. **slavery; DOK Level:** 2; **Content Topics:** I.USH.c.1, I.USH.c.2, I.CG.b.8, I.CG.d.2, II.G.b.1, II.G.c.2; **Practices:** SSP.1.a, SSP.1.b, SSP.2.a, SSP.2.b SSP.4.a, SSP.5.a, SSP.5.d.

3. **"the order of Providence." DOK Level:** 2; **Content Topics:** I.USH.c.1, I.USH.c.2, I.CG.b.8, I.CG.d.2, II.G.b.1, II.G.c.2; **Practices:** SSP.1.a, SSP.1.b, SSP.2.a, SSP.2.b, SSP.4.a, SSP.5.a, SSP.5.d. Essentially, Stephens is claiming that God would make the "problem" of slavery disappear.

4. **new [Confederate] government; DOK Level:** 2; **Content Topics:** I.USH.c.1, I.USH.c.2, I.CG.b.8, I.CG.d.2, II.G.b.1, II.G.c.2; **Practices:** SSP.1.a, SSP.1.b, SSP.2.a, SSP.2.b, SSP.4.a, SSP.5.a, SSP.5.d.

5. **not equal; DOK Level:** 2; **Content Topics:** I.USH.c.1, I.USH.c.2, I.CG.b.8, I.CG.d.2, II.G.b.1, II.G.c.2; **Practices:** SSP.1.a, SSP.1.b, SSP.2.a, SSP.2.b SSP.4.a, SSP.5.a, SSP.5.d.

LESSON 7, *pp. 34–35*

1. **C; DOK Level:** 3; **Content Topics:** I.USH.d.2, I.CG.c.5; **Practices:** SSP.1.b, SSP.2.a, SSP.2.b, SSP.3.b, SSP.4.a, SSP.6.b. Because Anthony served as a leader in the National Woman Suffrage Association, the most reasonable inference is that she traveled and lectured on the importance of woman suffrage. Anthony died in 1906, so she did not vote in the Presidential election of 1920. There is no information in the passage or the timeline to support the statement that Anthony opposed anti-slavery or temperance amendments, nor is any information given that provides where Anthony lived.

2. **Five or 5; DOK Level:** 2; **Content Topics:** I.USH.c.3, I.USH.d.1, I.CG.b.8, I.CG.d.2; **Practices:** SSP.1.b, SSP.2.a, SSP.2.b, SSP.3.b, SSP.4.a, SSP.6.b. The Fifteenth Amendment was ratified in 1870.

3. **1913; DOK Level:** 2; **Content Topics:** I.USH.c.3, I.USH.d.1, I.CG.b.8, I.CG.d.2; **Practices:** SSP.1.b, SSP.2.a, SSP.2.b, SSP.3.b, SSP.4.a, SSP.6.b.

4. **social equality or equality; DOK Level:** 2; **Content Topics:** I.USH.c.3, I.USH.d.1, I.CG.b.8, I.CG.d.2; **Practices:** SSP.1.b, SSP.2.a, SSP.2.b, SSP.3.b, SSP.4.a, SSP.6.b.

5. ***Plessy* v. *Ferguson*; DOK Level:** 2; **Content Topics:** I.USH.c.3, I.USH.d.1, I.USH.d.4, I.USH.d.5, I.CG.b.8, I.CG.d.2; **Practices:** SSP.1.b, SSP.2.a, SSP.2.b, SSP.3.b, SSP.4.a, SSP.6.b.

UNIT 2 REVIEW, *pp. 36–43*

1. **D; DOK Level:** 1; **Content Topics:** II.USH.f.3, II.USH.g.1; **Practices:** SSP.2.a, SSP.2.b. The U.S. objected to the spread of Communism on political and ideological grounds. The rise of the Red Army and the defeat of the White Army happened during the Revolution, not during its aftermath. The U.S. objected to Communism, not necessarily to the formation of the USSR.

2. **C; DOK Level:** 1; **Content Topics:** II.USH.f.3, II.USH.g.1; **Practices:** SSP.2.a, SSP.2.b. The establishment of the USSR as a Communist state led to the Cold War with the U.S. The beginning of WWI came before the beginning of the Russian Revolution. The Civil War was within Russia, not the U.S. WWII is not mentioned in the passage.

Answer Key

UNIT 2 (continued)

3. **A; DOK Level:** 1; **Content Topics:** II.USH.e, II.G.c.1, II.G.d.1, II.G.d.3; **Practices:** SSP.2.a, SSP.2.b. The chart shows that most immigrants originated from the region of Northern Europe.

4. **C; DOK Level:** 1; **Content Topics:** II.USH.e, II.G.c.1, II.G.d.1, II.G.d.3; **Practices:** SSP.1.a, SSP.1.b. Southern Europe had the smallest number of immigrants by 1890 and likely saw an increase in these numbers with the regional shift.

5. **B; DOK Level:** 3; **Content Topics:** II.USH.e, II.USH.f.4, II.USH.f.5, II.USH.g.3; **Practices:** SSP.1.a, SSP.1.b, SSP.2.a, SSP.2.b, SSP.6.b, SSP.7.a. Because Congress opposed the United States joining the League of Nations, and the United States is not listed in the table as a permanent member, you can infer that the United States never joined the League of Nations. Nations other than Allied and neutral countries could join, such as Germany. The table lists just the permanent members of the Council, not its entire membership. There is no information supporting the statement that Woodrow Wilson served as a member of the League of Nations World Court.

6. **D; DOK Level:** 3; **Content Topics:** II.USH.e, II.USH.f.4, II.USH.f.5, II.USH.g.3; **Practices:** SSP.1.a, SSP.1.b, SSP.2.a, SSP.2.b, SSP.6.b, SSP.7.a. Because the League of Nations was formed after World War I with the aim of preventing another world war, you can infer that it did not achieve its goal of preserving world peace. World War II and other international battles took place within 50 years of World War I. Member nations of the Council did not enjoy peaceful relations for many decades. The League of Nations was not taken over by the United States Congress.

7. **D; DOK Level:** 2; **Content Topics:** II.USH.f.2, II.USH.f.9, II.G.b.1; **Practices:** SSP.1.a, SSP.1.b, SSP.2.a, SSP.4.a, SSP.5.a, SSP.5.b, SSP.5.d. The main idea of this passage is found at the end, when the authors write "there are a thousand signs which point to Fascism as the characteristic doctrine of our time." Mussolini and Gentile write that Italy *is* rising again, not that the country *needs to* rise again. The authors do not state either that Fascism is the root cause of Italy's debasement and foreign servitude, or that the doctrine of Fascism is equal to decadence. Both of those answer options are, essentially, opposite of the main idea.

8. **D; DOK Level:** 3; **Content Topic:** II.USH.f.9; **Practice:** SSP.2.b. Germany was ruled by the Nazis and played a major role in the events of WWII. The other answer choices describe forms of democratic governments, which are not totalitarian.

9. **B; DOK Level:** 2; **Content Topics:** II.USH.f.2, II.USH.f.9, II.G.b.1; **Practices:** SSP.1.a, SSP.1.b, SSP.2.a, SSP.4.a, SSP.5.a, SSP.5.b, SSP.5.d. Mussolini makes errors in logic and reasoning because he makes absolute and universal claims, such as "Fascism is the doctrine best adapted to represent the tendencies and the aspirations of a people" and "there are a thousand signs which point to Fascism as the characteristic doctrine of our time." Mussolini does not make a reasoning error by appealing to the beliefs of his audience, or by focusing on the people of Italy. Nor does Mussolini make a reasoning error by defining the terminology that he uses to make his argument.

10. **A; DOK Level:** 1; **Content Topic:** II.USH.f.12; **Practices:** SSP.6.a, SSP.10.a. The U.S. holds only two colonial territories; France holds two; and New Zealand, one. The U.K. holds eleven.

11. **Romania; DOK Level:** 1; **Content Topics:** II.USH.f.9, II.USH.f.10; **Practices:** SSP.1.a, SSP.2.a, SSP.6.b.

12. **by rail lines or by railroads; DOK Level:** 2; **Content Topics:** II.USH.f.9, II.USH.f.10; **Practices:** SSP.1.a, SSP.2.a, SSP.6.b.

13. **as the final solution; DOK Level:** 3; **Content Topics:** II.USH.f.9, II.USH.f.10; **Practices:** SSP.1.a, SSP.2.a, SSP.6.b.

14. **espionage or spying; DOK Level:** 2; **Content Topics:** II.USH.f.11, II.G.d.2; **Practices:** SSP.1.a, SSP.2.a, SSP.6.b.

15. **western; DOK Level:** 2; **Content Topics:** II.USH.f.11, II.G.d.2; **Practices:** SSP.1.a, SSP.2.a, SSP.6.b.

16. **racism; DOK Level:** 3; **Content Topics:** II.USH.f.11, II.G.d.2; **Practices:** SSP.1.a, SSP.2.a, SSP.6.b.

17. **B; DOK Level:** 2; **Content Topics:** II.USH.f.13, I.CG.c.6, II.CG.f, I.E.a, I.E.b, II.E.f; **Practices:** SSP.1.a, SSP.2.a, SSP.2.b. Returning veterans from World War II would have flooded the job market and would have been under-educated, untrained, and without enough money for homes. The GI Bill was not caused by President Roosevelt bringing the United States into World War II. The Veterans Administration did not need to add employees to its workforce, nor were colleges and universities without sufficient numbers of students.

18. **C; DOK Level:** 2; **Content Topics:** II.USH.f.13, I.CG.c.6, II.CG.f, I.E.a, I.E.b, II.E.f; **Practices:** SSP.1.a, SSP.2.a, SSP.2.b. The major effect of the GI Bill was that returning veterans received educational, job, and housing assistance. The benefits are more important than the Administration. The educational tax benefit is small in relation to the other benefits. Roosevelt's election is not a benefit for veterans.

19. **D; DOK Level:** 2; **Content Topic:** II.USH.g.1, II.USH.g.5, II.USH.g.6; **Practice:** SSP.10.a. The U.S. tried to contain Communism by rebuilding Europe and fighting wars against Communist forces in Korea and Vietnam. The U.S. did not allow the Soviet Union to place missiles in Cuba or oppose the destruction of the Berlin Wall. The U.S. did not adopt an isolationist policy toward Europe and Asia.

ANSWER KEY

20. D; DOK Level: 2; **Content Topics:** II.USH.g.3, II.USH.g.5; **Practices:** SSP.1.a, SSP.2.a, SSP.2.b, SSP.4.a. Greece was fighting a civil war, and Turkey needed financial assistance. Both countries were geographically close to the Soviet Union and could fall under that nation's Communist government, thus further spreading communism throughout the world. There is no evidence that President Truman wanted the United States to take the place of Great Britain as a world power, or that the President wanted Greece and Turkey to become democratic countries. Greece and Turkey had not fallen to the Soviet Union.

21. B; DOK Level: 2; **Content Topics:** II.USH.g.3, II.USH.g.5; **Practices:** SSP.1.a, SSP.2.a, SSP.2.b, SSP.4.a. Government officials in the United States were worried that if one nation fell to communism, another close neighboring country who was weakened may also fall, thus spreading communism. They were not worried about supporting countries formerly supported by Britain. They did not believe that if one weakened country was given financial assistance from the United States, other weakened countries would expect aid. U.S. government officials and President Truman did not state that small countries such as Greece or Turkey could not govern themselves.

22. B; DOK Level: 2; **Content Topics:** II.USH.g.4, II.G.b.1, II.G.b.5, II.G.c.1, II.G.d.2, II.G.d.3; **Practices:** SSP.1.a, SSP.2.a, SSP.2.b, SSP.3.a, SSP.3.c. The Berlin Wall divided East (communist) from West Germany (democratic) and was a place where many east Germans lost their lives. Therefore, the Wall was not favored by many East Germans. There is no evidence that people in East Germany viewed West Germany as a hostile nation. East Germans eventually were able to escape through Hungary to West Germany, but that is not the main idea of the passage.

23. C; DOK Level: 2; **Content Topics:** II.USH.g.4, II.G.b.1, II.G.b.5, II.G.c.1, II.G.d.2, II.G.d.3; **Practices:** SSP.1.a, SSP.2.a, SSP.2.b, SSP.3.a, SSP.3.c. From 1961, when the communist government of East Germany constructed the Berlin Wall, to 1990, when East and West Germans were free to cross the boundary, is 29 years. It is not 38, nor 35, nor 25 years.

24. C; DOK Level: 2; **Content Topics:** II.G.b.1, II.CG.f, II.USH.g.2, II.USH.g.3, II.USH.g.4, II.USH.g.9, II.USH.h; **Practices:** SSP.1.a, SSP.1.b, SSP.2.a, SSP.2.b, SSP.3.a, SSP.3.c. Twenty eight countries presently form NATO; less the original twelve, the answer is sixteen. The article mentions twelve original countries and then lists an additional four by name, but the total is twenty eight.

25. D; DOK Level: 1; **Content Topics:** II.G.b.1, II.CG.f, II.USH.g.2, II.USH.g.3, II.USH.g.4, II.USH.g.9, II.USH.h; **Practices:** SSP.1.a, SSP.1.b, SSP.2.a, SSP.2.b, SSP.3.a, SSP.3.c. The formation of NATO was primarily in response to the Soviet blockade of Berlin, not the Berlin Airlift, in which the Allies helped supply the people of Berlin with needed food and goods, or the invasion of Czechoslovakia, which came in 1968. The signing of the Warsaw Pact was also conducted after the formation of NATO.

26. B; DOK Level: 2; **Content Topics:** II.USH.g.2, II.USH.g.3, II.USH.g.5; **Practices:** SSP.2.a, SSP.2.b. The U.S. adopted an isolationist policy at the end of WWI, but it changed to an inclusive policy at the end of WWII. The U.S. did not support the Soviet Union. The U.S. pledged to defend Western Europe.

27. A; DOK Level: 2; **Content Topics:** II.G.b.1, II.CG.f, II.USH.g.2, II.USH.g.3, II.USH.g.4, II.USH.g.9, II.USH.h; **Practices:** SSP.1.a, SSP.1.b, SSP.2.a, SSP.2.b, SSP.3.a, SSP.3.c. The last sentence of the passage states "Following the diminishing power of the U.S.S.R. in the 1980s, and the eventual fall of Communism, the Warsaw Pact was officially dissolved in 1991." The Warsaw Pact countries did not join NATO. The U.S.S.R. did not nullify the Warsaw Pact, nor did the invasion of Czechoslovakia nullify the Warsaw Pact.

28. A; DOK Level: 2; **Content Topics:** II.USH.g.3, II.USH.g.4, II.USH.g.9, II.USH.h, II.G.b.1; **Practices:** SSP.1.a, SSP.1.b, SSP.2.a, SSP.4.a, SSP.5.a, SSP.7.a. President Reagan wants to encourage Soviet leadership to acknowledge the importance of freedom. The rest of the speech is Reagan's way of challenging the Soviets to make this happen. Reagan is not proposing a treaty between the United States and the Soviet Union, nor is his main point to criticize Communist policies in Eastern Europe or proclaim American support for West Germany.

29. D; DOK Level: 2; **Content Topics:** II.USH.g.4, II.USH.g.9; **Practices:** SSP.2.a, SSP.2.b. President Reagan wants Gorbachev to "tear down" the Berlin Wall as a symbolic gesture toward freedom. He does not want false hopes or token gestures. The adoption of a new policy would not be symbolic.

30. A; DOK Level: 2; **Content Topics:** II.USH.g.3, II.USH.g.4, II.USH.g.9, II.USH.h, II.G.b.1; **Practices:** SSP.1.a, SSP.1.b, SSP.2.a, SSP.2.b, SSP.3.a, SSP.3.c. The information states that conservative Communist leaders tried to take back power from democratic reformers. Therefore, to refute the idea that all Eastern Europeans supported democratic reforms during this time, you can cite that conservative leaders staged a coup against the Soviet government. Gorbachev's reforms did allow opposition to grow, democratic governments did rise to power in nations such as Hungary and Poland, and the Soviet Union did choose not to intervene in outside conflicts. These do not refute, but substantiate, the idea that Eastern Europeans supported democratic reforms during this time.

31. B; DOK Level: 3; **Content Topics:** II.USH.g.3, II.USH.g.4, II.USH.g.9, II.USH.h, II.G.b.1; **Practices:** SSP.1.a, SSP.1.b, SSP.2.a, SSP.2.b, SSP.3.a, SSP.3.c. From the information, you can conclude that in general, the Soviet Union used military force to stop uprisings. The passage notes the fact that Gorbachev's reformist government chose not to intervene in countries such as Hungary, Poland, and Bulgaria. There is no evidence that the Soviet Union had provided financial backing to communists, although it is likely, and there is no evidence that they mediated peaceful resolutions to political unrest.

Answer Key

UNIT 3 CIVICS AND GOVERNMENT

LESSON 1, pp. 46–47

1. **D; DOK Level: 1; Content Topic:** I.CG.a.1; **Practices:** SSP.1.a, SSP.6.b. When examining a Venn diagram, such as the one on this page, be sure to note what each section of the diagram describes. In this diagram, you need to identify something that France did but England did not. The correct answer is D, because France claimed new territories from England. A and C are incorrect, because both England and France centralized their governments and increased wealth from new taxes. B is wrong because only England established a new justice system.

2.1. **C; DOK Level: 1; Content Topics:** I.CG.a.1, I.CG.b.1, I.CG.b.5, I.CG.b.8; **Practices:** SSP.1.a, SSP.6.b. The Enlightenment thinkers believed that people are born free, with natural **rights**.

2.2. **B; DOK Level: 1; Content Topics:** I.CG.a.1, I.CG.b.1, I.CG.b.5, I.CG.b.8; **Practices:** SSP.1.a, SSP.6.b. All of the men covered in the group believed that the power of government comes from the **people**.

2.3. **D; DOK Level: 1; Content Topics:** I.CG.a.1, I.CG.b.1, I.CG.b.5, I.CG.b.8; **Practices:** SSP.1.a, SSP.6.b. The belief was that a free people enter into an agreement with those who govern them, and this was called the **social contract**.

2.4. **A; DOK Level: 1; Content Topics:** I.CG.a.1, I.CG.b.1, I.CG.b.5, I.CG.b.8; **Practices:** SSP.1.a, SSP.6.b. If a ruler or government tries to take rights away from the people, the social contract has then been broken. In that case, the people have the right to rid themselves of the ruler or the government, by force if necessary, and **rebel**. Thomas Jefferson, who wrote the Declaration of Independence, was an admirer of Enlightenment thinkers such as Locke, and you can find this idea in the Declaration of Independence.

2.5. **A; DOK Level: 3; Content Topics:** I.CG.a.1, I.CG.b.1, I.CG.b.5, I.CG.b.8; **Practices:** SSP.1.a, SSP.6.b. **Hobbes** is the correct answer, because he is the only one of the four who believed in a strong central government with a powerful ruler.

LESSON 2, pp. 48–49

1. **C; DOK Level: 2; Content Topics:** I.CG.b.2, I.CG.b.3, I.USH.a.1; **Practices:** SSP.1.a, SSP.4.a. The term *domestic* in this excerpt means "within the nation." Therefore, "insure domestic tranquility" means to maintain peace within the nation. The phrase does not pertain to court systems, the rights of citizens, or the success of citizens.

2.1 **A;** 2.2 **C;** 2.3 **D;** 2.4 **A; DOK Level: 2; Content Topics:** I.CG.b.3, I.CG.b.5, I.CG.c.1, I.CG.c.3, I.CG.c.4, I.USH.a.1; **Content Practice:** SSP.1.a.

2.1 The President can sign bills into law, but the President cannot pass a bill. A bill needs to pass both Houses in **Congress** before it goes to the President.

2.2 Section 7 of Article I explains **how bills**—not just bills for raising revenue—**are passed**. It does not go into detail about how the President can veto a bill, and does not explain how amendments are added to the U.S. Constitution.

2.3 Section 7 of Article I states that "All bills for raising revenue shall originate in the House." Therefore, the Senate could not introduce a bill **that institutes a higher tax on gasoline**, since tax is revenue.

2.4 The last sentence in the excerpt explains that Congress can override the President's veto through **approval by two-thirds of both Houses**.

3. **D; DOK Level: 3; Content Topics:** I.CG.b.3, I.CG.b.8, I.CG.d.1, I.CG.d.2, I.USH.a.1; **Practices:** SSP.1.a, SSP.2.a. Amendment IX does not explain or mention all of the rights granted to citizens, inherent powers of the government, or states' authority to delegate rights. Instead, Amendment IX basically states that even though the Constitution describes certain rights, it does not mean that citizens do not have additional rights.

LESSON 3, pp. 50–51

1. **B; DOK Level: 2; Content Topics:** I.CG.a.1, I.CG.b.2, I.CG.b.7, I.CG.b.8; **Practices:** SSP.1.a, SSP.2.a, SSP.2.b, SSP.3.c. The correct answer is B, because the *Magna Carta*'s importance as an early document ensuring individual rights against a ruling authority is the main idea of the passage. The fact that the passage includes an excerpt from the *Magna Carta* on that subject is also an important clue that points to B. Neither C nor D is the answer because each is an incorrect statement. A is not correct because, while true, it is not the main idea of the passage.

2. **DOK Level: 3; Content Topics:** I.CG.a.1, I.CG.b.2, I.CG.b.3, I.CG.b.4, I.CG.b.8, I.CG.b.9, I.CG.d.1; **Practices:** SSP.1.a, SSP.2.a, SSP.2.b, SSP.3.c, SSP.9.b, SSP.9.c. A response earning 3 points would clearly identify the enduring issue as the beginnings of a stronger federal government with guarantees of individual rights. Summaries should include the following: In 1787, delegates met in Philadelphia to overhaul the Articles of Confederation. Instead, they created a new Constitution with a stronger federal government. When the document was submitted to the states for approval, many of them refused because the new Constitution did not protect individual rights from the power(s) of a stronger federal government. Eventually, the states passed the new Constitution, with the understanding that a "Bill of Rights" would be added to guarantee individual rights.

Social Studies Extended Response Traits: Explanation of Traits

Depth of Knowledge (DOK) Level 3: Composing an appropriate response for this item requires a variety of complex reasoning skills. Test-takers must present their ideas logically and support their claim with evidence. Accurately and adequately incorporating elements from the text into the presentation of one's own ideas demands complex reasoning and planning.

Trait 1: Creation of Arguments and Use of Evidence

2 points: generates a text-based argument that demonstrates a clear understanding of the relationships among ideas, events, and figures as presented in the source text(s) and historical contexts from which they are drawn; cites relevant and specific evidence from primary and secondary source texts that adequately supports an argument; or is well-connected to both the prompt and the source texts

ANSWER KEY

1 point: generates an argument that demonstrates an understanding of the relationships among ideas, events, and figures as presented in the source text(s); cites some evidence from primary and secondary source texts in support of an argument (may include a mix of relevant and irrelevant textual references); or is connected to both the prompt and the source text(s)

0 points: may attempt to create an argument but demonstrates minimal or no understanding of the ideas, events, and figures presented in the source texts or the contexts from which these texts are drawn; cites minimal or no evidence from the primary and secondary source texts; may or may not demonstrate an attempt to create an argument; or lacks connection either to the prompt or the source text(s)

Non-scorable Responses (Score of 0/Condition Codes): response exclusively contains text copied from source text(s) or prompt; response demonstrates that the test-taker has read neither the prompt nor the source text(s); response is incomprehensible; response is not in English, or response is not attempted (blank)

Trait 2: Development of Ideas and Organizational Structure

1 point: contains a sensible progression of ideas with understandable connections between details and main ideas; contains ideas that are developed and generally logical; multiple ideas are elaborated upon; or demonstrates appropriate awareness of the task

0 points: contains an unclear or no apparent progression of ideas; contains ideas that are insufficiently developed or illogical; just one idea is elaborated upon or demonstrates no awareness of the task

Non-scorable Responses (Score of 0/Condition Codes): See above.

Trait 3: Clarity and Command of Standard English Conventions

1 point: demonstrates adequate applications of conventions with specific regard to the following skills: 1) correctly uses frequently confused words and homonyms, including contractions; 2) subject-verb agreement; 3) pronoun usage, including pronoun antecedent agreement; and 4) pronoun case; 5) placement of modifiers and correct word order; 6) capitalization (e.g., proper nouns, titles, and beginnings of sentences); 7) use of apostrophes with possessive nouns; 8) use of punctuation (e.g., commas in a series or in appositives and other non-essential elements, end marks, and appropriate punctuation for clause separation); demonstrates largely correct sentence structure with variance from sentence to sentence; is generally fluent and clear with specific regard to the following skills: 1) correct subordination, coordination, and parallelism; 2) avoidance of wordiness and awkward sentence structures; 3) usage of transitional words, conjunctive adverbs, and other words that support logic and 4) clarity; 5) avoidance of run-on sentences, fused sentences, or sentence fragments; 6) standard usage at a level of formality appropriate for on-demand draft writing; may contain some errors in mechanics and conventions, but they do not interfere with understanding.*

0 points: demonstrates minimal control of basic conventions with specific regard to skills 1–8 as listed in the first section under Trait 3, Score Point 1 above; demonstrates consistently flawed sentence structure; minimal or no variance such that meaning may be obscured; demonstrates minimal control over skills 1–6 as listed in the second section under Trait 3, Score Point 1 above; contains severe and frequent errors in mechanics and conventions that interfere with comprehension; **OR** response is insufficient to demonstrate level of mastery over conventions and usage

*Because test-takers will be given only 25 minutes to complete Extended Response tasks, there is no expectation that a response should be completely free of conventions or usage errors to receive a score of 1.

Non-scorable Responses (Score of 0/Condition Codes): See above.

LESSON 4, *pp. 52–53*

1. **C; DOK Level:** 2; **Content Topics:** I.CG.b.7, I.CG.c.1, I.USH.c.4; **Practices:** SSP.1.a, SSP.2.a, SSP.2.b, SSP.3.d. The only correct statement is C, the plans featured different objectives. In this case, you should contrast (or find differences) between President Lincoln's plan and that of the Radical Republicans. Their plans featured different objectives for the process of Reconstruction. Both plans did not aim to rebuild the nation as quickly as possible, because the Radical Republicans' plan would have imposed harsh penalties on the Confederacy, making reuniting the nation a more drawn-out process. President Lincoln's plan did not include imposing harsh penalties on the Confederacy, and the two plans did not delegate the authority of Reconstruction to the states.

2. **A; DOK Level:** 3; **Content Topics:** I.CG.b.7, I.CG.c.1, I.USH.c.4; **Practices:** SSP.1.a, SSP.1.b, SSP.2.b, SSP.3.d. Radical Republicans and Freedmen are the groups whose interests you can compare and see that they were most aligned, not Andrew Johnson and the Radical Republicans, or the Freedmen and the carpetbaggers, or President Grant and the Freedmen.

3. **B; DOK Level:** 3; **Content Topics:** I.CG.b.7, I.CG.c.1, I.USH.c.4; **Practices:** SSP.1.a, SSP.1.b, SSP.2.b, SSP.3.d. Radical Republicans and President Johnson were the two whose interests differ the most, not Carpetbaggers and Freedmen, and not Northerners and President Grant, and not President Johnson and President Lincoln.

4. **C; DOK Level:** 2; **Content Topics:** I.CG.b.7, I.CG.c.1, I.USH.c.4; **Practices:** SSP.1.a, SSP.1.b, SSP.2.b, SSP.3.d. *Determination* can best be substituted for the word *resolve*, not *attempt*, *solution*, or *hesitation*.

5. **C; DOK Level:** 2; **Content Topics:** I.CG.b.7, I.CG.c.1, I.USH.c.4; **Practices:** SSP.1.a, SSP.2.a, SSP.2.b, SSP.3.d. C is correct because both generals had their troops collect supplies from local people. Neither general required troops to take loyalty oaths or assigned troops to build roads. Only General Lee had his troops take over railroad lines.

Answer Key

UNIT 3 (continued)

LESSON 5, pp. 54–55

1. **D; DOK Level:** 1; **Content Topics:** II.E.c.7, II.G.b.3; **Practices:** SSP.1.a, SSP.2.a, SSP.6.b, SSP.6.c, SSP.10.a, SSP.10.b. The line on the graph rises sharply between 1890 and 1900, showing that the number of manufacturing establishments increased dramatically in the 1890s. They did not increase slightly, nor decrease slightly, nor remain nearly the same.

2. **C; DOK Level:** 2; **Content Topics:** I.CG.c.1, I.CG.c.2, I.CG.c.6; **Practices:** SSP.1.a, SSP.1.b, SSP.2.b, SSP.3.a, SSP.3.c, SSP.6.b. The answer is not A, because the Pendleton Civil Service Reform Act was passed after Arthur became President, not before. B is wrong because Arthur was not elected to his first term. He succeeded to the office after the death of the President. D is also incorrect because the application for the job by Guiteau did not in itself cause any change in the presidency. So the answer is C, because it was the death of President Garfield that caused his Vice President, Chester Arthur, to become President.

3. **A; DOK Level:** 2; **Content Topics:** I.CG.c.1, I.CG.c.2, I.CG.c.6; **Practices:** SSP.1.a, SSP.1.b, SSP.2.b, SSP.3.a, SSP.3.c, SSP.6.b. The correct answer is A. Because a rejected federal job seeker killed the President, Congress supported passage of a law making many jobs obtainable only through merit. Jobs were still awarded after the Pendleton Civil Service Reform Act, not denied because of it. There is no information to support the claim that the Pendleton Civil Service Act was rejected by a very narrow margin, nor is it true that all federal jobs were obtained by political connections.

4. **D; DOK Level:** 3; **Content Topics:** I.CG.c.1, I.CG.c.2, I.CG.c.6; **Practices:** SSP.1.a, SSP.1.b, SSP.2.b, SSP.3.a, SSP.3.c, SSP.6.b. The correct answer is D, because usually graphs display numerical information. Flowcharts can show both numbers and text. But this flowchart's information is basically text that cannot be translated into numbers, making the use of a graph unfeasible. A and B are incorrect because graphs can show text and flowcharts do not contain *x*- or *y*-axes. C is incorrect because the problem with displaying this information on a graph is not that there is too much of it; it is because it is not numerical.

5. **A; DOK Level:** 2; **Content Topics:** I.CG.b.7, I.CG.b.8, I.CG.d.2, I.USH.d.4; **Practices:** SSP.1.a, SSP.1.b, SSP.2.b, SSP.3.b, SSP.3.c, SSP.6.b. The correct answer is A. The cause is located in the first box of the flowchart. Mr. Plessy intentionally sat in the railroad car reserved only for white people. B might seem to be the answer, because creation of cars for different ethnic groups was the initial cause of the confrontation. But it was Mr. Plessy's act of defying the unjust law that brought the case into court. The ruling of *Brown* v. *Board of Education* occurred much later, and the passage of the Fourteenth Amendment was not the cause that triggered the ruling in *Plessy* v. *Ferguson*.

6. **A; DOK Level:** 3; **Content Topics:** I.CG.b.7, I.CG.b.8, I.CG.d.2, I.USH.d.4; **Practices:** SSP.1.a, SSP.1.b, SSP.2.b, SSP.3.b, SSP.3.c, SSP.6.b. The law requiring separate cars for different ethnic groups was a state law, and might have been backed up by local laws. Plessy's attorneys stated that it conflicted with rights guaranteed in the U.S. Constitution. Because that set up a conflict between federal and state law, the correct answer is A. The other answer options are not correct.

LESSON 6, pp. 56–57

1. **B; DOK Level:** 1; **Content Topics:** I.CG.c.2, II.USH.f.4, II.USH.f.7; **Practices:** SSP.2.a, SSP.2.b. President Wilson campaigned on the fact that he had kept the United States out of war, and he won re-election. Therefore, you can infer that the American public supported Wilson's stance of neutrality for the United States. It is not a fair inference that most Americans believed that the United States should support Britain's blockade, or that Americans were angered by President Wilson's diplomatic approach to foreign policy. Nor is it a fair inference to state that most Americans hoped for the United States to avenge the loss of U.S. ships.

2. **B; DOK Level:** 3; **Content Topics:** I.CG.b.8, I.CG.c.5, I.CG.d.2, I.USH.d.2; **Practices:** SSP.1.a, SSP.1.b, SSP.2.b. The correct answer is B. As a leader of the women's suffrage movement, you can infer that Elizabeth Cady Stanton lectured on the topic. You can eliminate C because there are no facts in the passage that would support making that inference. D is not a logical inference because of the fact that Ms. Stanton worked with others in the campaign for women's suffrage, and there are no facts in the passage to indicate that she had difficulties working with others.

3. **C; DOK Level:** 3; **Content Topics:** I.CG.b.8, I.CG.c.5, I.CG.d.2, II.CG.e.2, I.USH.d.2; **Practices:** SSP.1.a, SSP.1.b, SSP.2.b. The answer is C. Because women had the right to vote in some states before they gained suffrage nationally, you can infer that women in some states were allowed to vote for their state's governor while women in other states would not have had that right. A is incorrect because the passage states that women had the vote in some states. B is also wrong because women did not have the right to vote throughout the United States, regardless of their ethnicity. The woman suffrage movement was still fighting to gain that right nationally for women. D is incorrect because, logically, certain activists could not gain the right to vote while the law denied that right to other women.

4. **A; DOK Level:** 3; **Content Topics:** I.CG.b.8, I.CG.c.5, I.CG.d.2, II.CG.e.2, I.USH.d.2; **Practices:** SSP.1.a, SSP.1.b, SSP.2.b, SSP.6.b. The correct answer is A. It is clear from the table that many of these women's suffrage advocates also worked for abolition of slavery. It is logical to assume that many other leaders of the women's suffrage movement did the same. You can eliminate B because it is impossible to make that inference based on the table. What's more, there is one example of these women working with men, in that Lucy Stone worked with Frederick Douglass to support passage of the Fifteenth Amendment. C is wrong because both women lived during roughly the same years, and it is unlikely that they never met. D is incorrect because, again, there is no evidence presented in the table that this is true. It is also illogical to infer that all women's suffrage supporters were in the North.

5. D; DOK Level: 3; **Content Topics:** I.CG.b.8, I.CG.c.5, I.CG.d.2, II.CG.e.2, I.USH.d.2; **Practices:** SSP.1.a, SSP.1.b, SSP.2.b, SSP.6.b. D is the correct answer because, given that the Constitutional Amendment granting women the right to vote nationally was ratified in 1920, none of these women would have lived to see it. Therefore, none of them ever had the right to vote nationally in a Presidential election. A is incorrect because the table states that only Susan B. Anthony was arrested for voting illegally. You cannot infer that any of the other women did the same. B is incorrect because women in only some of the states had the right to vote. Without knowing which states these women lived in, it is impossible to state or infer that any of them had the right to vote where they lived. C is also wrong because there is no indication in the table that these women did not support the right of all women to vote, regardless of ethnicity.

LESSON 7, *pp. 58–59*

1. B; DOK Level: 3; **Content Topics:** I.CG.d.2, II.CG.e.2, II.CG.e.3; **Practices:** SSP.1.a, SSP.1.b, SSP.2.a, SSP.2.b, SSP.5.a, SSP.5.b, SSP.6.b. B is the correct answer. In order to interpret this cartoon, you must look at how the image and the text work together to portray the cartoonist's point of view on Prohibition. The man with the axe represents the Prohibition Party. He is portrayed as strong, serious, and wielding the power of the vote, or the support of the American public. The text in the cartoon indicates that the cartoonist has disdain for politicians. The text to the left of the cartoon supports this positive image of the Prohibition Party, stating that the party "campaigned for several years" to achieve its goal. Therefore, you can assume that the cartoonist believes that the Prohibition Party is right in trying to outlaw alcohol, which makes B the most logical answer and eliminates C. D is incorrect because the politician is shown attacking Prohibition. A is wrong because the politician attacking Prohibition is shown as a silly-looking caricature protecting a source of patronage. The cartoonist clearly does not think politicians are right in attacking Prohibition.

2. B; DOK Level: 2; **Content Topics:** I.CG.c.3, II.CG.e.2; **Practices:** SSP.1.a, SSP.2.a, SSP.5.a, SSP.5.b, SSP.6.b. Because President Hoover is posting a detour sign to indicate the flow away from "Speculation Street" and onto "Business Boulevard," the cartoonist suggests that President Hoover is guiding the country's economy back to stability. The cartoon's depiction of Hoover is positive, as a leader guiding the nation down a path different from the one that caused the economic crisis. A and C are incorrect because the cartoon does not show the President as weak, ineffective, or unsure of himself. D is incorrect because President Hoover is shown guiding business, not particularly wary of it.

3. C; DOK Level: 2; **Content Topics:** I.CG.c.3, II.CG.e.2; **Practices:** SSP.1.a, SSP.2.a, SSP.5.a, SSP.5.b, SSP.6.b. C is correct, because the cartoon does blame speculation. The cartoonist shows this by depicting President Hoover having placed a barrier over "Speculation Street," as he guides the nation down a "detour" that goes in a different direction. The cartoonist does not blame President Hoover, labor, or a detour from regular business practices as the cause.

4. C; DOK Level: 3; **Content Topics:** I.CG.c.1, II.CG.c.3; **Practices:** SSP.1.a, SSP.2.a, SSP.5.a, SSP.5.b, SSP.6.b. Based on the information and the cartoon, President Roosevelt is portrayed as somewhat sad and dismayed. This is because he is shown looking at his proposed new plan to change the number of justices on the Supreme Court, and that plan, shown with bandages on it and with a sword thrust through it, is now essentially "killed" by both political parties. The President's demeanor cannot be characterized, based on the information and the cartoon, as hopeful. He, in fact, probably was angry, but this cartoon does not depict that. The President also is not portrayed as cold and calculating, based on the expression of the caricature drawn by the artist.

5. A; DOK Level: 3; **Content Topics:** I.CG.c.1, I.CG.c.3; **Practices:** SSP.1.a, SSP.2.a, SSP.5.a, SSP.5.b, SSP.6.b. Six months "flew by" from the time President Roosevelt proposed his new plan for increasing the number of U.S. Supreme Court justices, with no progress made. The text in the cartoon itself, "Six Wasted Months," indicates that the plan was not a good use of time, and those six months had "flown by" or "flown away." The wings on the calendar pages do not represent the passing away of the six justices who were turning 70 years old, whom the President wanted to step down or replace. Service on the U.S. Supreme Court is not fleeting; it is a lifelong appointment. The calendar pages and the wings also do not represent the President's strained relationship with the Republican and Democratic parties; there is no connection.

LESSON 8, *pp. 60–61*

1. D; DOK Level: 3; **Content Topics:** I.CG.c.1, I.CG.c.2, I.CG.c.3; **Practices:** SSP.1.a, SSP.3.c. The Speaker of the House and the President pro tempore of the Senate are elected officials, but the Cabinet members are appointed by the President. When the Cabinet members were first in line after the Vice President for succession to President, it presented a situation in which a person who was directly appointed by the President, and not elected in any way, could become President. This is a main reason why the Speaker of the House and President pro tempore of the Senate were put ahead of the Cabinet members in the line of succession. Whether any Cabinet member, Speaker of the House, or President pro tempore is any better qualified than another at any time is debatable.

2. DOK Level: 3; **Content Topics:** I.CG.c.1, I.CG.c.2, II.CG.e.2; **Practices:** SSP.1.a, SSP.1.b, SSP.2.a, SSP.2.b, SSP.9.a, SSP.9.b, SSP.9.c. With specific regard to this prompt about President Truman's actions and the subsequent rulings made by the U.S. Supreme Court, a response earning 3 points would clearly identify the enduring issue as an example of the U.S. government's system of checks and balances, specifically, how the Court limited the powers of the Executive branch. Before 1952 and the Supreme Court decision, the President had considerable power to seize private property.

ANSWER KEY

Answer Key

UNIT 3 (continued)

Social Studies Extended Response Traits: Explanation of Traits

Depth of Knowledge (DOK) Level 3: Composing an appropriate response for this item requires a variety of complex reasoning skills. Test-takers must present their ideas logically and support their claim with evidence. Accurately and adequately incorporating elements from the text into the presentation of one's own ideas demands complex reasoning and planning.

Trait 1: Creation of Arguments and Use of Evidence

2 points: generates a text-based argument that demonstrates a clear understanding of the relationships among ideas, events, and figures as presented in the source text(s) and historical contexts from which they are drawn; cites relevant and specific evidence from primary and secondary source texts that adequately supports an argument; or is well-connected to both the prompt and the source texts

1 point: generates an argument that demonstrates an understanding of the relationships among ideas, events, and figures as presented in the source text(s); cites some evidence from primary and secondary source texts in support of an argument (may include a mix of relevant and irrelevant textual references); or is connected to both the prompt and the source text(s)

0 points: may attempt to create an argument but demonstrates minimal or no understanding of the ideas, events, and figures presented in the source texts or the contexts from which these texts are drawn; cites minimal or no evidence from the primary and secondary source texts; may or may not demonstrate an attempt to create an argument; or lacks connection either to the prompt or the source text(s)

Non-scorable Responses (Score of 0/Condition Codes): response exclusively contains text copied from source text(s) or prompt; response demonstrates that the test-taker has read neither the prompt nor the source text(s); response is incomprehensible; response is not in English, or response is not attempted (blank)

Trait 2: Development of Ideas and Organizational Structure

1 point: contains a sensible progression of ideas with understandable connections between details and main ideas; contains ideas that are developed and generally logical; multiple ideas are elaborated upon; or demonstrates appropriate awareness of the task

0 points: contains an unclear or no apparent progression of ideas; contains ideas that are insufficiently developed or illogical; just one idea is elaborated upon or demonstrates no awareness of the task

Non-scorable Responses (Score of 0/Condition Codes): See above.

Trait 3: Clarity and Command of Standard English Conventions

1 point: demonstrates adequate applications of conventions with specific regard to the following skills: 1) correctly uses frequently confused words and homonyms, including contractions; 2) subject-verb agreement; 3) pronoun usage, including pronoun antecedent agreement; and 4) pronoun case; 5) placement of modifiers and correct word order; 6) capitalization (e.g., proper nouns, titles, and beginnings of sentences); 7) use of apostrophes with possessive nouns; 8) use of punctuation (e.g., commas in a series or in appositives and other non-essential elements, end marks, and appropriate punctuation for clause separation); demonstrates largely correct sentence structure with variance from sentence to sentence; is generally fluent and clear with specific regard to the following skills: 1) correct subordination, coordination, and parallelism; 2) avoidance of wordiness and awkward sentence structures; 3) usage of transitional words, conjunctive adverbs, and other words that support logic and 4) clarity; 5) avoidance of run-on sentences, fused sentences, or sentence fragments; 6) standard usage at a level of formality appropriate for on-demand draft writing; may contain some errors in mechanics and conventions, but they do not interfere with understanding.*

0 points: demonstrates minimal control of basic conventions with specific regard to skills 1–8 as listed in the first section under Trait 3, Score Point 1 above; demonstrates consistently flawed sentence structure; minimal or no variance such that meaning may be obscured; demonstrates minimal control over skills 1–6 as listed in the second section under Trait 3, Score Point 1 above; contains severe and frequent errors in mechanics and conventions that interfere with comprehension; **OR** response is insufficient to demonstrate level of mastery over conventions and usage

*Because test-takers will be given only 25 minutes to complete Extended Response tasks, there is no expectation that a response should be completely free of conventions or usage errors to receive a score of 1.

Non-scorable Responses (Score of 0/Condition Codes): See above.

LESSON 9, pp. 62–63

1. **B; DOK Level:** 2; **Content Topics:** I.CG.c.2, II.CG.f; **Practices:** SSP.1.a, SSP.1.b, SSP.5.a. Mr. Ford mentions that the two countries should continue to work together to expand knowledge and ensure peace and understanding among nations. The letter does not touch on any of the other answers.

2. **D; DOK Level:** 2; **Content Topics:** I.CG.b.6, I.CG.b.8; **Practices:** SSP.1.a, SSP.1.b, SSP.5.a. The excerpt best describes the point of view of the United Nations on rule of law. The first sentence refers to rule of law and what it means to the United Nations. Legal transparency, separation of powers, and human rights are all aspects that fall under the point of view of the United Nations on rule of law.

3. **B; DOK Level:** 2; **Content Topics:** I.CG.b.6, I.CG.b.8; **Practices:** SSP.1.a, SSP.1.b, SSP.5.a. The excerpt's purpose is to educate or inform. It is written in a matter-of-fact style, not meant to persuade, offer an opinion, or provide an editorial or commentary.

4. **C; DOK Level:** 2; **Content Topics:** I.CG.b.6, I.CG.b.8; **Practices:** SSP.1.a, SSP.1.b, SSP.4.a, SSP.5.a. In the excerpt, *adjudicated* is used to mean *legally decided*, or to have passed judgment about; not *negotiated*, *administered*, or *enforced*.

5. **C; DOK Level:** 2; **Content Topics:** II.CG.e.1, II.CG.e.3; **Practices:** SSP.1.a, SSP.1.b, SSP.5.a, SSP.5.b, SSP.7.a. The answer is C, because it is an endorsement of John Kerry for President. It provides the newspapers opinion, not a reportage of fact or news. This type of piece appears only on the Editorial or Opinion page of a newspaper. It would not appear in the Education section, the World News section, or in the Local News pages.

6. **D; DOK Level:** 2; **Content Topics:** II.CG.e.1, II.CG.e.3; **Practices:** SSP.1.a, SSP.1.b, SSP.5.a, SSP.5.b, SSP.7.a. The best answer is D. The author states the opposite of answer A. There is no indication that the author believes George W. Bush can give the nation a better future. Thus, both A and B are incorrect. C *may* be correct, in that the author may believe that Mr. Kerry makes his positions known.

LESSON 10, *pp. 64–65*

1. **C; DOK Level:** 2; **Content Topic:** I.CG.c.2; **Practices:** SSP.1.a, SSP.2.a, SSP.5.a. The author is biased toward Speaker Boehner. Although this information comes from a *.gov* website, it is from the website that represents the Speaker of the House. The website will portray the Speaker of the House in a favorable light. The excerpt highlights Speaker Boehner's accomplishments. The excerpt is not about the position of the Speaker of the House, but about a particular Speaker, so it is not biased toward the position of Speaker of the House. Speaker Boehner is a Republican, and the excerpt speaks highly of Speaker Boehner and Republican efforts, so it is biased toward, not against, Republicans. The author is not biased against John Boehner's record, but rather toward John Boehner's record, as he or she describes it in a positive light.

2. **A; DOK Level:** 2; **Content Topics:** I.CG.b.5, I.CG.c.1, I.CG.c.3; **Practices:** SSP.1.a, SSP.2.a, SSP.5.a. The information in this source is impartial. It is balanced and does not promote one side or another of an issue, so it is not biased. It is from an encyclopedia, which has the task of presenting factual information. The material is from 2013, so it is not dated. The information is written in an even tone, so it is not impassioned.

3. **D; DOK Level:** 3; **Content Topics:** I.CG.b.5, I.CG.c.1, I.CG.c.3; **Practices:** SSP.1.a, SSP.2.a, SSP.5.a. The answer is D, because the U.S. Supreme Court's website is the only choice that ends in *.gov*. It would be the most reliable source.

4. **B; DOK Level:** 1; **Content Topic:** I.CG.c.6; **Practices:** SSP.1.b, SSP.6.b. The source of information presented in the graph is a federal government agency—the U.S. Bureau of the Census. The job of this agency is to collect and maintain data about the nation's people and economy. You can find the source in the lower left corner of the graph. Since the source is listed on the graph, you can eliminate the other answer choices.

5. **C; DOK Level:** 3; **Content Topic:** I.CG.c.6; **Practices:** SSP.1.b, SSP.6.b. The idea that the decline in population was caused by an increase in violence by poor people is an example of a biased interpretation. The graph does show that the population was less in 2010 than in 1970, but it does not give any information as to why the population was lower. The other statements are all facts based on the passage.

LESSON 11, *pp. 66–67*

1. **C; DOK Level:** 2; **Content Topic:** I.CG.c.6; **Practices:** SSP.1.a, SSP.1.b, SSP.2.a, SSP.7.a, SSP.7.b. People without access to electricity typically live in poverty. This generalization is supported by the idea in the excerpt that if the people's need for electricity is ignored, we entrench, or perpetuate, their poverty. The information does not compare the energy produced in the United States to the energy produced in other countries, so a generalization cannot be made. The generalization that safe living environments are only available to those with electricity is too narrow. One can live safely without electricity. The generalization that the Bureau of Energy Resources works mainly in fossil fuels is contradicted by the information which refers mostly to clean, sustainable energy.

2. **B; DOK Level:** 3; **Content Topics:** I.CG.b.5, I.CG.c.1, I.CG.c.2, I.CG.c.3; **Practices:** SSP.1.a, SSP.1.b, SSP.2.a, SSP.7.a, SSP.7.b. The author makes the generalization that aggressive Presidents often take greater advantage of executive power. The excerpt discusses how the President at the time, George H. W. Bush, was arguing that he has the executive power to start a war whether or not Congress has declared war. The author refers both to "aggressive Presidents" and arguments for executive power. It is a valid generalization to link the two together. A President may not declare war, only wage war, so the generalization that Congressional approval is not necessary for the President to declare war is false. Congress is usually unwilling to declare war, according to the excerpt. The excerpt describes the President starting war before Congress has authorized it, so the generalization that the President may only start a war after Congress has authorized it is not valid.

3. **D; DOK Level:** 3; **Content Topic:** I.CG.c.3; **Practices:** SSP.1.a, SSP.1.b, SSP.2.a, SSP.7.a, SSP.7.b. The states all have constitutions similar to the U.S. Constitution. The excerpt explains that the legislatures approving state budgets and initiating legislation and articles of impeachment are part of a system of checks and balances that mirrors the federal system. This implies that the state governments operate very similarly to the federal government, which would mean their constitutions are also very similar. The passage does not describe different checks and balances systems. It describes most states as having bicameral, not unicameral, legislatures. Nebraska has a unicameral legislature, so the generalization that all states have bicameral legislatures is not valid.

4. **A; DOK Level:** 2; **Content Topic:** I.CG.c.3; **Practices:** SSP.1.a, SSP.1.b, SSP.2.a, SSP.7.a, SSP.7.b. The word *all* indicates that the statement is a generalization about all of the states. *Consider*, *introduced*, and *create* are not words that signal a generalization.

ANSWER KEY

Answer Key

UNIT 3 *(continued)*

LESSON 12, *pp. 68–69*

1. **B; DOK Level:** 2; **Content Topic:** I.CG.b.1 **Practices:** SSP.1.a, SSP.1.b, SSP.2.a. The main problem is illiquid assets. This is stated in the first sentence of the first paragraph. Home loans, school loans, and mortgage markets themselves are not the problems.

2. **D; DOK Level:** 2; **Content Topics:** I.CG.c.1, I.CG.c.3, I.CG.c.6; **Practices:** SSP.1.a, SSP.2.a. The main problem is loss of wilderness due to increasing growth and development. The first sentence states the need to assure that an increasing population does not modify all areas within the United States, meaning there is concern that a growing population and development will lead to loss of wilderness. The excerpt does not discuss the lumber industry, endangered wildlife, or logging regulations.

3. **B; DOK Level:** 2; **Content Topics:** I.CG.c.1, I.CG.c.3, I.CG.c.6; **Practices:** SSP.1.a, SSP.1.b, SSP.2.a, SSP.5.a. The legislation proposes to solve the problem by creating protected wilderness areas. The legislation does not imply that new national parks will be made, or that there will be specific efforts to protect species of wildlife. To build small communities in wilderness areas goes against the idea of protecting the areas from an increasing population and expanding settlement.

4. **C; DOK Level:** 3; **Content Topics:** I.CG.c.1, I.CG.c.3, I.CG.c.6; **Practices:** SSP.1.a, SSP.2.a, SSP.4.a. In the excerpt, *unimpaired* means *unspoiled*, or to be left as naturally as possible. In some contexts, the term *unimpaired* may mean *sober*, or *accessible*, or *unrestricted*, but the context in which the term is used determines its definition here.

5. **C; DOK Level:** 2; **Content Topics:** I.CG.b.3, I.CG.b.5, I.CG.c.1, I.CG.c.2; **Practices:** SSP.1.a, SSP.1.b, SSP.2.a, SSP.5.a. The amendment proposes a solution to the problem of the lack of term limits for the Presidency. It explicitly states for how long a President may serve. It does not address the order of succession to the Presidency. It also does not give any information about the level of power of the executive branch, or about disputes between the President and Congress.

6. **A; DOK Level:** 3; **Content Topics:** I.CG.b.3, I.CG.b.5, I.CG.c.1, I.CG.c.2; **Practices:** SSP.1.a, SSP.1.b, SSP.2.a, SSP.5.a. Franklin D. Roosevelt's Presidency prompted this amendment. President Roosevelt was the only President to serve more than two terms. The amendment was ratified in 1951, which was before John F. Kennedy, Richard M. Nixon, or Lyndon B. Johnson served as President, so none of them could have prompted the amendment.

7. **D; DOK Level:** 2; **Content Topics:** I.CG.b.3, I.CG.b.5, I.CG.c.1, I.CG.c.2; **Practices:** SSP.1.a, SSP.1.b, SSP.2.a, SSP.5.a. In the excerpt, *operative* means *enacted*, or to put into action. It does not mean *completed*, *operatic*, or *public*.

LESSON 13, *pp. 70–71*

1. **D; DOK Level:** 1; **Content Topics:** I.CG.c.1, I.CG.c.3; **Practices:** SSP.4.a, SSP.6.b. California is on the west coast of the United States, and includes the city of San Francisco. The map shows that California is in District 12, not Districts 5, 8, or 10.

2. **B; DOK Level:** 2; **Content Topics:** II.G.c.1, II.G.c.3, II.G.d.1, II.G.d.3; **Practices:** SSP.6.b, SSP.6.c. The population of each state is represented by the "person" icons in the key. Each icon stands for 1 million people. If you count the icons in each state, you will see that Illinois has the most, and therefore, the largest, population. Ohio, Michigan, and Wisconsin all have fewer icons, and thus, smaller populations.

3. **A; DOK Level:** 2; **Content Topics:** II.G.c.1, II.G.c.3, II.G.d.1, II.G.d.3; **Practices:** SSP.6.b, SSP.6.c. You have already determined that Illinois is the state with the largest population. The state that shares the northern border of Illinois is Wisconsin, not Minnesota, Michigan, or Indiana.

4. **C; DOK Level:** 2; **Content Topics:** II.G.c.1, II.G.c.3, II.G.d.1, II.G.d.3; **Practices:** SSP.6.b, SSP.6.c. The populations of Ohio and Michigan do add up to more than 20 million. Both A and B are incorrect, based on the number of "person" icons on the map for both states. D is also wrong because the two most populous states are Illinois and Ohio. They do not have a common border.

5. **C; DOK Level:** 2; **Content Topics:** I.CG.c.1, II.G.c.3, II.G.d.3; **Practices:** SSP.2.a, SSP.4.a, SSP.6.b. Based on the passage, the districts have approximately the same population. A is wrong, because even a quick glance at the map shows the districts are not the same in area. B is incorrect because, based on the map, they do not have the same number of important cities. D is incorrect, because we have no idea what the major industries are in each district, based on the map.

6. **D; DOK Level:** 3; **Content Topics:** I.CG.c.1, II.G.c.3, II.G.d.3; **Practices:** SSP.1.a, SSP.4.a, SSP.6.b, SSP.8.a. The passage explains the basis for the number of districts in a state; you cannot find that information on the map. Only the map shows the number of large cities and the number of districts, information not found in the passage. Neither the passage nor the map gives the basis for the census in districts.

LESSON 14, *pp. 72–73*

1. **A; DOK Level:** 2; **Content Topics:** II.CG.e.1, II.CG.e.3, II.CG.f; **Practices:** SSP.2.a, SSP.7.a, SSP.7.b. B, C, and D are all statements of fact that can be checked in a number of sources. A is the correct answer because it is the only answer that is an opinion or point of view that cannot be verified.

2. **B; DOK Level:** 3; **Content Topics:** I.CG.a.1, II.CG.e.3, II.CG.f; **Practice:** SSP.2.a. B is correct because the Electoral College makes it necessary for candidates to sometimes campaign in states that don't have the largest population, and that would otherwise get less attention if elections depended only on the popular vote. A is wrong because the fact that the Electoral College has failed to select the winner of the popular vote three times is not a compelling fact with which to defend it. C is incorrect because the time when the Electoral College was established isn't important here. D is wrong because the two-party system could exist without the Electoral College.

3. **C; DOK Level:** 2; **Content Topics:** I.CG.a.1, II.CG.e.3, II.CG.f; **Practice:** SSP.2.a. C is the correct answer, because many critics say the system has been around for centuries and has outlived its usefulness. A is wrong because bias is not one of the criticisms of the Electoral College. B is wrong because the Electoral College is not controlled by any particular party. D is wrong because expense has never been a criticism.

4. **A; DOK Level:** 2; **Content Topics:** I.CG.a.1, II.CG.e.3, II.CG.f; **Practice:** SSP.2.a. A is the correct answer, because the author restates the opinions of critics but does not state any personal opinions. All other answers are incorrect because the author does not state what he believes should be done.

5. **B; DOK Level:** 2; **Content Topics:** I.CG.a.1, II.CG.e.1, II.CG.e.3; **Practices:** SSP.2.a, SSP.5.b, SSP.7.a. The best answer is B. Opinions on posters such as this are there to appeal to voters' emotions. You can eliminate A because the opinion of experts has little to do with an ad such as this. C is wrong because Electoral College members are not the target for this, and even if they were, the poster would not be there to confuse them. Posters like this can sometimes be created to promote parts of a candidate's platform.

6. **A; DOK Level:** 2; **Content Topics:** I.CG.a.1, II.CG.e.1, II.CG.e.3; **Practices:** SSP.2.a, SSP.5.b, SSP.7.a. The opinion on the poster is basically that the Democratic ticket would promote peace and security. The only answer that addresses the opinion on the poster is A. The fact that Roosevelt took the country into World War II would tend to work against his claim of keeping the nation at peace. Roosevelt's age, how many terms he had served, or the identity of his Vice President are not relevant to the question.

7. **B; DOK Level:** 2; **Content Topics:** I.CG.a.1, II.CG.e.1, II.CG.e.3; **Practices:** SSP.2.a, SSP.5.b, SSP.7.a. B is correct because the National Museum of American History is a museum devoted to the study of the nation's history and would be the best source for facts about Roosevelt's administration, without a bias attached. All of the other possible source groups here betray some type of bias in their names. C and D are the names of groups affiliated with a political party. A is the name of a group that protests against war, and its view on Roosevelt might be colored by the choice he made to take the country into World War II.

LESSON 15, *pp. 74–75*
1. **A; DOK Level:** 2; **Content Topics:** I.CG.b.7, I.CG.b.8, I.CG.c.1, I.CG.d.2; **Practices:** SSP.5.a, SSP.7.a. The answer is clearly A, because it is the central example of faulty reasoning that caused Lilly Ledbetter to lose her gender discrimination case. Even the appeals court found discrimination. However, faulty reasoning led to a very narrow interpretation of the 180-day rule and actually defied logic: no one can file a case for discrimination before knowing the discrimination exists. B may be true, but it does not explain the faulty reasoning in this case. C is not true either, as it is too simplistic an answer and is not the reason for faulty reasoning in this case. D is not correct because it also is not the reason for faulty reasoning in this case.

2. **The American public, or the U.S. Government; DOK Level:** 2; **Content Topics:** I.CG.b.7, I.CG.b.8, I.CG.c.1, I.CG.d.2; **Practices:** SSP.5.a, SSP.6.b. The man wearing the striped hat and pants is an Uncle Sam-type figure, and stands for the United States or the American people.

---

3. **The Second Amendment guarantees that a well-regulated militia, not just a private citizen, may have the right to own guns; DOK Level:** 3; **Content Topics:** I.CG.b.7, I.CG.b.8, I.CG.c.1, I.CG.d.2; **Practices:** SSP.5.a, SSP.6.b. The cartoon suggests that the constitutional right relates to the need for a militia centuries ago. It suggests that people today who try to apply the right to the ownership of any gun at any time are applying faulty logic or reasoning.

4. **The Second Amendment guarantees that they can; DOK Level:** 3; **Content Topics:** I.CG.b.7, I.CG.b.8, I.CG.c.1, I.CG.d.2; **Practices:** SSP.5.a, SSP.6.b. Again, this faulty logic or reasoning equates a well-regulated militia with a private citizen.

5. **D; DOK Level:** 2; **Content Topics:** I.CG.b.7, I.CG.b.8, I.CG.c.1, I.CG.c.2, I.CG.d.2; **Practices:** SSP.5.a, SSP.7.a, SSP.7.b. The hasty generalization was that all people whose ancestry traces to an enemy nation are worthy of suspicion. This order was issued following the Japanese attack on Pearl Harbor. There was no reason for the government to assume that all Japanese Americans would spy for Japan. It is not a hasty generalization to require citizens to give up personal freedoms during periods of wartime, or that military commanders should receive absolute authority during times of war. It also is not a hasty generalization to state that the President can never establish military areas, simply because the excerpt states that the President is authorizing his Secretary of War to do so.

6. **B; DOK Level:** 2; **Content Topics:** I.CG.b.7, I.CG.b.8, I.CG.c.1, I.CG.c.2, I.CG.d.2; **Practices:** SSP.5.a, SSP.7.a, SSP.7.b. The faulty logic is that all rules are meant to be broken. This is a popular saying, and most people would probably agree that for the smooth functioning of a government or of society in general, there must be some rules. A majority of voters most often do select their elected officials; this is not faulty logic. Answer option C is a rule of physics, and is not faulty logic. The Articles of Confederation did precede the U.S. Constitution, and thus is not faulty logic.

LESSON 16, *pp. 76–77*
1. **D; DOK Level:** 2; **Content Topics:** II.CG.e.1, II.CG.e.3, II.CG.f; **Content Topics:** SSP.1.a, SSP.1.b, SSP.2.a, SSP.5.a, SSP.5.b. The answer is D because many general ideas for change are listed, but the list lacks specifics. There are no specific changes listed, so A is incorrect. B is also incorrect because there is no promise to consult the public. C should not be chosen because this excerpt does not ensure that any past policies will be continued.

2. **B; DOK Level:** 2; **Content Topics:** II.CG.e.1, II.CG.e.3; **Content Topics:** SSP.1.a, SSP.1.b, SSP.3.d, SSP.5.a, SSP.5.b. The correct answer is B, because the writer specifically singles out the "No Child Left Behind" Act for praise. A is incorrect because no landmark health care plan is mentioned. C is wrong because the writer states that there was no Kennedy-Kerry Education Act in an effort to mock Mr. Kerry. D is also wrong because the writer does not emphasize global assaults by Mr. Bush in his endorsement.

ANSWER KEY

Answer Key

UNIT 3 *(continued)*

3. **D; DOK Level:** 2; **Content Topics:** II.CG.e.1, II.CG.e.3; **Content Topics:** SSP.1.a, SSP.1.b, SSP.3.d, SSP.5.a, SSP.5.b. The main purpose of listing the failure of Mr. Kerry's policies and for the writer making it clear that he is voting for Mr. Bush is to persuade the reader also to vote for Mr. Bush. So the correct answer is D. A is wrong because the writer is obviously not endorsing Mr. Kerry and would therefore not have voted for him. B and C are also incorrect because each of these could be considered a part of the writer's purpose, but not his "main" purpose.

4. **C; DOK Level:** 2; **Content Topics:** II.CG.e.1, II.CG.e.3; **Content Topics:** SSP.1.a, SSP.1.b, SSP.3.d, SSP.5.a, SSP.5.b, SSP.7.a, SSP.7.b. C is correct because the author specifically cites two pieces of legislation sponsored by Mr. Kerry that did not get passed. A is incorrect because the fact that Mr. Kerry has been a discerning critic of Mr. Bush does not make Mr. Kerry unfit to be President. B is incorrect because Mr. Bush, not Mr. Kerry, sponsored the "No Child Left Behind" Act. And D is incorrect because the author is citing Mr. Bush's competitiveness about health care as positive, not negative.

5. **D; DOK Level:** 2; **Content Topics:** II.CG.e.1, II.CG.e.3; **Content Topics:** SSP.1.a, SSP.1.b, SSP.3.d, SSP.5.a, SSP.5.b, SSP.7.a, SSP.7.b. A quick analysis of the speech excerpt will show you that it consists entirely of opinions. The other answer options are incorrect.

6. **B; DOK Level:** 2; **Content Topics:** II.CG.e.1, II.CG.e.3; **Content Topics:** SSP.1.a, SSP.1.b, SSP.3.d, SSP.5.a, SSP.5.b, SSP.7.a, SSP.7.b. As you read the speech excerpt, it becomes clear that Mr. Obama is describing the hopes, and the American dream, of the American people during difficult times. He states that he is running to restore that dream. So the correct answer is B. The speech does not explain his program or describe his opponent's plan. Although the phrase "four more years of what we had for the last eight" is an indirect way of linking Mr. Obama's opponent to an unpopular President, it is not the main tactic used, so D is incorrect.

LESSON 17, *pp. 78–79*

1. **A; DOK Level:** 2; **Content Topics:** I.CG.c.2, II.CG.e.1, II.CG.e.3, II.CG.f; **Practices:** SSP.1.a, SSP.2.a. The correct answer is A. Although Mr. Clinton does use some facts in this excerpt, putting in additional facts about the way President Obama's policies have helped the economy can only strengthen the argument. B is incorrect because strengthening the notion that Mr. Obama is a nice person would not bolster the argument that he should lead the country. C is wrong because the successes of the Clinton administration are not necessarily transferable, and listeners/people would understand that. D is incorrect because ridiculing Mr. Obama's opponent might be amusing to the audience, but unless there are facts that support an argument against the opponent as well, it would not make a good argument for Mr. Obama.

2. **DOK Level:** 3; **Content Topics:** I.CG.c.1, I.CG.c.2; **Practices:** SSP.1.a, SSP.1.b, SSP.2.a, SSP.5.a, SSP.5.d, SSP.7.b, SSP.9.a, SSP.9.b, SSP.9.c. With specific regard to this prompt about the effect of President Johnson's policy in Southeast Asia, a response earning 3 points would clearly identify the issue that neither senator backs up his arguments with an abundance of facts about what the resolution would authorize the President to do. In particular, Senator Fulbright bases his argument in support on believing that the President would do only what is "reasonable" in the situation, while Senator Gruening argues in opposition by listing recent troubling activities of the U.S. Armed Forces in Southeast Asia and hostile actions from North Vietnam. Senator Gruening fears the resolution would allow the President to expand these activities and escalate military action, and he is able to use facts in support of it. His argument seems more logical and well-reasoned. Senator Fulbright's argument seems based mostly on his opinion that the President will be cautious, but he has no facts to back that up, and freely admits that he really does not know what will happen.

Social Studies Extended Response Traits: Explanation of Traits

Depth of Knowledge (DOK) Level 3: Composing an appropriate response for this item requires a variety of complex reasoning skills. Test-takers must present their ideas logically and support their claim with evidence. Accurately and adequately incorporating elements from the text into the presentation of one's own ideas demands complex reasoning and planning.

Trait 1: Creation of Arguments and Use of Evidence

2 points: generates a text-based argument that demonstrates a clear understanding of the relationships among ideas, events, and figures as presented in the source text(s) and historical contexts from which they are drawn; cites relevant and specific evidence from primary and secondary source texts that adequately supports an argument; or is well-connected to both the prompt and the source texts

1 point: generates an argument that demonstrates an understanding of the relationships among ideas, events, and figures as presented in the source text(s); cites some evidence from primary and secondary source texts in support of an argument (may include a mix of relevant and irrelevant textual references); or is connected to both the prompt and the source text(s)

0 points: may attempt to create an argument but demonstrates minimal or no understanding of the ideas, events, and figures presented in the source texts or the contexts from which these texts are drawn; cites minimal or no evidence from the primary and secondary source texts; may or may not demonstrate an attempt to create an argument; or lacks connection either to the prompt or the source text(s)

Non-scorable Responses (Score of 0/Condition Codes): response exclusively contains text copied from source text(s) or prompt; response demonstrates that the test-taker has read neither the prompt nor the source text(s); response is incomprehensible; response is not in English, or response is not attempted (blank)

Trait 2: Development of Ideas and Organizational Structure

1 point: contains a sensible progression of ideas with understandable connections between details and main ideas; contains ideas that are developed and generally logical; multiple ideas are elaborated upon; or demonstrates appropriate awareness of the task

0 points: contains an unclear or no apparent progression of ideas; contains ideas that are insufficiently developed or illogical; just one idea is elaborated upon or demonstrates no awareness of the task

Non-scorable Responses (Score of 0/Condition Codes): See above.

Trait 3: Clarity and Command of Standard English Conventions

1 point: demonstrates adequate applications of conventions with specific regard to the following skills: 1) correctly uses frequently confused words and homonyms, including contractions; 2) subject-verb agreement; 3) pronoun usage, including pronoun antecedent agreement; and 4) pronoun case; 5) placement of modifiers and correct word order; 6) capitalization (e.g., proper nouns, titles, and beginnings of sentences); 7) use of apostrophes with possessive nouns; 8) use of punctuation (e.g., commas in a series or in appositives and other non-essential elements, end marks, and appropriate punctuation for clause separation); demonstrates largely correct sentence structure with variance from sentence to sentence; is generally fluent and clear with specific regard to the following skills: 1) correct subordination, coordination, and parallelism; 2) avoidance of wordiness and awkward sentence structures; 3) usage of transitional words, conjunctive adverbs, and other words that support logic and 4) clarity; 5) avoidance of run-on sentences, fused sentences, or sentence fragments; 6) standard usage at a level of formality appropriate for on-demand draft writing; may contain some errors in mechanics and conventions, but they do not interfere with understanding.*

0 points: demonstrates minimal control of basic conventions with specific regard to skills 1–8 as listed in the first section under Trait 3, Score Point 1 above; demonstrates consistently flawed sentence structure; minimal or no variance such that meaning may be obscured; demonstrates minimal control over skills 1–6 as listed in the second section under Trait 3, Score Point 1 above; contains severe and frequent errors in mechanics and conventions that interfere with comprehension; **OR** response is insufficient to demonstrate level of mastery over conventions and usage

*Because test-takers will be given only 25 minutes to complete Extended Response tasks, there is no expectation that a response should be completely free of conventions or usage errors to receive a score of 1.

Non-scorable Responses (Score of 0/Condition Codes): See above.

UNIT 3 REVIEW, *pp. 80–87*

1. **B; DOK Level:** 2; **Content Topics:** I.CG.b.8, I.CG.d.2, II.USH.g.1; **Practices:** SSP.1.a, SSP.1.b, SSP.2.a, SSP.2.b. B is the correct answer, because information about senatorial traditions might be interesting, but it is a minor detail in terms of the story of Senator McCarthy's infamous hearings. It would not belong in a summary. A, C, and D are all key information that helps communicate the main idea of the passage.

2. **C; DOK Level:** 2; **Content Topics:** I.CG.b.8, I.CG.d.2, II.USH.g.1; **Practices:** SSP.1.a, SSP.1.b, SSP.2.a, SSP.2.b, SSP.4.a. The meaning of the word *censure* is to condemn or criticize. If you know the meaning of the word, you will see that the answer is C. However, even if you do not know the meaning of the word, you can figure it out using context clues. A reading of the passage indicates that Senator McCarthy encountered increasing resistance as he became more reckless with his accusations. You can infer that the hearings did not end on a positive note for him.

3. **B; DOK Level:** 2; **Content Topics:** I.CG.c.2, I.CG.d.2, II.CG.e.1, II.G.b.1, I.USH.c.1, I.USH.c.2, I.USH.c.4; **Practices:** SSP.1.a, SSP.1.b, SSP.2.a, SSP.2.b, SSP.6.b. B is correct because President Lincoln's plan allowed former Confederates to participate in the rebuilding process. He did this by offering reconciliation, offering pardons to former Confederates who agreed to support the Constitution and the United States, by allowing southern states to elect former Confederates to Congress, and by allowing Confederate states to rejoin the Union if they established anti-slavery governments. A is incorrect because President Lincoln's plan did not make it simple for former Confederate states to rejoin the Union. C is incorrect because President Lincoln's plan didn't establish the Freedmen's Bureau, and D is incorrect because it was the Radical Republicans' plan that sought to punish Confederates.

4. **D; DOK Level:** 2; **Content Topic:** II.CG.e.1; **Practices:** SSP.1.a, SSP.5.a, SSP.7.a. This source is an encyclopedia, which contains facts presented in an unbiased and scholarly way. So the only one of the four that would not be in the article is D, because it is opinion rather than fact. Names of Democratic Party members are known facts, as is the history of how the Party was formed. It also can be proved how the Party stands on certain issues.

5. **B; DOK Level:** 3; **Content Topics:** II.USH.f.1, II.USH.f.8, II.USH.g.3; **Practices:** SSP.1.a, SSP.2.b. The correct answer is B. The passage states that the French and British command was not impressed with the fighting skills of the Americans. Yet Americans were continuing to arrive in Europe to fight. So you can infer that they were only there because the British and French were so desperate for help that they were willing to accept soldiers who they did not believe would be up to the task. A is not correct because the British commanders did not respect the American doughboys. C is incorrect also because there is no information proving that General Pershing was a much better commanding officer than any of the British or French commanders. D is also incorrect because American troops fought with British and French soldiers against the German soldiers.

Answer Key

UNIT 3 *(continued)*

6. **B; DOK Level: 1; Content Topics:** I.CG.a.1, I.CG.b.3, I.CG.b.7, I.CG.b.8, I.USH.a.1; **Practices:** SSP.1.a, SSP.2.b. A careful reading of the passage shows that the answer is B. There are three main qualifications listed: 1) a person must be a natural-born citizen, not naturalized; 2) a person must be at least 35 years old; and 3) this person must have lived in the United States for at least 14 years. In other words, he or she could not be a natural-born citizen, age 35, who had lived abroad for most of his or her life. The other answer options are not correct as written.

7. **D; DOK Level: 2; Content Topics:** II.E.c.4, II.E.c.7, II.E.c.10, II.E.d.3; **Practices:** SSP.1.a, SSP.6.b, SSP.10.a. The correct answer is D, because the line graph clearly shows an increase in accommodation and food services.

8. **D; DOK Level: 3; Content Topics:** II.G.b.1, II.USH.g.9; **Practices:** SSP.1.a, SSP.1.b, SSP.2.a, SSP.2.b. The correct answer is D. Because Mr. Gorbachev's policy of *glasnost* was generally aimed at changing existing Soviet policies, you can assume that Communist leaders would have generally opposed *glasnost*. *Glasnost* was embraced by artists, scientists, and journalists.

9. **B; DOK Level: 2; Content Topics:** II.CG.f, II.USH.h; **Practices:** SSP.1.a, SSP.2.a, SSP.2.b, SSP.5.a, SSP.7.a. B is the only answer that works here, because it is the only answer that basically summarizes the author's point. A and D contain ideas that the author believes and he mentions them, but neither is the main idea of this editorial. C is incorrect because the author does not state or imply that President Obama does not keep his promises.

10. **C; DOK Level: 2; Content Topics:** II.CG.f, II.USH.h; **Practices:** SSP.1.a, SSP.2.a, SSP.2.b, SSP.5.a, SSP.7.a. C is the only answer that is correct. The writer does not use any of the other methods of supporting his point of view.

11. **D; DOK Level: 2; Content Topics:** I.CG.c.1, I.CG.c.3; **Practices:** SSP.1.a, SSP.5.a, SSP.6.b. The right answer is D. The U.S. economy is the sick patient, and President Roosevelt is the doctor about to cure him with his new programs. The title of the cartoon is encouragement to the American public to have faith in President Roosevelt, and to give him the chance to make his new programs work. The other answer options are incorrect.

12. **B; DOK Level: 2; Content Topic:** II.USH.f; **Practices:** SSP.1.a, SSP.1.b, SSP.2.a, SSP.5.a, SSP.6.b. B is the correct answer because December 7, 1941, is the date on which the Japanese bombed Pearl Harbor, forcing the United States into World War II. It does not refer to the end of World War II, nor to the dropping of the atomic bomb, nor to the D-Day invasion.

13. **A; DOK Level: 2; Content Topics:** I.CG.b.1, I.CG.b.2, I.CG.d.2, I.USH.a.1; **Practices:** SSP.1.a, SSP.1.b, SSP.5.a. The statement with which both would agree most is A, that all powers of government flow from a naturally free people. Mr. Jefferson states that governments derive their power from the consent of the governed. Mr. Locke states that people are born in a state of "perfect freedom," owing obedience to no other person. Mr. Jefferson might agree with B, but Mr. Locke probably would not. Neither man would agree with C or D.

14. **C; DOK Level: 2; Content Topics:** I.CG.b.1, I.CG.b.8, I.USH.a.1; **Practices:** SSP.1.a, SSP.1.b, SSP.5.a. The only one of the four terms that is even remotely close to what both men would agree on is C, *limited*. Both men believe human beings have natural rights, which means that government can only be by the people, and therefore limited. Neither man would want a strong or militaristic government, so A and B are incorrect. There is no indication that either man would want a government ruled by religious leaders, so D is also wrong.

15. **B; DOK Level: 3; Content Topics:** I.CG.b.1, I.CG.b.8, I.USH.a.1; **Practices:** SSP.1.a, SSP.1.b, SSP.5.a. B is correct, because "without asking leave," means "without asking for permission." The words do not mean to be excused, nor to go outside the country freely, nor do the words mean that one may choose to form his or her own government.

16. **A; DOK Level: 2; Content Topics:** I.CG.b.4, I.CG.b.7, II.CG.e.1, II.CG.e.3; **Practices:** SSP.1.a, SSP.7.a. A is correct, because Mr. Gore's statement shows that he thinks the only way to get a true count is with a hand count. He is prepared to wait for those results because it is "the best way to know the true intentions of the voters...". B is wrong because Mr. Gore believes getting the correct count is more important than speeding up the process. The fact that Mr. Gore wants the votes recounted obviously means that C is incorrect. D might be true, but Mr. Gore does not express this opinion. He notes that machines can make mistakes, but sees a hand recount as the best way to remedy that.

17. **C; DOK Level: 2; Content Topics:** I.CG.b.4, I.CG.b.7, II.CG.e.1, II.CG.e.3; **Practices:** SSP.1.a, SSP.7.a. The only statement that expresses a fact is C. The other answer options express feelings and opinions.

18. 18.1 **A**; 18.2 **B**; 18.3 **C**; 18.4 **D; DOK Level: 2; Content Topics:** I.CG.c.1, II.G.c.3, II.G.d.3; **Practices:** SSP.1.a, SSP.6.b. For **18.1**, the map shows that more of the population is in the **eastern** part of the country. The region with the most light-colored areas, indicating low population density, is in the **Central Plains**, making the answer to **18.2 B**. Of the states listed for **18.3**, the one with the most light-colored areas is **Alaska**. Population density there is low. For **18.4**, of the states listed as answer options, only **D, Wyoming**, shows more population density than Alaska, Montana, or Idaho, all of which have very low population densities.

19. **B; DOK Level: 2; Content Topics:** I.CG.b.8, I.CG.c.1, I.CG.d.2, II.E.c.4; **Practices:** SSP.1.a, SSP.2.b, SSP.3.b, SSP.3.c. The answer is B. In the last part of the excerpt, Justice Ginsburg states that the ball is in Congress' court, and that Congress may have to act to correct the Court's decision, which she clearly believes is wrong. Justice Ginsburg believes that if the majority on the U.S. Supreme Court will not order redress of the discrimination Ledbetter suffered because they state that the law does not allow it, then she challenges Congress to change the law. Justice Ginsburg does not urge a change in the Court justices, nor does she state that Ledbetter should sue Goodyear again. Neither does Justice Ginsburg insist that Title VII does not allow suits for discrimination.

20. C; DOK Level: 3; **Content Topics:** I.CG.a.1, I.CG.b.3, I.CG.b.7, I.CG.b.8, I.CG.d.1, I.CG.d.2; **Practices:** SSP.1.a, SSP.2.a. The rights listed in A, B, and D are in Amendment V. The only one not listed is the right to trial by jury. Note that the right to have a grand jury hear evidence in a serious criminal case is a right spelled out in Amendment V. However, the more basic right to be tried in court by a jury of one's peers is actually in Amendment VI.

21. B; DOK Level: 2; **Content Topics:** I.CG.c.2, II.USH.g.8; **Practices:** SSP.1.a, SSP.1.b, SSP.2.a, SSP.2.b, SSP.3.c. The answer is B, because President Nixon states that he is resigning in the wake of the Watergate matter and it is consuming so much of his time that he would not be able to carry out his Presidential duties. Mr. Nixon does not say in this excerpt that he is resigning because public sentiment was against him, or that Congress is pushing him out the door. He also does not say he does not want to work full-time as President.

22. D; DOK Level: 2; **Content Topics:** I.CG.c.2, II.USH.g.8; **Practices:** SSP.1.a, SSP.1.b, SSP.2.a, SSP.2.b, SSP.3.c. The answer is D, remorseful. President Nixon does not use a defiant, joyful, or stubborn tone in this speech.

23. C; DOK Level: 2; **Content Topics:** I.CG.d, II.G.c.1, II.G.d.3; **Practices:** SSP.1.a, SSP.6.b. C is correct. A majority of the places listed on the chart are in the West: Hawaii, California, Arizona, Colorado, and Montana. Most of the people age 85 and over do not live in the Southeast, Northeast, or Midwest, according to the table.

24. B; DOK Level: 3; **Content Topics:** I.CG.d, II.G.c.1, II.G.d.3; **Practices:** SSP.1.a, SSP.6.b. B is correct. You can infer that older people prefer the warmer climates of the Western region, especially states such as Hawaii, California, and Arizona.

25. D; DOK Level: 3; **Content Topics:** I.CG.b.4, I.CG.b.8, I.CG.c.6, I.CG.d.2, II.CG.e.2, II.CG.e.3, I.USH.d.3; **Practices:** SSP.1.a, SSP.1.b, SSP.2.a, SSP.4.a, SSP.5.a, SSP.5.b, SSP.5.c, SSP.6.b. D is correct, because the figures in the cartoon seem to be in charge of giving a literacy test, yet cannot themselves read the word *literacy*. These figures demonstrate faulty logic because an honest literacy test would prevent them from voting. They do not demonstrate faulty logic because they cannot agree on the best method for testing voters, or have oversimplified the qualifications for voting, nor have they made a hasty generalization that only opposing party members would be affected by the literacy tests.

26. A; DOK Level: 3; **Content Topics:** I.CG.b.4, I.CG.b.8, I.CG.c.6, I.CG.d.2, II.CG.e.2, II.CG.e.3, I.USH.d.3; **Practices:** SSP.1.a, SSP.1.b, SSP.2.a, SSP.4.a, SSP.5.a, SSP.5.b, SSP.5.c, SSP.6.b. A is correct, because literacy tests were just one way that Southern states tried to prevent African Americans from voting before the success of the Civil Rights movement. Often white voters were given very simple tests, while African Americans who attempted to vote would be given extremely difficult ones. By pointing out the unfairness of this, the cartoonist is making a statement about civil rights, not about government spending, presidential elections, or democratic reforms.

27. C; DOK Level: 2; **Content Topics:** I.CG.b.8, I.CG.d.2, I.USH.b.1; **Practices:** SSP.3.a, SSP.3.b, SSP.6.b. The key to answering this question correctly is finding the correct sequence of events in the flowchart. A, B, and D are in the wrong sequence. Only C is in the correct sequence, with the Boston Massacre occurring first, in 1770, and the Committees becoming important in 1772. So C is correct. The Committees could have been formed, at least in part, because of events such as the Boston Massacre.

28. D; DOK Level: 3; **Content Topics:** I.CG.b.8, I.CG.d.2, I.USH.b.1; **Practices:** SSP.3.a, SSP.3.b, SSP.6.b. There is a bit of inference involved in answering this correctly. You should infer that more people will become involved each year, as the tension between the colonies and Britain heightens and there are more incidents between them. Therefore, choose the latest year, which is D, 1773.

29. D; DOK Level: 3; **Content Topics:** I.CG.b.8, I.CG.d.2, I.USH.b.1; **Practices:** SSP.3.a, SSP.3.b, SSP.6.b. The only answer that could be true is D, the signing of the Declaration of Independence. If you do not remember that it happened in 1776, you should reason that the Declaration is the document in which the colonies finally broke with Britain and decided to go to war. So it had to come before any of those other events. Look at the listed events and draw conclusions about the sequence in which they would unfold. It cannot be C, because the Constitution was not written until the war was over and the new nation had been formed. It is not B, because Yorktown was the British surrender at the end of the war, and it is not A, because the peace treaty came well after that.

30. A; DOK Level: 3; **Content Topics:** II.USH.f.9, II.USH.g.1, II.USH.g.9, II.G.b.1; **Practices:** SSP.1.a, SSP.2.b, SSP.3.b, SSP.3.c. A is the correct answer. When Mr. Gorbachev made the decision to allow democratic reform in the Soviet Union's satellite states in Eastern Europe, and to allow dissent in the Soviet Union itself, he unleashed forces that eventually he could not control. This led to the fall of the government of the Soviet Union. The fall of the Soviet Union cannot be generalized, based on the passage, by Mr. Yeltsin causing Mr. Gorbachev to resign, or that democracy in Eastern Europe led the Soviet Union to adopt democracy, too. Nor can the fall of the Soviet Union be generalized by stating that Communist leaders dissolved the government to resist Boris Yeltsin.

UNIT 4 ECONOMICS

LESSON 1, *pp. 90–91*
1. B; DOK Level: 2; **Content Topic:** II.E.d; **Practices:** SSP.4.a, SSP.6.b. The fact that a can of frozen orange juice costs $2.09 at the supermarket is an example of microeconomics. It gives very specific information about the price of one can of frozen orange juice at the supermarket. The other three options are examples of macroeconomics because they involve the entire economy of the United States or the economy of Florida.

Answer Key

UNIT 4 *(continued)*

2. **A**; **DOK Level:** 2; **Content Topics:** II.E.c.1, II.E.d.1; **Practices:** SSP.4.a. Competition among sellers encourages prices to be held at about the same level in a market. High demand for the goods may induce sellers to increase prices. Incentives for the consumer will not keep prices held at similar levels. The quantity of the available goods also may tend to induce sellers to raise or lower their prices, not keep them similar to other sellers' prices.

3. **C**; **DOK Level:** 2; **Content Topics:** II.E.c.1, II.E.c.3; **Practices:** SSP.1.a, SSP.1.b, SSP.2.a, SSP.4.a. A monopoly can occur when one company sells a good that has no good substitutes and other companies are blocked from entering the market. The information discusses a cucumber seller having a monopoly if he or she is the only cucumber seller and others cannot enter the market. A small number of companies controlling the market for a good still have competition among them. If companies are producing slightly different goods, then they are not competing. If several companies are producing the same product, there is competition.

4. **D**; **DOK Level:** 3; **Content Topics:** II.E.d.6, II.E.d.9; **Practices:** SSP.1.a, SSP.1.b, SSP.2.a. An investor is most likely to invest in U.S.-based companies if the GDP of the United States is consistently increasing. This is a leading economic indicator and, therefore, a good predictor of the future economy. The investor would not be as likely to invest in foreign-manufactured goods or sell investments in foreign companies based on the strength of the U.S. economy. The investor is less likely to sell investments in U.S. businesses because the U.S. economy is doing well.

5. **B**; **DOK Level:** 1; **Content Topic:** II.E.d.10; **Practices:** SSP.2.a, SSP.2.b. Unemployment is a lagging indicator as employment may not increase for two or three quarters after an economic improvement. The stock market, money supply, and building permits are leading indicators.

LESSON 2, *pp. 92–93*

1. **B**; **DOK Level:** 3; **Content Topic:** II.E.d.8; **Practices:** SSP.6.a, SSP.6.b, SSP.10.a. B is correct because the graph shows that this period has the highest rate of inflation and the information in the passage presents these factors as direct effects of inflation. All of the other answer options include factors (increased value of money, increased demand for goods, deflation) that are exactly opposite to what would be true.

2. **DOK Level:** 3; **Content Topics:** II.E.d.1, II.E.d.2, II.E.d.8; **Practices:** SSP.3.c, SSP.6.c, SSP.10.a. At prices above the equilibrium point, demand goes down and supply goes up. At prices below the equilibrium point, supply goes down and demand goes up.

3. **D**; **DOK Level:** 2; **Content Topics:** II.E.d.1, II.E.d.2, II.E.d.8; **Practices:** SSP.3.c, SSP.6.c, SSP.10.a. According to the information, supply, demand, and inflation are each influenced by many causes. They are not each basic causes of economic activity, they do each influence the economy, and they do not operate independently of one another.

4. **A**; **DOK Level:** 2; **Content Topics:** II.E.d.1, II.E.d.2, II.E.d.8; **Practices:** SSP.3.c, SSP.6.c, SSP.10.a. Supply and demand require competition to function freely. Competition helps regulate prices and the supply of goods. Also, if demand is higher, more companies will start producing an item, which can help drive prices down to the equilibrium point. Supply and demand do not require government regulation of prices, inflation, or a growing economy to function freely.

LESSON 3, *pp. 94–95*

1. **A**; **DOK Level:** 3; **Content Topic:** II.E.e.1; **Practices:** SSP.6.a, SSP.6.c, SSP.10.a, SSP.10.b. An upswing in the economy is the most likely reason for the increase in nonrevolving consumer credit beginning in 2009. When people are optimistic about their financial future, they will make more substantial purchases, such as a car or a home, each of which usually involves nonrevolving credit. In addition, revolving consumer credit became fairly flat just after 2009. The shift does not indicate increased fear of an economic downturn, or the beginning of a recession, or a decrease in the amount of credit available.

2. **C**; **DOK Level:** 3; **Content Topics:** II.E.c.5, II.E.e.2; **Practices:** SSP.6.a, SSP.6.c, SSP.10.a, SSP.10.b. C is correct because interest on savings is low, and interest on payments is higher; therefore, people are paying down revolving debt. A is incorrect because savings are dependent on income, particularly on disposable income. B is incorrect because people spend what they *have to*, with disposable income remaining. D is incorrect because personal income and disposable personal income *are* related.

3. **C**; **DOK Level:** 2; **Content Topic:** II.E.c.5; **Practices:** SSP.6.a, SSP.6.c, SSP.10.a. The opportunity cost for Country B to produce 10 tons of corn is 6 tons of wheat.

4. **D**; **DOK Level:** 2; **Content Topic:** II.E.c.5; **Practices:** SSP.6.a, SSP.6.c, SSP.10.a, SSP.10.b. D is the correct answer. Country A should produce wheat and Country B should produce corn because Country A has the lowest opportunity cost for wheat and Country B has the lowest opportunity cost for corn. All of the other answer options include incorrect statements.

LESSON 4, *pp. 96–97*

1. **C**; **DOK Level:** 2; **Content Topics:** II.E.c.8, II.E.c.11; **Practices:** SSP.6.a, SSP.6.b, SSP.10.a. According to the pictograph, the value of trade between the United States and Japan is just over two symbols' worth. Each symbol is worth $100 billion, so the value of trade between the United States and Japan is about $200 billion. The other answer choices are not close enough to the value of the symbols for Japan.

2.1 **C**; 2.2 **C**; 2.3 **D**; **DOK Level:** 2; **Content Topics:** II.E.c.8, II.E.c.9, II.E.c.10; **Practices:** SSP.6.a, SSP.6.b, SSP.10.a, SSP.11.a.

2.1 According to the pictograph, Iowa's value of production was more than twice that of **Indiana**. Iowa's value of production was 11.7 billion. The only state that had a value of production less than half of that was Indiana, with a value of production of 4.9 billion.

ANSWER KEY

2.2 The median value is the middle value in a data set when you arrange the data from least to greatest. The data in order from least to greatest are $4,939 million; $6,719 million; $7,860 million; $10,707 million; $11,735 million. Thus, the median value of the data is **$7,860 million.**

2.3 You can assume from this information that **Wisconsin**, since it is listed after Ohio among the states rounding out the top 10 corn-producing states in the nation, had a production total less than Ohio's. Iowa, Illinois, and Indiana are listed in the top five corn-producing states; therefore, their production would not be less than Ohio's.

LESSON 5, pp. 98–99

1. B; DOK Level: 2; **Content Topics:** II.E.e.1, II.E.e.3; **Practices:** SSP.6.a, SSP.6.b, SSP.6.c, SSP.10.a, SSP.10.c. Based on the bar graphs, the only correct statement among the answer options is B: The average prime interest rate in 2008 was about 6 percent.

2. C; DOK Level: 2; **Content Topics:** II.E.d.4, II.E.d.5; **Practices:** SSP.6.a, SSP.6.b, SSP.6.c, SSP.10.a, SSP.10.c. The value of M2 is greater than that of M1. This statement will always be true because M2 includes all of M1, in addition to other items, so it must be greater than M1. The value of M1 does not always exceed $300 billion. The value of M2, according to the graph, is not increasing steadily. The value of M1 may or may not be approximately one-half the value of M2, but is not always so.

3. B; DOK Level: 2; **Content Topics:** II.E.d.4, II.E.d.5; **Practices:** SSP.6.a, SSP.6.b, SSP.6.c, SSP.10.a. The approximate value of M1 in 2010 was $200 billion. The point on the graph is higher than $100 billion and lower than both $300 billion and $400 billion.

4. D; DOK Level: 2; **Content Topics:** II.E.d.4, II.E.d.5; **Practices:** SSP.1.a, SSP.6.a, SSP.6.b, SSP.6.c, SSP.10.a. The economy probably had the most liquidity in 2010. Liquidity is measured in how easily items can be turned into cash. The M1 value contains the most liquid assets, so the economy had the most liquidity when the M1 value was the highest. It was the highest in 2010, not 1980, 1990, or 2000.

5. B; DOK Level: 3; **Content Topic:** II.E.c.4; **Practices:** SSP.1.a, SSP.6.a, SSP.6.b, SSP.6.c, SSP.10.a, SSP.10.c. It is true that age is not a factor in whether federal employees telecommute. According to the graph, in nearly every age group, the percentage of employees telecommuting is about the same as the percentage of all federal employees in that age group. Older employees are more likely, not less likely, to telecommute. The percentage, and therefore the number, of younger employees is less than the number of older employees, so there are not more younger employees telecommuting. The percentage of employees that telecommute increases, not decreases, with age, except for those who are over 60 years of age.

1. C; DOK Level: 3; **Content Topics:** II.E.d.1, II.E.d.2, II.E.d.4, II.E.d.7; **Practices:** SSP.3.c, SSP.6.a, SSP.6.b. The purchasing power of U.S. consumers grew increasingly weak during the early 1930s. The information states that if people's purchasing power is weakened, an economic depression can get worse. This is evident in the table by the decreasing GDP. There is no data in the table for the 1920s besides 1929, so you cannot conclude that the United States had been in a recession at that time. The production of war supplies helped increase the GDP and bring the country out of the Great Depression. The passage states that 1929 was a high point in GDP so government intervention would not likely have been necessary during the 1920s.

2. A; DOK Level: 3; **Content Topic:** II.E.d.10; **Practices:** SSP.6.a, SSP.6.b, SSP.10.a. You could have predicted that unemployment in the United States would gradually decrease in the years following 1939. World War II began in Europe in 1939, leading to an increasing demand for industrial goods, which led to an increase in jobs and a decrease in unemployment. The rise in GDP indicates decreasing, not growing, bankruptcies; and increases, not decreases, in demand; and improving, not depressed, conditions.

3. C; DOK Level: 2; **Content Topic:** II.E.d.8; **Practices:** SSP.3.c, SSP.6.a, SSP.6.b, SSP.10.a. The table shows the U.S. GDP in year-2005 dollars because of inflation. By adjusting for inflation, economists and historians can make accurate comparisons. Overproduction, unemployment, and supply and demand do not have an effect on whether or not the GDP is shown in current or year-2005 dollars.

4. D; DOK Level: 2; **Content Topic:** II.E.d.8; **Practices:** SSP.3.c, SSP.4.a, SSP.6.a, SSP.6.b. *Volatility* in this context means **instability**, or unpredictability. Currency values that are volatile move about erratically and are unstable. *Volatility* does not mean fullness, ambulatory, or loudness.

5. B; DOK Level: 2; **Content Topic:** II.E.d.8; **Practices:** SSP.3.c, SSP.4.a, SSP.6.a, SSP.6.b. *Stimulate* in this context means **motivate or encourage**, as governments will want to "shake up" or arouse investors from an economic crisis. *Stimulate* does not mean explode, inflate, or to bring to an abrupt halt.

6. B; DOK Level: 3; **Content Topics:** II.E.d.4, II.E.d.5; **Practices:** SSP.3.c, SSP.6.a, SSP.6.b, SSP.10.a. The approval of a federal budget that produces a surplus dedicated to paying money owed to other nations would guarantee a reduction in the debt. The other three answer options are likely to cost the government money and therefore increase the debt.

7. C; DOK Level: 3; **Content Topics:** II.E.d.4, II.E.d.5; **Practices:** SSP.3.c, SSP.6.a, SSP.6.b, SSP.10.a. This pictograph can be tricky. The circles represent $100 billion, whereas the blocks represent $1 trillion. By analyzing the pictograph carefully, you can determine that the national debt level has continued to rise since 1975. It is not true that the U.S. national debt exceeded $600 billion by 1975; it exceeded $500 billion. Also, it is untrue that the U.S. national debt decreased between the years 1980 and 1985; it increased. It also is not true that the U.S. national debt expanded more between 1995 and 2000 than it did between 2000 and 2005; in fact, it expanded less.

UNIT 4 *(continued)*

8. D; DOK Level: 2; **Content Topic:** II.E.c.10; **Practice:** SSP.3.c. Increased productivity from teleworkers can be expected based on the information that enhanced worker effectiveness is a benefit of telework. The information states that telework helps with retaining a workforce, so there will not be large turnover. The information also discusses a reduction in costs, so higher overhead costs would not be expected. The information references security incidents, but does not discuss security clearance.

9. C; DOK Level: 2; **Content Topic:** II.E.c.4; **Content Practices:** SSP.3.c, SSP.6.b. The work of your employees falls under the category of labor. Labor describes human effort. Money is capital. Your ability to manage your employees is not a factor of production. The property on which your company is located is land.

10. D; DOK Level: 2; **Content Topic:** II.E.c.4; **Content Practices:** SSP.2.b, SSP.3.c, SSP.6.b. Your willingness to start your own business and manufacture products is entrepreneurship. An entrepreneur is a person who starts a business. Labor is human effort, capital is wealth and resources, and profit is the amount of money a company makes.

11. B; DOK Level: 3; **Content Topic:** II.E.c.4; **Practices:** SSP.2.b, SSP.3.c, SSP.6.b. According to the information in the flowchart, firms generate revenue (earn money) by selling goods and services to people in households. They do not generate revenue from buying goods and services, from buying factors of productions, or by avoiding the markets for goods and services and factors of production.

12. C; DOK Level: 3; **Content Topic:** II.E.c.4; **Practices:** SSP.2.b, SSP.3.c, SSP.6.b. All four corners of the flowchart show examples of how all transactions between firms and households contribute to the nation's GDP. The other three answer options contain information that is not correct, based on the flowchart and the information.

13. A; DOK Level: 2; **Content Topic:** II.E.e.1; **Practice:** SSP.1.a. The revolving credit graph shows a low, steady line during 2010 to 2012, while the non-revolving credit graph shows a sharp spike upward during these years. There are drops in both graphs in earlier years, 2008 and 2009. There is never an upward spike in the revolving credit graph.

14. A; DOK Level: 3; **Content Topic:** II,E,e,1; **Practices:** SSP.6.a, SSP.6.b, SSP.10.a. During a recession people are less likely, not more likely, to make big purchases, such as cars and homes. Credit card balances are examples of revolving, not non-revolving, credit.

15. A; DOK Level: 2; **Content Topic:** II.E.d.6; **Practices:** SSP.6.b, SSP.6.c, SSP.10.a, SSP.10.c. The statement that many investors made money on their investments in 1995 is most likely true. The Dow Jones Industrial Average showed a positive change of more than 30%. This large positive change makes it likely that many investors made money. There is no indication that most people shied away from investing in 2005. The return on investments in 2000 was negative, so it could not be considered healthy. The table does not indicate what type of stocks people invested in, so you cannot say that investors invested heavily in technology in 2010.

16. D; DOK Level: 3; **Content Topics:** II.E.c.9, II.E.c.10, II.E.c.11; **Practices:** SSP.6.b, SSP.6.c, SSP.10.a, SSP.10.c. A nationwide drought could have caused the changes shown on the graphs. The citrus production decreased, and the number of wildfires increased. Only a nationwide drought could have this effect. A greater demand for agricultural products would not affect the number of forest fires. A decrease in productivity per hour would also not affect the number of forest fires. More farmers specializing in citrus would also not affect the number of forest fires.

17. C; DOK Level: 3; **Content Topic:** II.E.c.6; **Practices:** SSP.6.b, SSP.6.c, SSP.10.a. Citrus production declined during the years with the most wildfires. You can conclude that a decrease in citrus production would lead to a decrease in profits. Profits would not double, remain the same, or increase from previous years. They would decline.

18. C; DOK Level: 2; **Content Topic:** II.E.c.6; **Practices:** SSP.6.b, SSP.6.c, SSP.10.a. The graph shows that wildfires were the third highest in 2004 within the five-year span shown in the graph.

19. B; DOK Level: 2; **Content Topic:** II.E.c.6; **Practices:** SSP.6.b, SSP.6.c, SSP.10.a. The line graph shows that the greatest increase in U.S. wildfires occurred between 2005 and 2006, not in the other years shown in the other answer options.

20. C; DOK Level: 3; **Content Topic:** II.E.d.9; **Practices:** SSP.6.a, SSP.6.b, SSP.6.c, SSP.10.a. The period from 2011 to 2015 would likely feature little change in GDP and per capita income for each state based on the graphs. The per capita income for Arkansas is about 50% that of Ohio, but the GDP for Arkansas is much less than 50% of the GDP for Ohio. The rate of increase for Ohio on both graphs is more than that for the other two states. GDP and per capita income are related, as seen by how they follow the same trends in both graphs.

21. D; DOK Level: 3; **Content Topic:** I.E.d.9; **Practices:** SSP.6.a, SSP.6.b, SSP.6.c, SSP.10.a. You can conclude that Connecticut has a smaller population than Ohio. *Per capita* means "per person", so the second graph takes the entire income of each state and divides it by the population of that state. The first graph shows that Ohio has a much higher GDP than Connecticut, but in the second graph, Connecticut has a much higher per capita income. Therefore, you can conclude that Connecticut has a smaller population than Ohio. The graph does not show imports. If the population of Arkansas were expanding at a higher rate than that at which its wages are increasing, the per capita income would decrease. The GDP of Arkansas and Connecticut are not likely to reach the same level.

22. A; DOK Level: 2; **Content Topic:** I.E.d.9; **Practices:** SSP.6.a, SSP.6.b, SSP.6.c, SSP.10.a. The multi-line graph takes the population of each state into account when measuring data. That is why it is called "Per Capita Income by State." The multi-bar graph does not take each state's population into account. The other answer options are all incorrect, based on the two graphs.

23. C; DOK Level: 2; **Content Topic:** I.E.c.2; **Practice:** SSP.3.c. A $50.00 check to open a new checking account is a positive economic incentive. The bank rewards you with $50.00 for bringing your business to it. Having an interest charge on your credit card statement, or a late fee for an overdue library book, or an extra charge for extra minutes on your cell phone statement are all negative economic incentives. These fines discourage certain actions.

24. **Your Obligation:** Managing Credit; **Credit Bureau's Obligations:** Compliance Under the Act, Error Investigation; **Obligations of Both:** Accuracy, Privacy, Working with Lenders. **DOK Level:** 3; **Content Topics:** II.E.d.3, II.E.e.3; **Practices:** SSP.1.a, SSP.2.b, SSP.3.d, SSP.6.a, SSP.6.b, SSP.10.a. It is your obligation to **manage** your credit. You do this by accessing your credit report, understanding what it contains, responding to any incident of denied credit or any error in your report. It is the Credit Bureau's obligation, not your obligation, to **be in compliance** with the Fair Credit Reporting Act. It is both your obligation and the Credit Bureau's obligation to ensure **accuracy**, **privacy** of data, and to **work with lenders.**

25. **D; DOK Level:** 2; **Content Topic:** II.E.c.1; **Practice:** SSP.4.a. There must be more than a single seller or buyer for a market to be competitive. In a competitive market, there is competition among sellers for buyers and competition among buyers for products. A market does not need to be international to be competitive. A market with government control over prices would not be competitive. A market with only one company to sell each product is also not competitive.

26. **B; DOK Level:** 2; **Content Topic:** II.E.c.3; **Practice:** SSP.4.a. A monopolistic market is one in which consumers only have one seller from which to purchase a product. The seller is a monopoly—the only provider of a good or service in a market. A monopolistic market does not have multiple sellers. It also does not have only one type of good. A monopoly may produce and sell several products, but it is the only company selling those products. Consumers have less power, not more power, than sellers in a monopoly because the consumers have no choice.

27. **A; DOK Level:** 2; **Content Topics:** II.E.c.1, II.E.c.3; **Practices:** SSP.1.a, SSP.1.b, SSP.2.a, SSP.2.b, SSP.3.c. By choosing which products to buy, consumers choose which businesses succeed and which fail. Consumers do not support monopolies, which profit at the expense of consumers. While consumers may pay higher prices for convenience or shop for the best values, these criteria relate to which products consumers buy and which they do not, which ultimately determines the winners and losers in the business world.

ANSWER KEY

Index

A

Absolute location, 4
Afghanistan War, 21, 82
African Americans
  enslaved laborers, 32–33
  Great Migration of, 23
  Jim Crow laws, 35
  during Reconstruction, 53, 80
  segregation, 35, 53, 55
Agriculture
  citrus production, 104
  corn production in U.S., 97
  failures following stock market crash, 59
Albania, 18, 42
Altitude, 2
Amendments to the Constitution
  Bill of Rights, 51
  fifteenth, 57
  fifth, 85
  fourteenth, 55
  nineteenth, 34, 57
  ninth, 49
  number to date, 48
  second, 75
  twenty-second, 69
American Equal Rights Association, 57
American Expeditionary Force, 81
American Revolution
  Declaration of Independence, 27
  events leading to, 87
  ideas influencing, 47
  preparations for, 25
  unification of colonies, 32
American Woman Suffrage Association, 34, 57
Amos, Wally, 88
Analyzing Information Sources, 64–65
Anthony, Susan B., 34, 57
Anti-Federalist Letters from the Federal Farmer to the Republican, 29
Anti-Federalists, 28
Anti-Semitism, 39
Arguments
  analyzing effectiveness of, 78–79
  facts supporting, 72
Arkansas, congressional districts in, 71
Arthur, Chester A., 55
Articles of Confederation, 51
Assembly line, 97
Author's purpose, 76
Average annual mortgage, 98
Axes of graphs, 54

B

Balance of powers, 47
Balkan peninsula, 18
Bankruptcies, 100
Banks, 59, 99

Bar graphs, 98–99, 104, 105
Battle of Tippecanoe, 31
Benchmark dates (on timelines), 34–35
Berlin Airlift, 42
Berlin Wall, 41, 43
Bias, 64, 76
Biden, Joseph, Jr., 77, 82
Bill of Rights, 51
Bills, process of passing, 49
Boehner, John, 64
Bolsheviks, 36
Borders, 8–9
Boston Massacre, 87
Boston Tea Party, 87
Botswana, 16
Britain/British
  American Revolution, 25, 27
  control of Oregon Country, 31
  government system, 46
  losses during World Wars I and II, 41
  Magna Carta, 46, 62
  support of Russian White Army, 36
  taxation of colonies, 87
  U.S. trade with, 96
  War of 1812, 31
  World War I, 56
British colonies in America
  call for independence, 26, 27
  events leading to American Revolution, 87
  Federalists and Anti-Federalists in, 28, 29
  Jamestown Colony, 10
  origins of migrations to, 25
  population of, 25
Brown v. Board of Education, 55
Bulgaria, 42, 43
Bush, George W., 63, 67, 77

C

Calculator directions, xii
Canada, 14, 96
Capital (monetary), 102
Captions, 64
Cardinal directions, 4
Caricature, 58
Carpetbaggers, 53
Categorize, 28–29
Cause and effect, 32–33, 40, 92–93
Charts, interpreting, 52, 54–55
Checks and balances, 67
Cherokee Nation, 30
China, 11, 96
Circuit Court of Appeals Act, 65
Citizens' responsibilities, 45
Citrus production, 104
Civics and government
  analyze effectiveness of arguments, 78–79
  analyze information sources, 64–65
  Articles of Confederation, 51
  Bureau of Energy Resources, 66
  checks and balances, 67

compare and contrast, 52–53
contributors to American political thought, 47
declaration of war, 67
democracy, 45
determine point of view, 62–63
draw conclusions, 60–61
Electoral College system, 73
evaluate information, 76–77
fact and opinion, 72–73
Fair Credit Reporting Act, 106
Fascism, 38
faulty logic and reasoning, 74–75
Federal Reserve Districts, 70
financial system, 68
generalize, 66–67
GI Bill, 40
Glasnost in Soviet Union, 81
House of Representatives, 71
identify problem and solution, 68–69
interpret charts, graphs, and flowcharts, 54–55
interpret diagrams, 46–47
interpret political cartoons, 58–59
interpret the Constitution, 48–49
Japanese internment camps, 39, 75
judicial system, 65, 85
limitation of terms of Presidents, 69
Magna Carta, 46, 62
make inferences, 56–57
National Infrastructure Reinvestment Bank, 76
National Wilderness Preservation System, 69
Pendleton Civil Service Act, 55
presidential campaigns/elections, 63, 73, 76, 77, 78, 83
Presidential Succession Act, 60
process of passing bills into law, 49
Prohibition Party, 58
rule of law, 63
Speaker of the House, 64
special-purpose maps, 70–71
state legislatures, 67
summarize, 50–51
Telework Enhancement Act (2010), 101
United Nations, 63
voting rights, 34, 45, 57, 86
women's rights, 34, 57, 74, 85
See also **Amendments to the Constitution; Congress; Constitution of the United States; President of the United States; Supreme Court of the United States**
Civil Rights Movement, 80
Civil War, 32–33, 52, 53
Clear key, xii
Climate, 2, 6–7, 15, 16, 19
Clinton, Bill, 78
Clinton, Hillary, 77
Cold War, 36, 40
Columns in tables, 24
Commerce, 100
Committees of Correspondence, 87
Common law, 46

INDEX

Index

Index

Q

Question types on GED® Test, x–xi
  drag-and-drop, 93, 106
  drop-down, 47, 49, 97
  extended response, 51, 61, 79
  fill-in-the-blank, 23, 25, 27, 33, 35, 75
  hot spot, 3, 7

R

Radical Republicans, 52, 53, 80
Reagan, Ronald, 43
Reasoning, 74–75
Recession, 100
Reconstruction, 52, 53, 80
Recovery Act, 78
Relative location, 4–5
Rent, 102
Retton, Mary Lou, 20
Revolving consumer credit, 94, 103
Rights of the people, 47, 83
Roosevelt, Franklin D., 39, 40, 59, 82
Roosevelt, Theodore, 76
Rousseau, Jean-Jacques, 47
Rows (in a table), 24
Rule of law, 63
Russia
  civil war in, 36
  Truman Doctrine and, 41, 42
  See also **Soviet Union**
Russian Revolution, 36

S

Satire, 58
Savings as percentage of disposable income, 95
Scales (on a map), 4–5, 8
Scientific notation key, xii
2nd key, xii
Second Amendment, 75
Secondary sources, 64
Second Congress, 60
Segregation, 35, 53, 55
Self-incrimination, 85
Senate, 49. See also **Congress**
Sequence, 30–31
Services, 102
Shaping America's Global Energy Policy **(Bureau of Energy Resources)**, 66
Sherman, William T., 53
Sign key, xii
Silk Road, 11
Slavery, 32–33, 35, 80
Social Studies test, x–xi
Sources, analyzing, 64–65

Soviet Union
  control of East Germany, 41, 42
  fall of communism, 42, 43, 87
  Glasnost, 81
  space program, 62
  See also **Russia**
Spain, 29, 42
Specialization, 95, 97
Special-purpose maps, 10, 70–71
Speeches (as sources of information), 64
Spotlighted Items, x–xi
  drag-and-drop, 93, 106
  drop-down, 47, 49, 97
  extended response, 51, 61, 79
  fill-in-the-blank, 23, 25, 27, 33, 35, 75
  hot spot, 3, 7
Square key, xii
Stamp Act, 87
Stanton, Elizabeth Cady, 57
State legislatures, 67
States' rights, 32–33
Steel industry, 61
Steel-Seizure Case, 61
Stephens, Alexander, 33
Stock market, 59, 91, 103
Stone, Lucy, 57
Study skills, xiv
Suffrage for women, 34, 45, 57
Summarizing, 50–51
Supply and demand, 93, 100
Supporting details, 26–27
Supreme Court of United States
  checks and balances, 67
  Circuit Court of Appeals/Judiciary Acts, 65
  Ledbetter v. Goodyear Tire and Rubber Company, 74, 85
  Roosevelt's appointments, 59
  ruling on seizure of steel industry, 61
  rulings on segregation, 55
Symbols
  on maps, 4–5, 6–7, 10, 70
  on pictographs, 96
  in political cartoons, 58

T

Tables, interpreting, 24–25, 27, 28, 100, 103
Taxes, 46, 76, 78, 87
Tea Act, 87
Telework Enhancement Act (2010), 101
Territorial colonies, 38
Test-Taking Tips, xiii
  analyze effectiveness of arguments, 78
  determine point of view, 62
  differentiating between micro- and macroeconomics, 90
  evaluate information, 76
  headings of rows/columns, 24
  interpret diagrams, 46
  interpret special-purpose maps, 70
  interpret the Constitution, 48

main idea and details, 26
map components, 8
map key, 10
recognizing bias, 64
Thirteen colonies, 24–25
TI-30XS calculator, xii
Timelines, interpreting, 34–35
Title
  of diagrams, 46
  of graphs, 54
  of maps, 4–5, 22
  of sources, 64
  of tables, 24
Toggle key, xii
Tonkin Gulf Resolution, 79
Topic sentence, 26
Townshend duties, 87
Tracking marketing, 107
Trade, 11, 96, 100
Trotsky, Leo, 36
Truman, Harry S., 41, 42, 61
Truman Doctrine, 41, 42
Turkey, 41, 42
Twenty-Second Amendment, 69
Two Treatises of Government **(Locke)**, 83

U

Unemployment rate, 91, 100. *See also* **Employment**
United Kingdom. *See* **Britain/British**
United Nations, 38, 63
United States
  agriculture in, 59, 97, 104
  citizens' responsibilities, 45
  geography/climates of, 15
  national debt, 101
  population density, 84
  space program, 62
  taxes, 76, 78
  trade partners, 96
  unemployment rate, 91, 100
  voting rights, 34, 45, 57, 86
  See also **British colonies in America; Constitution of the United States; Federal government; United States history**
United States history
  Afghanistan War, 21, 82
  American Revolution, 25, 27, 32, 87
  Articles of Confederation, 51
  Berlin Airlift, 42
  categorize, 28–29
  cause and effect, 32–33
  Circuit Court of Appeals Act, 65
  Civil Rights Movement, 80
  Civil War, 32–33, 53
  Constitution, 47, 48–49
  Declaration of Independence, 27, 47, 83
  desegregation, 55
  establishment of government, 28, 29
  European immigration, 37

Fair Credit Reporting Act, 106
GI Bill, 40
Great Migration, 23
inflation rates, 92
interpret tables, 24–25
interpret timelines, 34–35
Iraq War, 21
isolationism, 42
Japanese internment camps, 39, 75
Jim Crow period, 35
League of Nations, 37
Lilly Ledbetter Fair Pay Act, 74, 85
main idea and details, 26–27
McCarthyism, 80
National Infrastructure Reinvestment
   Bank, 76
Pendleton Civil Service Act, 55
Presidential Succession Act, 60
Prohibition Party formation, 58
Reconstruction, 52, 53, 80
Recovery Act, 78
Relate geography and history, 22–23
role of military, 21
segregation, 35, 53, 55
sequence, 30–31
slavery, 32–33
stock market crash/Great Depression,
   59
Telework Enhancement Act (2010), 101
Thirteen colonies, 24–25
Trail of Tears, 30
Truman Doctrine, 41, 42
Vietnam War, 79
War of 1812, 31
Watergate, 85
westward expansion, 23, 29–31
women's rights, 21, 34, 45, 57, 74
World War I, 41, 56, 81
World War II, 39, 40, 41
   See also **Amendments to the
      Constitution; Civics and
      government; Constitution of the
      United States**
Using Logic
   categorize information, 28
   compass rose, 4
   countries on equator, 2
   distinguish fact and opinion, 72
   identify problem and solution, 68
   interpret graphs, 54
   interpret timelines, 34
   key words for cause and effect, 32
   make inferences, 56
   summarize, 50
   valid/invalid generalizations, 66
U.S.S.R. *See* **Soviet Union**

V

Venn diagram, 46, 106
Vietnam War, 79
Viewpoint, 62–63, 64. *See also*
   Opinions
Virginia Colony, 24

Visuals
   compare and contrast, 52, 94–95
   interpret charts, graphs, and
      flowcharts, 54–55
   interpret diagrams, 46–47
   interpret political cartoons, 58–59, 75,
      82
   interpret posters, 82
   interpret tables, 24–25
   interpret timelines, 34–35
   See also **Graphs; Maps**
Voting
   literacy tests (political cartoon), 86
   machine errors in counting votes, 83
   suffrage for women, 34, 57

W

Wages, 74, 85, 102
War of 1812, 31
Wars
   in Afghanistan, 21, 82
   American Revolution, 87
   civil war in Russia, 36
   Civil War in U.S., 32–33, 52, 53
   declaration of, 67
   Iraq War, 21
   Vietnam War, 79
   War of 1812, 31
   World War I, 41, 56, 81
   World War II, 39, 40, 41
Warsaw Pact, 42
Watergate, 85
Websites (as sources of information),
   64
Westward expansion, 23, 29–31
Wilson, Woodrow, 37, 56
Women's Army Corps (WAC), 21
Women's Rights, 34
World War I, 41, 56, 81
World War II, 39, 40, 41

X

x-**axis**, 54

Y

y-**axis**, 54
Yeltsin, Boris, 43, 87

INDEX